SELECTED READINGS FOR THE
INTRODUCTION TO THE TEACHING PROFESSION

Milton Muse
Editor
University of Houston

McCutchan Publishing Corporation
2526 Grove Street
Berkeley, California 94704

ISBN: 0–8211–1218–X
Library of Congress Catalog Card Number: 77–130502

PREFACE

These selected readings have been assembled to help beginning education students become aware of the major aspects in current educational theory and practice. In particular, this volume is not intended as basic resource material, rather it supplements and parallels other experiences afforded by introductory courses. We hope that these readings will assist prospective teachers in increasing their ability to understand and interpret situations they will face in the classroom, in the school, and in the community, as well as in helping them recognize the theoretical concepts upon which the understanding and interpretations are based.

The planning and teaching of the course is a team effort just as the search, selection, and final choice of content represents the combined product of team members. The members are:

Faculty	Teaching Fellows
James Boyer	Jane Flavin
Howard Jones	Thomas Hewitt
Nelda Lawrence	Lucilla Koppany
Milton Muse	Donna Livingston
Robert Stewart	Anitra Lourie
William Yost	Bryan Myers
	Harold Prochnow

During the past three years, working with all who have served on the team has been a rewarding experience for me. With sincere respect and steadfast affection—thank you, teammates.

We wish to acknowledge our appreciation for the cover design by Anita Harrell.

We dedicate this publication to the Future Teachers from the University of Houston.

Milton Muse
May, 1970

CONTENTS

1

THE PLACE OF SCHOOL IN SOCIETY TODAY

THE AMERICAN COMMITMENT

John W. Gardner

I believe that large numbers of Americans—and I count myself among them—
have in recent years come to some kind of decision as to the sort of society they
really want.

We found ourselves in a period of unprecedented affluence, and we decided
that affluence wasn't enough. We found ourselves in a period of extraordinary
technical achievements, and we decided that technical proficiency wasn't enough.
We decided that what we really wanted was a society designed for people:

- a society in which every young person could fulfill the promise that was in
  him;
- a society in which every person, old or young, could live his life with some
  measure of dignity;
- a society in which ignorance and disease and want could tyrannize no longer;
- a society of opportunity and fulfillment.

I'm speaking of something that has happened fairly recently, but these are
not new themes in our national life. They represent a rebirth, a rededication to
values that were always at the heart of the American commitment.

Unfortunately, some of our fellow citizens do not honor those ends. But
many others do. Many live by the American commitment and live to further that
commitment.

It can be honored only by deeds. If we say one thing and do another, then we
are dealers in illusions and not a great people.

No one should underestimate the great scope and difficulty of the tasks we
are undertaking (and by "we" I mean people in and out of government)—the
elimination of poverty, the redesign of our cities, the drastic upgrading of state and
local government, the creation of a genuinely humane environment for older

Americans, the raising of our schools to a new level of quality.

All of these tasks are complex, most are costly, some are painful. They cannot be accomplished without a great burst of energy and concern on the part of millions of Americans.

I believe that such concern and commitment will be forthcoming when enough Americans realize how intimately our current efforts are tied to the basic values that give meaning and continuity to our life as a people.

Basic to any widespread release of human potential are equality of opportunity and equal access to the benefits of the society.

Every child should enjoy the advantages that make healthy growth and development possible. The avenues of individual fulfillment should be open to everyone. No one should be shut out from the life of the society.

It is an ideal to which we have been grievously unfaithful.

The idea of the worth and dignity of the individual is thousands of years old. But embedding that idea in social and political institutions has been a painfully slow process. It is still slow.

Our own history is instructive. No nation had ever before expressed so clear a concern for individual freedom and fulfillment as was expressed in our founding documents.

Yet it was not until 1863 that we freed the slaves. It was not until the early years of this century that we outlawed child labor. It was not until 1920 that women were allowed to vote. It was not until 1954 that the Supreme Court outlawed segregation in the schools. And degrading poverty and discrimination still exist in this free and prosperous land.

Don't let anyone tell you we're confused. We know the values to which we are being unfaithful. You may ask, "What difference does it make that we agree on our values if we aren't faithful to them?" I would answer that from the standpoint of therapy it always makes a difference what the patient is suffering from. This patient is not suffering from confusion but from infidelity.

Back of every great civilization, behind all the panoply of power and wealth, is something as powerful as it is insubstantial: a set of ideas, attitudes, convictions and the confidence that those ideas and convictions are viable.

No nation can achieve greatness unless it believes in something--and unless that something has the moral dimensions to sustain a great civilization.

If the light of belief flickers out, then all the productive capacity and all the know-how and all the power of the nation will be as nothing, and the darkness will gather.

In Guatemala and southern Mexico one can observe the Indians who are without doubt the lineal descendants of those who created the Mayan civilization. Today they are a humble people, not asking much of themselves or the world, and not getting much. A light went out.

The geography and natural resources are virtually unchanged; the genetic make-up of the people is no doubt much the same. They were once a great people. Now they do not even remember their greatness. What happened?

I suspect that in the case of the Mayans the ruling ideas were too primitive to sustain a great civilization for long.

What about our own ideas? Can they sustain a great civilization?

The answer depends on what ideas we are talking about. Americans have valued and sought and believed in many different things: freedom, power, money, equality, justice, technology, bigness, success, comfort, speed, peace, war, discipline, freedom from discipline and so on.

I like to believe that most Americans would agree on which of those values might serve as the animating ideas for a great civilization, but it's not my intention to review here the moral undergirding of our society.

I deal with a side of American society in which the existence of certain ruling ideals is visible and inescapable. I see children being taught, the sick healed, the aged cared for, the crippled rehabilitated, the talented nurtured and developed, the mentally ill treated, the weak strengthened.

Those tasks are not done by unbelieving people. I believe that when we are being most true to ourselves as Americans we are seeking a society in which every young person has the opportunity to grow to his full stature in every way, a society in which no one is irreparably damaged by circumstances that can be prevented.

The release of human potential, the enhancement of individual dignity, the liberation of the human spirit—those are the deepest and truest goals to be conceived by the hearts and minds of the American people.

And those are ideas that can sustain and strengthen a great civilization—if we believe in them, if we are honest about them, if we have the courage and stamina to live for them.

Such ideas cannot be said to be alive unless they live in the acts of men. We must build them into our laws and our institutions and our ways of dealing with one another. That is slow, arduous, painful work, and you don't get many cheers while you're doing it.

But it is the great work of our generation. Each preceding generation had its great work to perform—founding the nation, conquering the wilderness, settling the land. Ours is to make this a livable society for every American.

THE IMPENDING INSTRUCTION REVOLUTION

Harold E. Mitzel

First, let me explain my choice of the above title. It is fashionable in these days of rhetorical excess to describe change as revolutionary in scope. The mass media remind us daily that revolutions are occurring right under our noses. We hear of (and see) the Social Revolution, the Sexual Revolution, the Technology Revolution, the Student Revolt, the Faculty Revolt, and so on. Apparently any complete or sudden change in the conduct of human affairs, with or without a violent confrontation or an exchange of power, may properly be called a revolution.

It is my thesis that the last three decades of the twentieth century will witness a drastic change in the business of providing instruction in schools and colleges. Change by the year 2000 will be so thoroughgoing that historians will have no difficulty in agreeing that it was a revolution. You will note the omission of words like "teaching" and "learning" in describing the coming revolution. Teaching connotes for most of us an inherently person-mediated activity and the vision of the "stand-up" lecturer comes most immediately to mind. One of the concomitants of the impending change is a major modification of the role of teacher. It is likely that future terms for teacher may be "instructional agent" or "lesson designer" or "instructional programmer." As for learning, we take the position that the word is not a way of describing an *activity* of the student, but rather a way of characterizing change in the student's behavior in some desired direction between two definite time markers. Pask has pointed out that teaching is "exercising control of the instructional environment by arranging scope, sequence, materials, evaluation, and content for students." In other words, instruction is the general term for the process and learning is the product.

My objective is to challenge you with the shape of the instruction revolution, to point out how you as a teacher or administrator can cooperate and cope with it, and to suggest some of the social changes which are currently fueling this revolution.

*Reprinted, with permission, from *Engineering Education.* Copyright 1970 by the American Society for Engineering Education.

Individualized Instruction

At the secondary school level, American educators, beginning with Preston W. Search in the late nineteenth century, have been interested in the goal of individualization. Between 1900 and 1930, disciples of Frederick Burk (see Brubacher and Parkhurst) devised and implemented several laboratory-type plans for self-instruction in the lower schools. These were self-pacing plans for the learner and demanded a great deal of versatility on the part of the teacher. Additional impetus for the theoretical interest of educators in individualization stemmed from the mental testing movement, beginning with the seminal work of Binet about 60 years ago. Early intelligence tests clearly showed differences in speed of task completion among pupils, and these differences were easily confirmed by a teacher's own observations of mental agility. At the practical level, a great deal of individualization took place in rural America's one-room schools. Fifteen to 25 children spread unevenly through ages 6 to 14 necessarily committed the teacher to large doses of individual pupil direction, recitation, and evaluation. With population increases and school consolidations, most village and rural schools began to look like rigidly graded city schools. Teachers found themselves responsible for larger and larger groups of children of approximately the same age and about the same physical size. It is little wonder that some of the zest, enthusiasm, and obviousness of need for individualized teaching was lost. When teachers complained about too-large classes, the lack of time to spend with individual pupils, the wide diversity in pupil ability levels, many not-so-smart administrators introduced "tracking" or "streaming" strategies. Separating children into homogenoues classes according to measured mental ability within age groups has been shown conclusively to fail to increase the achievement levels of groups as a whole. Homogeneous ability grouping has, on the other hand, seriously exacerbated social problems connected with race and economic levels by "ghettoizing" classrooms within the schools, even though the schools served racially and economically mixed neighborhoods.

Whereas the common schools have *some* history of experimentation with individualized instruction methods, higher education, led by the large state universities, has pushed the development of mass communication methods in instruction. The large-group lecture and the adaptation of closed-circuit television are examples of higher education's trend away from individualized instruction. Of course, the outstanding accomplishments of American university graduate schools could never have been achieved without the cost-savings introduced by mass communications techniques in their undergraduate colleges.

Interest in individualized instruction had a surge about 15 years ago when Harvard's B. F. Skinner advocated an education technology built around the use of rather crude teaching machines. It soon became apparent that there was no particular magic in the machines themselves, since they contained only short linear series of questions and answers to word problems called "frames." These programs were quickly put into book form and the programmed text was born. Although it enjoyed initial success with some highly motivated learners, the programmed text has not caught on in either the lower schools or in higher education as a major instructional device. Industry and the military forces seem to have made the best use of programmed texts, perhaps because of a high degree of motivation on the part of many learners in those situations.

Most recently, an educational technique for the lower schools has been developed out of the work of the Learning Research and Development Center at the University of Pittsburgh. The method, called "individually programmed instruction" or IPI, is described by Lindvall and Bolvin, by Glaser, and by Cooley and Glaser. Behind the method lies the careful development of a technology based on precise specification and delineation of educational objectives in behavioral terms. Pupils work individually on a precisely scaled set of materials with frequent interspersed diagnostic quizzes.

It must be clear, even after this sketchy review of the history of individualized instruction, that the concept has been pursued in a desultory fashion. I have heard hour-long conversations on individualization by educators who have only the vaguest notion of what is encompassed by the concept. Let me review five *different* concepts of individualization and acknowledge that I am indebted to Tyler for some of these distinctions.

First, most educators agree that instruction is "individual" when the learner is allowed to proceed through content materials *at a self-determined pace that is comfortable for him.* This concept of self-paced instruction is incorporated into all programmed texts and is perhaps easiest to achieve with reading material and hardest to achieve in a setting that presents content by means of lectures, films, and television. Oettinger, in his witty but infuriating little book, *Run, Computer, Run,* refers to this self-pacing concept of individualization as "rate tailoring."

A second concept of individualized instruction is that the learner should be able *to work at times convenient to him.* The hard realities of academic bookkeeping with the associated paraphernalia of credits, marks, and time-serving schedules make this concept difficult to implement in colleges or in the common schools.

That a learner should *begin instruction in a given subject at a point appropriate to his past achievement* is a third way of looking at individualization. This concept makes the assumption that progress in learning is linear and that the main task is to locate the learner's present position on a universal continuum. Once properly located, he can then continue to the goal. These notions seem to have their optimum validity for well-ordered content like mathematics or foreign languages. In fact, the advanced placement program, which provides college credit for tested subject matter achievement during secondary school, is a gross attempt to get at this kind of individualization.

A fourth concept of individualization is the idea that *learners are inhibited by a small number of easily identifiable skills or knowledges.* The assumption is that the absence of these skills is diagnosable and that remedial efforts through special instructional units can eliminate the difficulty. Colleges and universities seeking to enroll a higher proportion of their students from among the culturally disadvantaged and the economically deprived will be forced to bring this concept to bear if they wish to maintain current academic standards.

A fifth concept is that individualization can be achieved by *furnishing the learner with a wealth of instructional media from which to choose.* Lectures, audio tapes, films, books, etc., all with the same intellectual content, could theoretically be made available to the learner. The underlying notion is that the learner will instinctively choose the communication medium or combination of media that enable him to do his best work. The research evidence to support this viewpoint and practice is not at all strong. Perhaps even more persuasive than the lack of evidence is the vanity of instructors who cannot understand why a student would choose a film or an audio tape in preference to the instructor's own lively, stimulating, and informative lectures.

I have reviewed five concepts of individualization which have some credence in education, but by far the most prevalent interpretation is the one of self-pacing, or rate tailoring. These notions lead us directly to the idea of adaptive education in responsive environments, which I want to discuss shortly. But first, one more distinction. "Individual instruction," where one studies in isolation from other learners, should probably be distinguished from "individualized instruction," where the scope, sequence, and time of instruction are tailored in one or more of the five ways I have just described. "Individualized instruction" can still be in a group setting and, in fact, was commonly practiced in rural one-room schools, as mentioned earlier. On the other hand, "individual instruction" can be singularly rigid, monotonous, and unresponsive to the needs of the learner. You could, for instance, take programmed text material which is designed for individualized instruction and put it into an educational television format. Each frame could be shown to a large group of students for a short time, allowing the students to pick a correct option and then going on to another frame. This procedure would be individual instruction with a vengeance. But it forces a kind of lockstep on students of varying abilities and interests that is the antithesis of "individualized instruction."

Adaptive Education

I predict that the impending instruction revolution will shortly bypass the simple idea of individualizing instruction and move ahead to the more sophisticated notion of providing *adaptive education* for school and college learners. By adaptive education we mean the tailoring of subject matter presentations to fit the special requirements and capabilities of each learner. The ideal is that no learner should stop short of his ultimate achievement in an area of content because of idiosyncratic hang-ups in his particular study strategies.

We have seen how the concept of individualized instruction has been pretty well arrested at the level of encouraging the learner to vary and control his task completion time. Many additional, more psychologically oriented variables will have to be brought into play to achieve the goals of adaptive education, as well as the adoption of individualizing techniques. We know a great deal about individual differences among people in regard to their sensory inputs, their reaction times, their interests, their values and preferences, and their organizational strategies in "mapping" the outside world. What we do not know very much about is the extent to which, or how, these easily tested, individual difference variables affect the acquisition and retention of new knowledge. Psychological learning theory has been preoccupied with the study of variables in extremely simple stimulus-response situations, and investigations of meaningful learning phenomena have clearly dealt with human subjects as if they were all cut from the same bolt. The exception to this observation is, of course, the variable of measured mental ability, which has been shown to be related to achievement and has been carefully controlled in many learning experiments involving human subjects.

Essential to the idea of adaptive education is the means of utilizing new knowledge about individual differences among learners to bring a highly tailored instructional product to the student. As long as we are dealing with static or canned linear presentations such as those contained in books, films, video tapes, and some lectures, there seems to be little incentive to try to discover what modifications in instructional materials would optimize learning for each student. To plug this important gap in the drive toward vastly improved learning, the modern digital computer seems to have great promise. About a decade ago, Rath, Anderson, and Br ainerd suggested the application of the computer to teaching tasks and actually programmed some associative learning material. In the intervening decade, a number of major universities, medical schools, industries, and military establishments have been exploring the use of the computer in instruction. Five years ago we instituted a computer-assisted instruction laboratory at Penn State and have been trying to perfect new instructional techniques within the constraints of available hardware and computer operating systems. There are, according to my estimate, some 35 to 40 active computer-assisted instruction (CAI) installations operating in the world today, and fewer than 100 completed, semester-length courses or their equivalent. Almost none of these courses have been constructed according to the ideals I mentioned for adaptive education. Indeed, many of them look like crude, made-over versions of programmed textbooks, but this does not disturb me when I recall that the earliest automobiles were designed to look like carriages without the horses. The fact is that the modern computer's information storage capacity and decision logic have given us a glimpse of what a dynamic, individualized instruction procedure could be, and some insight into how this tool might be brought to bear to achieve an adaptive quality education for every student. We do not claim that the achievement of this goal is just around the corner or that every school and college can implement it by the turn of the century. We do believe that progress toward a program of adaptive education will be the big difference between our best schools and our mediocre ones at the end of the next three decades.

What individual difference variables look most promising for adapting instruction to the individual student via CAI? At Penn State we are testing the idea that a person learns best if he is rewarded for correctness with his most preferred type of reinforcement. Thus some students will, we believe, learn more rapidly if they receive encouragement in the form of adult approval. Others will perform better if they receive actual tokens for excellence in the program, the tokens being exchangeable for candy, cokes, or other wanted objects. Still others respond to competitive situations in which they are given evidence of the superiority or inferiority of their peers. It is a fairly simple matter to determine a learner's reward preference in advance of instruction and to provide him with a computer-based program in which the information feedback is tailored to his psychological preference.

Perhaps the most dynamic and relevant variable on which to base an adaptive program of instruction is the learner's immediate past history of responses. By programming the computer to count and evaluate the correctness of the 10 most recent responses, it is possible to determine what comes next for each learner according to a prearranged schedule. For example, four or fewer correct out of the most recent 10 might dictate branching into shorter teaching steps with heavy prompting and large amounts of practice material. A score of five to seven might indicate the need for just a little more practice material, and eight or more correct out of the 10 most recent problems would suggest movement onto a fast "track" with long strides through the computer-presented content. The dynamic part of this adaptive mechanism is that the computer constantly updates its performance information about each learner by dropping off the learner's response to the tenth problem back as it adds on new performance information from a just-completed problem.

There are two rather distinct strategies for presenting subject matter to learners. One is *deductive,* in which a rule, principle, or generalization is presented, followed by examples. The other strategy is *inductive* and seeks, by means of a careful choice of illustrative examples, to lead the learner into formulating principles and generalizations on his own initiative. In the lower schools, inductive method is called "guided discovery" and has been found useful by many teachers. Our belief at the Penn State CAI Laboratory is that these two presentation strategies have their corollaries in an individual differences variable and that, for some students, learning will be facilitated by the deductive approach; others will learn more rapidly and with better retention if an inductive mode is adopted. A strong program of adaptive education would take these and other identifiable learner variables into account in the instructional process.

Evaluation and Student Appraisal

One of the important concomitants of the instruction revolution will be a drastic revision in the approach to learner evaluation and grading practices by faculty. Even the moderate students on campus are saying that letter grades are anachronistic. On many campuses, including our own, students have petitioned for, and won, the right to receive "satisfactory" and "unsatisfactory" evaluations of their work in certain non-major courses. Other students have attacked all grades as a manifestation of a coercive, competitive, materialistic society. Without admitting to be a tool of a sick society, we should change this part of the business of higher education as rapidly as possible.

It seems to me that most formal instruction has been predicated on the notion that a course is offered between two relatively fixed points in time. In addition, the tools of instruction, such as lectures, textbooks, references, and computer services, are all relatively fixed and are the same for all learners. To be sure, the students do vary the amount of time they spend with these tools. Even there, the college catalogue tells the students that they should all study three hours outside of class for every hour in class. At the close of the period of instruction or end of the course, usually the end of the term, we give the students an achievement test that is constructed in a way that will maximize the *differences* among their scores. To get this seemingly important differentiation between our students in achievement, we have to ask extremely difficult questions. Sometimes we even go so far as to ask questions about footnotes in the text. In fact, we often have to ask questions on topics or objectives that we have made no attempt to teach. Our rationalization for this tactic is that we want the students to be able to *transfer* their knowledge. After obtaining the achievement examination results, we consult the trusty "normal curve" and assign A's, B's, C's, D's, and F's according to our interpretation of the grading mores of the institution. With time and materials fixed, we are essentially capitalizing upon the same human abilities that are measured by intelligence tests. Thus it is not surprising that intelligence and teacher-assigned grades tend to be highly correlated.

We could, as collegiate educators, do society and ourselves a big favor by making a fundamental shift in our approach to teaching and examining. (Incidentally, we might generate some relevance "points" with our students.) First, we should say (and mean) that our job is helping each of our students to achieve *mastery* over some operationally defined portion of subject matter. Furthermore, failure by any student putting forth an effort is a failure on our part as teachers, or a breakdown of the selection system. Now, to do this job we will have to get rid of a lot of the present practices and irrelevancies of higher education. There is no point in maintaining an *adversary* system in the classroom, with the students against the instructor and each of the students against each other. Society may think that it wants us to mark our students on a competitive scale, but how much more sensible it would be if we could say, on the basis of accumulated examination evidence, that John Jones has achieved 85 percent of the objectives in Engineering 101, rather than say that he got a "B." If our job is to help the student master the subject matter or come close—say, achieve 90 percent or greater of the objectives—then we are going to have to adapt our instruction to him. As a starter, we could individualize by letting the student pace his own instruction. We know, for example, from preliminary work with class-sized groups in computer-assisted instruction, that the slowest student will take from three to five times as long as the fastest student in a rich environment of individualized teaching material. During a recent computer-mediated in-service teacher education course presented by Penn State in Dryden, Virginia, to 129 elementary school teachers, the average completion time was 21 clock hours. The fastest student finished in 12 hours and the slowest took 58 hours.

Student evaluations should also be based on the concept that an achievable mastery criterion exists for each course. We should no longer engage in the sophistry of classical psychometrics, in which we prepare a test or examination deliberately designed to make half the students get half of the items wrong. It is true that such a test optimally discriminates among the learners, which we justify by claiming need for competitive marking information. If, however, 50 percent of the students get 50 percent of the items wrong, then either we are asking the wrong questions or there is something seriously wrong with our non-adaptive instructional program.

Under optimum circumstances, we might get an enlightened view of the faculty's need to adopt mastery-type student evaluation procedures and we might get professors to talk less, but we would still be faced with the psychological problem of instructor dominance or instructor power. The power over students which the "giving" of grades confers on professors would not be yielded easily by many in college teaching today. As Pogo says: "We have met the enemy and he is us."

If we, as faculty and administrators in higher education, embraced the notion of teaching for student mastery by means of individually adaptive programs, then these are some of the concomitants:

1. Instructors would have to state their course objectives in behavioral terms.

2. Achievement tests keyed to course objectives would have to be constructed and used as both diagnostic placement and end-of-course determiners.

3. The bachelor's degree might take from two to eight years instead of the

traditional four, because of the wide variability in mastery achievement.

4. Instead of telling three times a week, instructors might have to spend their time listening to students individually and in small groups where progress toward subject mastery required careful monitoring.

5. Instead of being primarily concerned with a discipline or with a specialization, those who profess for undergraduates would have to make the student and his knowledge their first concern.

6. Evaluation for promotion and salary increments for college teachers would be based on measured amounts of growth exhibited by their students and on numbers of students who achieved a specific mastery criterion.

If professors and deans ignore the reasoned demands for reform of undergraduate instruction which come from the students, the government, and a concerned citizenry, then the revolution will be ugly and wrenching. The so-called "free universities," with their obvious shortcomings, are already harbingers of the chaos into which traditional higher education could slip if there is no responsiveness on the part of a majority of academicians to the need for change.

In the current wave of student unrest, many of the best articulated issues are local in nature, like the quality of food in the cafeteria or the relaxation of dormitory visiting rules for members of the opposite sex. Underneath these surface issues, however, lies the *one big issue,* which the students themselves haven't spelled out clearly. This is the issue of the relevance of contemporary collegiate instruction for students' lives. It seems to me students are saying, albeit not very clearly, that they want some wise adult to care about them, to pay attention to them, to listen and to guide them. We sit on our status quo's and ignore their cry for help at our peril.

Increasing Heterogeneity

Part of the fuel breeding the revolution in instruction is the increasing heterogeneity in mental ability and scholastic preparation among college students. The combined power of the teaching faculty, regional accrediting agencies, and shortage of spaces for students has, until recently, enabled many public universities to become increasingly selective. In fact, prestige among higher education institutions has been closely correlated with the norms for entrance test scores. Even the great state universities, which began under the land-grant aegis as people's colleges, have a kind of "elitist" aura about them. Rising aspirations of minority groups, particularly blacks, have pointed up the fact that the poor, the disadvantaged, and the dark-skinned of our society do not share equally in whatever benefits a postsecondary college experience confers. A recent study and report by John Egerton for the National Association of State Universities and Land-Grant Colleges was based on 80 public universities which enroll almost one-third of the nation's college students. He found that less than two percent of the graduate and undergraduate students were Negro in these institutions and that less than one percent of the faculty were black. Yet approximately 11 percent of the total U.S. population is black. It seems irrefutable that, with society's new awareness of the inequality in higher education, university entrance standards will have to be lowered for sizeable groups of blacks who have been poorly educated in the nation's secondary schools. Accounts of City University of New York's open admissions plan for fall, 1970, provide ample proof of the beginning of this trend, and Healy's recent article firms up the humanitarian and social theory for the change in this great university. The lowering of entrance requirements will inevitably increase the heterogeneity of scholastic skills which makes the conventional teaching job so difficult.

Another source for increasing individual differences among college undergraduates is their stiffening resistance to required courses. Students clearly want more freedom of choice in devising their educational programs. They want to determine what subjects are relevant to their lives and are increasingly impatient with elaborate prerequisites and multi-course sequences. Although the activists are not likely to win a complete victory on this score, the pressure which they generate will serve to breach the walls and gates around courses that have carefully been built by faculty over the years in order to make the conventional job of teaching somewhat more manageable. In addition to the student rejection of required courses, there is a corresponding need for the teaching of interdisciplinary subjects. Students see, perhaps more clearly than the faculty, that solution of the nation's problems such as urban decay, congestion, air and water pollution, and war and peace are not going to be solved by the unitary application of knowledge from traditional disciplines. For purposes of this discussion, the drive toward more interdisciplinary courses of study can only increase the heterogeneity among students which the faculty has labored to minimize.

Conclusion

I have argued that we are now living with the early stages of a revolution in instruction which will be more or less complete by the turn of the century. The major changes will be primarily characterized by individualization of instruction leading to sophisticated systems of adaptive education. Two concomitants of the revolution which seriously concern college faculty and administrators are the need for new fundamental concepts of student appraisal and adaptation to increasing heterogeneity among the students in our charge.

THE SCHOOLS VS. EDUCATION

John I. Goodlad

The years from 1957 to 1967 constituted the Education Decade for the United States. It began with Sputnik and the charge to education to win the cold war; it ended with a hot war and the growing realization that education is a long-term answer to mankind's problems and must not be confused with short-termed social engineering. The danger is that we are becoming disillusioned with education, without realizing that we are only beginning to try it.

During the Education Decade, the school years were extended upward and downward, the school curriculum was revised from top to bottom, the Elementary and Secondary Education Act of 1965 brought the federal government into education as never before, the schools became both a focal point for social protest and a vehicle for social reform, and schooling joined politics and world affairs as leading topics of social discourse. "Innovation" and "revolution" were used interchangeably in discussing the changes taking place in the schools.

But the education scene today remains confusing. Put on one pair of glasses and the schools appear to be moving posthaste toward becoming centers of intense, exciting learning, marked by concern for the individual. Put on another, and they appear to be mired in tradition, insensitive to pressing social problems, and inadequate to the demands of learning.

Where are the schools today? How widespread have been the changes during the decade since Sputnik? What kind of changes are needed in the 1970s, and what lies ahead for the balance of the century?

While conducting studies of new approaches to school curricula during the early 1960s, I visited many schools and classrooms. Although the Education Decade was well underway, the reforms it espoused were not conspicuously present. Was the sample of schools visited inadequate, or were proposed changes losing their momentum before reaching their target? Several colleagues joined me in an effort to probe more deeply as we visited some 260 kindergarten through third-grade

*John L. Goodlad, "The Schools vs. Education," from *Saturday Review,* April 19, 1968, pp. 59-61, 80-1. Copyright 1969 Saturday Review, Inc. Reprinted by permission of *Saturday Review* and the author.

classrooms in 100 schools clustered in or around the major cities of thirteen states.

If the most frequently discussed and recommended educational practices of the Education Decade were already implemented, what would constitute a checklist of expectations? The following would seem reasonable. First, teaching would be characterized by efforts to determine where the student is at the *outset* of instruction, to diagnose his attainments and problems, and to base subsequent instruction on the results of this diagnosis. Second, learning would be directed toward "learning how to learn," toward self-sustaining inquiry rather than the memorization and regurgitation of facts. Third, this inquiry would carry the student out of confining classrooms and into direct observation of physical and human phenomena. Fourth, classrooms would be characterized by a wide variety of learning materials—records, tapes, models, programed materials, film strips, pamphlets, and television—and would not be dominated by textbooks. Fifth, attention to and concern for the individual and individual differences would show through clearly in assignments, class discussions, use of materials, grouping practices, and evaluation. Sixth, teachers would understand and use such learning principles as reinforcement, motivation, and transfer of training. Seventh, visitors would see vigorous, often heated, small and large group discussions, with the teacher in the background rather than the forefront. Eighth, one would find rather flexible school environments—marked by little attention to grade levels— and extensive use of team-teaching activities involving groups of teachers, older pupils, parents, and other persons in the teaching-learning process. And, certainly, it would be reasonable to expect to find innovative ways of dealing with special educational problems such as those presented by environmentally handicapped children.

Although these expectations seemed reasonable at the outset of our visits to schools, they did not constitute an accurate description of what we found. We were unable to discern much attention to pupil needs, attainments, or problems as a basis for beginning instruction, nor widespread provision for individual opportunities to learn. Most classes were taught as a group, covering essentially the same ground for all students at approximately the same rate of speed. Teaching was predominantly telling and questioning by the teacher, with children responding one by one or occasionally in chorus. In all of this, the textbook was the most highly visible instrument of learning and teaching. If records, tapes, films, film strips, supplementary materials, and other aids to learning were in the schools we visited, we rarely saw them. When small groups of students worked together, the activities engaged in by each group member were similar, and bore the mark of the teacher's assignment and expectations. Rarely did we find small groups intensely in pursuit of knowledge; rarely did we find individual pupils at work in self-sustaining inquiry. Popular innovations of the decade—non-grading, team teaching, "discovery" learning, and programed instruction—were talked about by teachers and principals alike but were rarely in evidence.

On a more general and impressionistic level, teachers and students did not appear to be intensively involved in their work. Only occasionally did we encounter a classroom aura of excitement, anticipation, and spontaneity; when we did, it was almost invariably a kindergarten class. This is not to say that classroom inhabitants were uninvolved but rather to suggest that it may be erroneous to assume that teaching and learning in the schools, more than other human enterprises, are characterized by excitement and enthusiasm. On the positive side, however, the teachers we observed were warm and supportive, and not sadistic as some polemicists have pictured them to be.

From the data, we were unable to differentiate practices in schools enrolling a high proportion of disadvantaged or minority group children from practices in other schools. Our descriptions of classrooms enrolling predominantly Mexican-American children, for example, were not distinguishable from our descriptions in general. Nor were there marked differences in our respective descriptions of classrooms in the inner city, on the fringe of the urban environment, and in suburbia.

It is dangerous to generalize about something as large, complex, and presumably diverse as schooling in the United States, or even about the first four years of it. As far as our sample of schools is concerned, however, we are forced to conclude that much of the so-called educational reform movement has been blunted on the classroom door.

Yet, the responsibility for this situation does not rest entirely with schoolteachers and principals. The elementary schools were anything but the "palaces" of an affluent society. In fact, they looked more like the artifacts of a society that did not really care about its schools, a society that expressed its disregard by creating schools less suited to human habitation than its prisons. These artifacts reflect the strange notion that learning proceeds best in groups of thirty, that teachers are not to converse with each other, that learning should be conducted under rather uncomfortable circumstances, and that schools proceed best with their tasks when there is little or no traffic with the outside world.

We had hoped to conduct sustained interviews with the teachers we observed, but there were rarely quiet, attractive places to confer. We held our interviews on the run or, more favorably, when we were able to have breakfast or dinner together. These teachers wanted to talk about education: what "good" things we had observed elsewhere; what we thought about current innovations; whether we had any suggestions for improving the teaching we had just observed; and on and on. Interestingly, those with whom we talked had a rather favorable image of what they were doing in the classroom; they thought they were individualizing instruction, teaching inductively, and encouraging self-propelled learning. Neither principals nor teachers were able to articulate clearly just what they thought to be most important for their schools to accomplish. And neither group was very clear on changes that should be effected in the near future.

Both our observations alone and those with teachers lead to several disquieting conclusions. Public schooling probably is the only large-scale enterprise in this country that does not provide for systematic updating of the skills and abilities of its employees and for payment of the costs involved. Teachers are on their own as far as their in-service education is concerned, in an environment designed for "telling" others, yet one that is grossly ill-suited to intellectual pursuits with peers. Teachers, we presume, can readily cast aside their old, inappropriate ways and acquire markedly different ones through some process of osmosis.

Sixteen or more years of schooling should educate teachers and others for self-renewal—and this frequently is the case. But general failure to do so for large numbers of people constitutes the greatest failure of our educational system. In the colleges as well as in the lower schools, the processes and fruits of human experience are so cut up in the curriculum and so obfuscated by detail that cohesiveness, relationships, and relevance are obscured.

Another aspect of our educational malaise is that an enormous amount of energy goes into merely maintaining the system. Studies have shown that administrators favor teachers who maintain orderly classrooms, keep accurate records, and maintain stable relations with parents and the community. Other studies reveal that middle managers in the educational system, such as principals and supervisors, tend to be recruited from among teachers who demonstrate these orderly qualities. Because they are rewarded for maintaining the system, administrators are not likely either to challenge it or to reward subordinates who do.

Just as teachers and principals appear to be uncertain as to what their schools are for, the communities they serve provide no clear sense of direction or guidelines. There is evidence to suggest that parents are somewhat more favorably disposed toward educational change than are teachers or school administrators, but legions of educators who push at the forefront of innovative practice stand ready to show their community-inflicted scars. Many parents are more interested in changes in the abstract or for someone else than in changes involving their own children. Social change is a formidable enterprise under the best of conditions; schooling too often presents only the worst of circumstances, with resistance being built into both the setting and the internal structure.

It should come as no surprise, then, that comprehensive experiments in schooling are the rarest of all educational phenomena. Small wonder that teachers practice so little individualizing instruction, inductive teaching, non-grading, team teaching, or other recently recommended practices. They have not seen them. If teachers are to change, they must see models of what they are going to change to; they must practice under guidance the new behaviors called for in the exemplary models. If teachers are to change, the occupation itself must have built into it the necessary provisions for self-renewal. The creation of these conditions is an important agenda item for the decade ahead.

Seers of bygone decades occasionally asked whether our schools had outlived their usefulness—and we laughed. The question is no longer funny. The schools are conspicuously ill-suited to the needs of at least 30 per cent of their present clientele: the large numbers of children from minority groups who live in harsh environments; the tens of thousands who suffer from crippling mental, physical, and emotional handicaps; and a few whose rare gifts separate them sharply from their peers. But the lack of "fit" between school and client extends into other realms until one is forced to ask whether our educational system serves even 50 per cent of its clientele in reasonably satisfying ways. Learning disabilities evidenced in the primary grades often go undiagnosed, persisting throughout life and seriously limiting human relations participation. Talents in music, art and creative writing lie largely outside the school's scope and are usually brought to fruitition in the home where parents can afford to, or not at all where parents cannot. The human models in these fields, so necessary to refinement of childhood talent, are inaccessible to the school because of teacher certification restrictions or sheer failure to recognize their powerful role in educating the young.

It is also questionable whether those students who appear to be adjusting well are acquiring desirable traits and repressing undesirable ones. Success in school seems to assure further success in school; good grades predict good grades. But academic success neither assures nor predicts good work habits, good citizenship, happiness, compassion, or other human virtues. The incidences of dropouts, non-promotion, alienation, and minimal learning reinforce our apprehension that schools have become or are fast becoming obsolete. They appear to have been designed for a different culture, a different conception of learning and teaching, and a different clientele.

The task of rehabilitating the schools, then, is indeed formidable. We dare not ask whether we *should* rehabilitate our schools, although this is a good question. Impotent and irrelevant though much schooling may be, the schools are at present the only educational institution deliberately created and maintained for inculcating something of man's heritage, for developing the basic tools of literacy, and for instilling some powers of rational thought and criticism. Although our civilization abounds in educational institutions and media, from scuba diving to television, none is centrally committed to this basic, cultural role. By seeking to rehabilitate the *educational* role of the school, rather than its various ancillary functions (baby-sitting, social stratification, economic investment, etc.), perhaps we will keep the meaning of education before us, experiment with improved means, and ultimately transfer the process to new and better institutions should the schools fail us and we them.

A brief analysis of television serves both to illustrate what I mean by rehabilitating the *educational* role of the school and to project us into the varied possibilities of an electronic educational future. Some of us still remember those wonderful evenings of intellectual discourse with friends, before that glass-faced monster took over. At first, exposure to the glass face meant only a few hours' diversion each week, watching the favorite programs we had only heard before. But now there are "hot" and "cool" stimuli, Marshall McLuhan's non-linear communication, and a television generation. From birth to high school graduation, today's young man or woman spends an average of 15,000 hours before television sets and just over 12,000 hours (1,000 hours each year) in school. I do not believe that these hours of schooling provide anything like an antidote for the formidable array of violence, cruelty, dishonesty, prejudice, and inhumanity to man provided by newspapers, magazines, movies, and television.

Our schools have not adopted television; nor has television adopted the schools. An occasional educational television program becomes a "tack-on" to the curriculum. During the Education Decade, a national network occasionally found it mildly profitable to feature a "special" on the schools. Meanwhile, however, television has gone about its business and the schools have gone about theirs. Television has not yet taken on the essentially educational function of humanizing the content of experience for teaching and learning. It seeks only to entertain, to hold the viewer. But neither have the schools been markedly successful in producing an intensely human environment in which children are caught up in man's adventure, whether in the arts, politics, the sea, or outer space.

Herein lies our dilemma. On one hand, a powerful medium has caught the attention—indeed, the very lives—of our children. But it lacks significant substance to nurture a civilization and appears to care not, despite its protestations, whether it uplifts or debases. On the other hand, the only institution charged specifically with the performance of educational functions fails to grip a significant portion of its clientele. Unfulfilled educational promise lies between.

In schools run by humans, we have not succeeded in developing intensely humanistic learning environments—not in process, not in content, and not in perspective. The schools do not, in general, foster man's most creative traits, nor grapple with his great ideas, nor relate these ideas and talents to the contemporary environment where man's dramas are continuously re-enacted. The schools are bogged down with routine, trivialities, and the lesser literacies. In the rat race to cover what is in the textbook, schooling has lost sight of education as an end in itself and has become instrumental to the next textbook, the next grade, higher education, and the Gross National Product. And now—at a critical time in the history of schools, education, and man—an electronic teacher of great power, the computer, comes into this human-based environment. The instructional era now on the horizon is one of man-machine interaction. Will the computer dehumanize learning and teaching even more? The choice is ours.

On an experimental basis, computers are demonstrating their usefulness in teaching spelling, mathematics, reading, and a host of cognitive skills. Tapes, video-screens, records, and other devices are combined with computer memory to produce an unique instructional system of sight, sound, and touch. Current writings on computer-aided instruction present a picture of instructional efficiency and the freeing of human teachers to do those truly *human* educational things. But what are these things? And have teachers been prepared to engage in them?

Already it is clear that computers, unlike television, are more efficient by far than humans in performing routine instructional tasks and in assuring error-free performance on the part of learners in those basic skills to which teachers devote so much time. It is clear, then, that computers have a viable, albeit threatening, role in the schools. The critical problem is how computers and people are to live together productively in the school environment. If educators continue to confuse instruct ion in the basic skills with education, then teachers will merely monitor the computer and, in time, become its servant. Under such circumstances, in due time, there would be no need for schools as other than custodial agencies, since computer terminals might more readily and profitably be placed in homes. St ate and local budgets, together with some transportation problems, would be substantially relieved.

A happier alternative, however, is that there will be a separation of those instructional tasks most appropriate for electronic teachers from those educational activities most appropriate for human teachers. Efficiently taught in the basic tools of their culture, young people would have much more time than is now the case to pursue education as a way of life. With the processes of providing these tools freed from the restraints of the human time and energy for teaching them, they would become readily accessible to all. But this alternative, too, destroys or drastically changes the school as we have known it.

The tireless computer is fully capable of working twenty-four hours a day every day. It can recall the same material and teach the same lesson over and over, and it can provide subject matters singly or in various combinations and sequences. No need, then to confine teaching to the hours between 9 in the morning and 3 in the afternoon; nor to delay certain subjects until high school or college; nor to complete sixteen units of work in four years. Suddenly, we come to realize that schools as we know them are largely the product of limitations and conventions in the use of human energy. Introduce a new source of ,instructional energy and learning is unshackled.

But still to be accounted for in schooling are "those educational activities most appropriate for *human* teachers." Their human character demands libraries, seminar rooms, museums, studios, art galleries, courts of law, government offices, airports, housing developments, fields, ponds, counseling centers, hospitals, quiet study corners, work experiences, visits with exemplary models of accomplishment, and on and on. Take the educational environment beyond school and classroom and learning can be humanized.

With fundamental learning effectively taken care of, perhaps we can then correct our myopic perspective that equates education with schooling, and go beyond the utilitarian boundaries we have set for both ideas. We can then tend to the urgent need to value education for its own sake, to grapple with education's first question: What kinds of human beings do we seek? But even before looking toward what we want to be, perhaps we should ask fundamental questions about where we are. To what extent is each individual being provided with opportunities to develop his unique potentialities? To what extent is each individual developing a deep sense of personal worth—the kind of selfhood that is prerequisite to self transcendence? To what extent are our young people coming into critical possession of their culture? And to what extent are our people developing a mankind identity—an identity that transcends all men in all times and in all places?

2

OBSERVER AIDES

AT THE TEACHER'S RIGHT HAND

William Rioux

Each weekday morning for nine months of the year, more than 43 million Americans meet for another round of give and take—43 million students taking what 1.6 million teachers have to give in the Nation's elementary and secondary schools.

On the face of it, the 25 to 1 student-teacher ratio doesn't seem too bad. Under ideal conditions a teacher should accomplish quite a lot in a six-hour school day—if, that is, the teacher could devote those hours only to teaching, to awakening the curiosity of the student to the world about him.

But much of what America's teachers have to do during a school day bears little relationship to the awakening of student curiosity. Far too much of the teacher's time is taken up by endless chores that are essential but inconsequential: supervising playgrounds; lugging a slide projector and screen into class and setting them up; acting as observer of several hundred children distributing what seem like equal portions of food to their mouths and to the floor; arranging for a bus to carry children to the zoo (and sometimes driving the bus); phoning parents to arrange a meeting about a child's poor work; and marking endless pages of multiple-choice questions.

All of these tasks must be done and many others, too. But why take a teacher's time away from teaching to do them? If we are reorganizing our efforts to improve education, we cannot afford to pass lightly over the fundamental need of matching jobs to skills, of giving teachers the maximum time and opportunity to teach.

Lawyers have secretaries and clerks, doctors have nurses and technicians, college professors have graders and assistants. Teachers have only themselves. And that is not enough.

Help for harried teachers could well come through an aide or assistant trained to function at a level below the professional and under the professional's direct

*From William J. Rioux, "At the Teacher's Right Hand," in *Principles and Practice of Teaching: Selected Readings,* edited by John F. Ohles, reprinted from *American Education,* Vol. 2, Dec. 1965-Jan. 1966. Reprinted by permission.

supervision. These "subprofessionals," handling non-teaching functions, can serve as the teacher's secretary and good right arm. Their employment in the schools will permit far more effective use of the professional teacher and increase the schools' resources.

Thus far, America's low-income areas, where the need to improve schooling is critical, have benefited most from the use of subprofessionals in the schools. Last summer some 46,000 teacher aides were used in preschool programs throughout the country:

- In Akron, Ohio, 33 teacher aides were recruited to assist teachers in classroom activities. High school students were selected as tutors to work with children under a teacher's direction.
- In Chicago, Illinois, 22 teacher aides were used to assist teachers with preschool children.

We need a corps of subprofessionals to back up the thin line of professionals, to perform the hundreds of routine tasks which now diminish America's teaching time.

How should they be used? I offer the following list of roles with no attempt to be comprehensive. Superintendents, principals, and especially teachers can readily extend the list.

Assisting as a teaching team member. The aide takes attendance, corrects true-false or multiple-choice test papers, duplicates materials, assigned books and lockers, obtains library materials for use under the teacher's direction, helps students on special projects, and supports the teacher's authority and maintains discipline in the classrooms.

Monitoring study centers. The aide attends to details of room organization, attendance, and student behavior.

Managing audiovisual equipment. The increasing use of classroom equipment —tape recorders, teaching machines, slide projectors—calls for one aid in a medium-sized school of 500 to 800 pupils, two for a school of 1,000 or more. The aide answers requests for audiovisual equipment, instructs students in its use, understands maintenance and minor repairs, and keeps time-use records. While the teacher is busy lecturing on the slides about to be shown, for example, the aide sets up the equipment, plugs in the projector, and adjusts the screen. After the teacher has used the equipment, the aide takes it to storage or to the next class.

Assisting on field trips. On trips to museums, zoos, historical sites, and other community resources, the aide makes arrangements in accord with regulations of the institution to be visited. The aide also keeps attendance records, maintains discipline, and gets the children in and out of buses and buildings. The aide may attend orientation sessions on community resources and recommend field trips to teachers.

Helping on playgrounds. The aide manages, controls, and distributes playground equipment. Under the teacher's general supervision, the aide conducts exercises and games and polices the area after play period.

Helping school nurses and doctors. The aide assists in arranging medical examinations, provides basic maintenance of clinical facilities, helps in emergencies, and handles other duties assigned by the school nurse or doctor.

Advising case workers and gathering information. The aide, informed about the school neighborhood, may advise administrators or case workers about detrimental home situations that may have escaped professional attention. The aide may also gather information for surveys or research projects aimed at promoting a better understanding of the area served by the school.

Strengthening school-community relations. The aide explains school programs, rules, plans, services, and policies to parents in an attempt to increase parental support and involvement in school affairs.

Assisting the preschool program. The aide, working under a trained teacher of preschool children, hands out materials to the children and collects them when the project is finished. The aide conducts storytelling sessions, enabling the teacher to divide the class into more effective groups.

Counseling. The aide helps counseling staffs make appointments and cares for children of parents being interviewed. The aide follows up cases to make sure that referrals to community agencies are made.

Where are these teachers' aides to come from?

Thus far, the largest potential pool for subprofessional talent has been in the low-income group, which has supplied teachers' aides under recent educational programs for combatting poverty. Students in late junior high school and high school, as well as adults (housewives and college students), served admirably in last summer's programs.

For a continuity of effort, however, the hard facts of recruitment and training must be faced. Many candidates will not have graduated from high school, perhaps not even from junior high school. In converting these candidates into valuable subprofessionals, schools must establish criteria. What will they be?

Shall we say that no person with less than an eighth-grade education will be considered? Or will we consider attainment as low as the fifth grade and devise training programs suited to this level? What kind of programs would they be?

Many large, urban school systems have the facilities to train subprofessionals. Certainly this possibility should be considered. Each school should carefully weigh the goals, programs, procedures, and policies before determining whether or how it will train subprofessionals. It is entirely possible, for example, for a school in this work to engage in basic literacy training.

Generally, it would seem better to train subprofessionals in some place other than public schools. A survey might well be made of physical facilities and personnel available in colleges, universities, and industries. The best training grounds might prove to be community and junior colleges, technical institutes, and semi-professional schools.

Once the training of the first teaching assistants is finished, where will they be employed? Forward-looking school systems will very likely be happy to have them —as long as money is available and aides demonstrate the value of their contribution.

Many systems, of course, may be reluctant to employ subprofessionals, a reluctance that may permeate the staff until its members recognize that these aides would relieve a teacher of time-consuming details and permit better fulfillment of his professional task. The school administration would wisely rely on teachers to suggest what jobs could be handled by teachers' aides. This list would undoubtedly contain chiefly the mechanical chores that have burdened teachers for years.

Only as teachers and administrators see at first hand the contributions that can be made by subprofessionals, only as professionals are freed to be more professional, only as they witness the reliability of teaching aides, will headway be made in destroying the myth that subprofessionals usurp teachers' prerogatives and that all classroom-related functions require professional training.

As it succeeds, this initial experience will encourage professional staff members, teachers, and administrators to examine again their day-to-day routine in search of more jobs that can be assigned to aides. Some teachers will be ready for this second stage two months after the start of the program; others not until the end of the first year. Security bred in the first experience will trigger the release of a flood of opportunities.

Efforts might now be made to begin massive subprofessional programs in large city school systems. The experiences of their administrators and teachers would be useful in influencing those in other districts who are reluctant and doubtful. To have the best chance to succeed, however, the program will need to have standards and procedures for selection of subprofessional personnel, inservice training programs, and handling of personnel problems. A school system of any appreciable size—roughly an enrollment of 20,000 students or more—should appoint a full-time person to run the program. Systems of 100,000 or more pupils may require four or five staff members.

Introducing a program of subprofessional help will not be easy in any school system. The problems of recruitment, training, and assignment, as well as latent reluctance to change, will make the first year a trying period. The benefits outweigh the difficulties.

If we are to give our children—*all* our children—a first-rate education, we must give our teachers the best chance to make this desire a reality. This means teachers must give their pupils personal and thoughtful attention.

3

THE NATURE OF STUDENT-TEACHER REACTIONS

A PERCEPTUAL VIEW OF THE ADEQUATE PERSONALITY

Arthur W. Combs

There are two ways we may approach the question of what it means to be a truly healthy, adequate, self-actualizing person. We may attempt to describe what such people are like or we can seek to discover the dynamics of how such people get to be that way. Each of these approaches is, of course, important to our understanding of such people. To provide the professional worker in human relations fields with effective guides for action, however, we need to know particularly the nature of the processes producing adequate personalities. When we understand these "causes," we may be in a favorable position to establish the conditions by which an increasing number of persons can be helped to achieve richer, more satisfying lives.

There are a number of ways in which the problems of causation might be approached. My own favorite frame of reference is to view these problems from a perceptual orientation. Perceptual psychologists have stated, as a basic axiom, that all behavior is a product of the perceptual field of the behaver at the moment of action. That is to say, how any person behaves will be a direct outgrowth of the way things seem to him at the moment of his behaving. To change behavior in this frame of reference requires that we understand the nature of the individual's perceptual field. Knowing the meanings that exist for a particular person, we may then be able to create the conditions which will facilitate changes in his behavior and personality.

Looking at the problem from this frame of reference, I will attempt, in the pages to follow, to describe the truly adequate, self-actualizing person in terms of his characteristic way of seeing himself and the world. How do such persons see themselves and the world in which they live? What is the nature of their perceptual organization and how does this differ from their less fortunate fellows? I have sought the answers to these questions in psychological research and theory, on the one hand, and from my own experience as counselor, teacher, and observer of human relations, on the other. In the course of this study I find myself brought back repeatedly to four characteristics of the perceptual field which always seem to underlie the behavior of truly adequate persons. These characteristics are: (a) a positive view of self, (b) identification with others, (c) openness to experience and acceptance, and (d) a rich and available perceptual field.

A Positive View of Self

Extremely adequate, self-actualizing persons seem to be characterized by an essentially positive view of self. They see themselves as persons who are liked, wanted, acceptable, able; as persons of dignity and integrity, of worth and importance. This is not to suggest that adequate people never have negative ways of regarding themselves. They very well may. The total economy of such persons, however, is fundamentally positive. They see themselves as adequate to deal with life. As Kelley has put it, they see themselves as "enough." Adequate persons have few doubts about their own worth and value and have so large a reservoir of positive regard that negative perceptions are unable to distort the totality. They seem to say, when it is so, "Yes, I have not been as honest, or fair, or good as I should have been," without such self-perceptions destroying the remainder of the personality structure. Negative aspects of self can be taken in stride. Indeed, it is even this essentially positive structure of self that seems to make *possible* the admission of negative self-references.

When we describe the truly adequate person as seeing himself in essentially positive ways, we are speaking of the individual's self concept, not his self-report. We mean by the self concept, the ways in which an individual characteristically sees himself. This is the way he "feels" about himself. The self-report, on the other hand, refers to the way in which an individual *describes* himself when he is asked to do so. These are by no means identical. What a person *says* he is and what he *believes* he is may be very far apart. Indeed, the person who finds it most necessary to claim a positive self may even turn out to be the least adequate. When we describe the adequate personality as feeling essentially positive about himself, it is his self concept we are talking about, not his self-report. It is what he *feels* about himself, not what he says of himself, that determines his behavior.

We are beginning to discover that the kind of self concepts an individual possesses determines, in large measure, whether he is maladjusted or well adjusted. For example, it is not the people who see themselves as liked, wanted, acceptable, worthy and able who constitute our major problems. Such people usually get along fine in our culture and make important contributions both to themselves and to the societies in which they live. It is the people who see themselves as unliked, unwanted, unworthy, unimportant or unable who fill our jails, our mental hospitals and our institutions. These are the maladjusted: the desperate ones, against whom we must protect ourselves, or the defeated ones, who must be sheltered and protected from life. It is the people who feel inadequate, who succumb to brainwashing, who feel so little faith or strength within themselves that they are fair game for any demagogue, who offers security and strength from without. The movement toward personality health is an expression of increased strength of self, just as bodily health is the product of strength of physique. Psychotherapists have repeatedly observed that improvement in mental health is correlated with a stronger, more positive view of self.

Positive View of Self Expressed in Action

A positive view of self gives its owner a tremendous advantage in dealing with life. It provides the basis for great personal strength. Feeling positively about themselves, adequate persons can meet life *expecting* to be successful. Because they expect success, they behave, what is more, in ways that tend to bring it about. "The rich get richer and the poor get poorer." With such a basic security, life can be met straightforwardly. Courage comes naturally. Indeed, behavior which seems courageous to their fellows often to very adequate people seems to be only the "normal" thing.

Because they feel essentially sure about themselves, self-actualizing persons can feel a higher degree of respect for their own individuality and uniqueness. As a consequence they are less disturbed or upset by criticism. They can remain stable in the midst of stress and strain. Positive feelings of self make it possible to trust themselves and their impulses. They can utilize themselves as trustworthy, reliable instruments for accomplishing their purposes. They have less doubts and hesitation about themselves. Small wonder that weaker persons are often drawn to them or that adequate people are likely to gravitate into leadership roles.

With a self about which he can be fundamentally sure, a person is free to pay much more attention to events outside the self. When the house is in good shape and food is set by for the winter, one is free to go adventuring. A strong self can be forgotten on occasion. A weak self must be forever buttressed and cared for. It intrudes in every situation. With a strong self, problems can be dealt with more objectively because self is not at stake. Solutions can be sought solely as "good" answers to the problem at hand, rather than in terms of their immediate contribution to the enhancement of self. Adequate persons can afford to behave unselfishly because the self is already basically fulfilled.

An essentially positive view of self permits adequate people to be effective without worry about conformity or nonconformity. For them, conformity is not a goal or even a way of dealing with life, but only an artifact of the process of problem solving. They can behave in terms of what seems best to do, and let the chips fall where they may. When the goal is problem solution without the necessity for personal aggrandizement, then, whether one conforms or not is merely an outsider's judgment of what happened, not a governing motivation in the behaver.

Having a positive view of self is much like having money in the bank. It provides a kind of security that permits the owner a freedom he could not have otherwise. With a positive view of self one can risk taking chances; one does not have to be afraid of what is new and different. A sturdy ship can venture farther from port. Just so, an adequate person can launch himself without fear into the new, the untried and the unknown. This permits him to be creative, original and spontaneous. What is more, he can afford to be generous, to give of himself freely or to become personally involved in events. Feeling he is much more, he has so much more to give.

Development of a Positive Self

The self concept, we know, is learned. People *learn* who they are and what they are from the ways in which they have been treated by those who surround them in the process of their growing up. This is what Sullivan called "learning about self from the mirror of other people." People discover their self concepts from the kinds of experiences they have had with life; not from telling, but from experience. People develop feelings that they are liked, wanted, acceptable and able from *having been* liked, wanted, accepted and from *having been* successful. One learns that he is these things, not from being told so, but only through the experience of *being treated as though he were so.* Here is the key to what must be done to produce more adequate people. To produce a positive self, it is necessary to provide experiences that teach individuals they are positive people.

It is a common fallacy among many lay people and some teachers that, since the world is a very hard place and people sometimes fail, children should be introduced to failure early. The logic of this position, at first glance, seems unassailable and in harmony with the goal of education to "prepare for life." But the position is based on a false premise. Actually, the best guarantee we have that a person will be able to deal with the future effectively is that he has been essentially successful in the past. People learn that they are able, not from failure, but from success. While it may be true that toughness and adequacy come from successfully dealing with problems, the learning comes not from experiencing failure but from successfully avoiding it. Similarly, to feel acceptable one must experience acceptance. To feel lovable one must have been loved. A positive view of self is the product of fulfillment, of having been given. The product of deprivation is a diminished self, and even, if carried to extreme, a depraved self.

Identification with Others

A second major characteristic of the truly adequate personality seems to be his capacity for identification with his fellows. The self concept, we know, is not confined to the limits of the physical body alone. It is capable of contraction or expansion so that the self may be defined so narrowly as to virtually exclude the physical body or expanded so greatly as to include many other people and things. Psychologists have pointed out that infants are highly egocentric and only with growth and maturity achieve an increasing degree of altruism. Some people, unfortunately, never achieve such feelings and remain to the end of their days capable of concern for little more than their own welfare. Others, among them the most adequate men and women in history, seem to reach a point where they can identify with great blocks of mankind, with *all* mankind, without reference to creed, color or nationality. Truly adequate people have a greatly expanded feeling of self.

This feeling of oneness with their fellows does not mean that adequate personalities are necessarily charming hosts or hostesses or even that they like to be surrounded with people. We are not talking of "togetherness" or a frantic need to be with people. Identification has to do with a *feeling* of oneness with one's fellows. This feeling can exist without demanding that a particular individual be a "hail fellow well met" or "life of the party." It is even conceivable that he might not like parties or might preper to spend much of his time alone in individual pursuits. Searching for a new cure for cancer all alone in a laboratory, for example, may be a profound demonstration of concern for others.

The feeling these truly adequate persons have has also been described as a feeling of "belonging." Unfortunately, this term has come to mean, for some people, "joining," being a member of, or "keeping up with the Joneses." The feeling of belonging characteristic of these adequate people is a far cry from that. It is a feeling of unity or oneness, a feeling of sharing a common fate, or of striving for a common goal. It represents a real extension of the self to include one's fellows.

Expression of the Feeling of Identification

The feeling of oneness with one's fellows produces in the truly adequate person a high degree of responsible, trustworthy behavior, There is reason for this response. When identification is strong, one cannot behave in ways likely to be harmful or injurious to others, for to do that would be to injure one's self. As a consequence, adequate persons are likely to manifest a deep respect for the dignity and integrity of other people and a strong sense of justice and moral probity. A self which truly encompasses others is incapable of "selfishness," in the usual sense. This is a kind of enlightened selfishness in which the boundaries between self and others disappear. One cannot behave in ways which ignore and reject others when self and others are one. It should not surprise us, therefore, that adequate persons usually possess a deep sense of duty or responsibility or that they are likely to be democratic in the fullest sense of the word.

The feeling of identification also seems to produce a deep sensitivity to the feelings and attitudes of others. The motives of adequate persons are much more likely to be others-centered. Pity and compassion are far more a part of their daily lives and experience. Warmth and humanity come easily to these people as a logical outgrowth of their feeling of oneness with their fellows. This sensitivity also finds its expression in what Maslow has described as a "non-hostile sense of humor."

Because they have strong feelings of identification, adequate persons can work harmoniously with others in either a leader or follower role. Feeling adequate, they do not *have* to lead in order to prove their strength and power. Leadership for them is not a way of proving superiority, but a way of organizing to accomplish desirable ends. The feeling of identification produces such trust in others that adequate persons can lead or not as the situation demands and be satisfied in either role.

How Identification Is Acquired

Identification, like the self concept, is learned. It is the product of the individual's experience and an outgrowth of the essentially positive view of self we have already described. One learns to identify with others, depending upon the nature of his contacts with the important people in his life. As people are friendly and helpful, it is easy and natural to extend one's self to include them or to feel at one with them. As people are harmful and rejecting, on the other hand, one's need to protect himself produces an organization from which such people must be excluded. It is a natural reaction to build walls against those who hurt and humiliate us. On the other hand, it is possible to lower defenses when we can be sure of the friendly behavior of others.

Truly adequate people are able to go further. They can often identify even with those who are antagonistic to them. To do this requires that one feel so strong within himself as to be confident he can withstand the attacks of others. The insecure self can identify only with those who make him feel safe and secure. The more positive the individual's feelings about self, the easier it is to identify with an ever broader sample of mankind. The capacity for identification appears to be a product of an essentially positive view of self and of successful, satisfying experiences in interaction with other people. Here is a place where a child's experiences in school can be made to count.

Openness to Experience and Acceptance

Truly adequate persons possess perceptual fields maximally open to experience. That is to say, their perceptual fields are capable of change and adjustment in such fashion as to make fullest possible use of their experience. Truly healthy persons seem capable of accepting into awareness any and all aspects of reality. They do not find it necessary to defend themselves against events or to distort their perceptions to fit existing patterns. Their perceptual fields are maximally open and receptive to their experiences.

This capacity to confront life openly and without undue defensiveness has sometimes been called acceptance. Acceptance, however, should not be confused with resignation. The openness to experience we are describing refers to the ability to admit evidence into awareness. One cannot deal effectively with what he is unable to conceive exists. The admission of evidence to awareness is the first necessary step to effective action. Being willing to confront the facts, however, does not mean one is defeated by them. On the contrary, it is the only basis upon which any action can safely be premised.

The capacity for acceptance is directly related to the individual's freedom from the experience of threat. We know that when people feel threatened: (a) their perceptions become narrowed to the threatening events, and (b) they are forced to the defense of their existing perceptual organizations. These unhappy concomitants of threat are the very antithesis of the openness to experience we have been describing as characteristic of the truly adequate personality. Whether an individual feels threatened, furthermore, is a product of two factors we have already discussed; namely, the positive self and identification. The more secure the individual's self, the less he will feel threatened by events and the more open he can be in relating to the world about him. Similarly, the more the individual is identified with other people, the less threatened he will feel by those who surround him and the more he will be able to accept his experience with others with equilibrium and profit. Openness to experience and acceptance, it thus appears, are related to the individual's freedom from threat, and this freedom in turn is a product of a positive self and identification.

To this point we have spoken of the adequate person's acceptance of events outside himself. But the openness to experience and acceptance we have been describing refer equally to the individual's perceptions of self. Adequate persons are more accepting of themselves. Feeling fundamentally positive about self makes it less necessary to be defensive or to bar from perceptual organization what is true about self. Adequate persons are less likely to be at war with themselves and so see themselves more accurately and realistically.

Effect of Acceptance upon Behavior

A greater openness to experience offers many advantages. It provides adequate people with more data and, with more data, they are much more likely to be right. Maslow found, for example, that his self-actualizing people were not only connatively right, they were cognitively right as well. A more open perceptual field can encompass more. Adequate people are thus more likely to include the generic as well as the specific aspects of problems or to perceive events or details that would be missed or would seem unimportant to others. This is another way of saying adequate persons behave more intelligently, for what else is intelligence but the ability to behave more effectively and efficiently?

A broader, more accurate perception of the world permits adequate persons to behave more decisively. Decisions can be made with more certainty when one feels he is in command of the data and feels sufficiently sure of self to be unafraid to commit himself to action. Decisions made on the basis of more data are likely to be better ones. On the other hand, the straightforward, uncomplicated relationship these people have with reality also makes it possible for them to live comfortably *without* a decision when this is called for. They are characterized by what Frenkel-Brunswik called a "toleration of ambiguity." That is, they find it possible to live comfortably with unsolved problems. They do not *have* to have an answer when there is none yet, so are less likely to adopt spurious or expedient explanations.

The accurate, realistic assessment of self resulting from acceptance makes possible the use of self as a dependable, trustworthy instrument for achieving one's purposes. These people do not kid themselves. They can permit themselves to be what they are while working to become the best they can be. They do not have to fight what they are. As a consequence, they are free to devote their energies to what is positive and constructive. With a more accurate conception of self, they can and do set more realistic goals for themselves. Their levels of aspiration are more likely to be in line with their capacities. Because goals are more realistic, they are more likely to achieve them. And, of course, the more often goals are achieved, the more positively they feel about self and the more acceptance of and openness to experience become possible for them.

Increased capacity to accept self, we know, permits greater acceptance of others as well. Adequate people are, therefore, less disturbed and upset by the errors and transgressions of their fellows. They are able to take them, too, as they are. They can be more sympathetic and less judgmental. Because they do not demand of others that they be what they are not, they can have greater patience and forbearance in dealing with human foibles. With a greater openness to and acceptance of other people, human relationships are likely to be more successful, since they derive from broader, more accurate perceptions of what other people are like. Disillusionment and despair in human relationships are the product of inaccurate assessment of what people are like and what can be expected of them. A clear conception of possibilities and limitations is more likely to produce more realistic goals. These in turn provide the bases for success experience and good morale.

The capacity for openness to experience and acceptance makes life more pleasant and exciting for adequate persons. It permits them to feel a greater wonder and appreciation of events. Without the necessity for defensiveness, the world can be met openly and gladly. Life can be experienced and savored without fear or hesitation. It can be lived "to the hilt." Such people experience more of what Maslow has called "peak experiences." What is more, adequate persons seem to remain more imaginative and creative even when well along in years.

Dynamics of Openness and Acceptance

Openness and acceptance are not innate characteristics. They are learned. Adequate persons develop these capacities as a function of an essentially positive self and identification. An essentially positive self and a strong feeling of identification with one's fellows make it possible for adequate persons to operate freer from the inhibiting and crippling effects of the experience of threat. What contributes to the child's feelings of security and integrity and to his feelings of oneness with his fellow human beings makes possible a greater acceptance of and openness to his experience.

A third factor contributing to acceptance of and openness to experience is the existence of a value system that prizes openness. Perceptual psychology has presented us with a vast body of research demonstrating the effect of values on the perceptual field. It seems clear that persons who have developed attitudes of valuing new experience, of seeking personal growth, or of the testing of idea against idea are likely to develop perceptual fields more open and accepting. Values of this sort, moreover, can be learned and can be taught. The individual's search for personal adequacy can end, as it does for many, in attempts to protect the precious self, to ring it round with defensive works and to reject or ignore what might cause disruption or change. Or, fulfillment may be found in an approach to life which flirts with danger, actively seeks for challenge, enjoys the testing of one's mettle or the satisfaction of achieving a new goal or objective. The kind of experience provided to people in their most formative years will determine which kinds of values they espouse.

Acceptance is learned. Clinical evidence shows that children can accept even the most formidable handicaps if these handicaps can be accepted by those who surround them. Accurate, realistic concepts of self are essential bases for growth and fulfillment and are in turn the products of one's experience. It is characteristic of the neurotic that he is unable to accept either himself or his fellows. In the protocols of psychotherapy one can perceive how neurotics reject themselves and their associates. It is apparent in these protocols, too, that as clients get better, they become increasingly able to accept themselves and the people and events which surround them. Apparently one learns to accept himself and others as a function of having *experienced* acceptance. It is not surprising, therefore, that modern psychotherapy stresses the acceptance of the client by the therapist as an essential for progress. But the experience of acceptance is by no means limited to the relationship of therapist and client. Acceptance can be experienced in the relationship of the child with his family, his peer group or his teachers in the public schools.

A Rich and Available Perceptual Field

To this point we have described the adequate personality in terms of his perceptions of self, of others, and of the openness of the perceptual field to experience. In the complex society in which we live one cannot be both adequate and stupid simultaneously. The truly adequate person must also be well informed. Indeed, the minimum level of what everyone needs to know just to exist continues to rise year by year as we become ever more specialized and dependent upon technical know-how. One need not know everything to be adequate, but one must certainly have a field of perceptions, rich and extensive enough to provide understanding of the events in which he is enmeshed and available when he needs them. Adequate people have such perceptual fields.

This does not mean that their perceptions are necessarily of an abstract, intellectual character or gained solely from formal schooling. Rich perceptual fields may be derived from quite informal sources through firsthand involvement in human relations, in business, in recreation, or in performing a trade or occupation. On the other hand, with the rapid rise of specialization and technology in our world, perceptions of a technical and abstract character become increasingly necessary for successful action and are less and less available from informal sources. Whatever their origin, however, the fields of adequate people are rich and extensive.

The mere existence of perceptions within the perceptual field is not enough, however, to assure effective behavior. We have already observed that the fields of adequate people are open to their experience. This facilitates the development of a rich and extensive field. The richest field, however, is of little account unless perceptions are available when they are needed for action. This availability, too, seems characteristic of the fields of adequate persons. They not only possess more information or understanding; they are more able to produce these when needed and to put them to effective use.

Some Effects of a Rich and Available Perceptual Field

Clearly, if behavior is a function of perceptions, then a rich and available perceptual field makes possible more effective, efficient behavior. One can do a better job when he has a fine array of tools immediately at hand than he can when he is limited to the use of a hammer and screw driver for every task no matter what its character. Just so, with wider choices open to them, adequate persons can and do operate in ways more satisfying and productive both for themselves and for the world in which they live. They show better judgment and are more often right in their observations and decisions. This is simply another way of saying they behave more intelligently.

How Rich and Available Fields Are Acquired

People get their perceptions, we have seen, as a consequence of their experience. Rich and extensive perceptual fields are a product of the kinds of opportunities an individual has been exposed to. Other things being equal, the richer the opportunity, the more likely the development of a rich and extensive field. It is such opportunities that educators have long sought to provide for children. Unfortunately, other things are seldom equal and, as any teacher is aware, mere exposure to an event is no guarantee that the event will be perceived by the individual or be available on later occasions.

Something more than confrontation with events is necessary to insure inclusion of perceptions in the field and their availability on later occasions. This availability seems dependent upon at least two factors: (a) the individual's discovery of personal meaning, and (b) the satisfaction of need.

The degree to which any perception will affect behavior depends upon its personal meaning for the individual. Perceptions may exist at any level of meaning —from isolated bits of information that pass through our consciousness, like the bits of news we read at the foot of a newspaper column, to those perceptions having deep personal meanings for us, like our feelings about a daughter or son, or those concerned with matters in which we are deeply interested, as a business project, hobby or the like. These varying levels of personal meaning are expressed in the words we use to describe such perceptions. Arranged in order of increasing meaning, we speak, for example, of looking, seeing, knowing; of understanding, belief, conviction. The deeper, more personally significant the perception, moreover, the more likely it is to affect behavior.

Adequate people seem to have many more such personal meanings. As a consequence, much more of their knowing affects behaving. They are less easily swayed and much more precise and efficient because the relationship and pertinence of perceptions are clearer and more available when needed. Such meanings, of course, are a result of the nature of the individual's experience. One learns the meaning of events. Whether perceptions exist as isolated knowings or as deep personal understanding will depend upon the opportunities, stimulation and encouragement a person has had, the values he has acquired, the freedom he has had to explore and discover meaning, and the existence of a positive self.

The availability of perceptions in the field will also be vitally affected by the individual's achievement of need satisfaction. Need has a focusing effect upon perception. We perceive what we *need* to perceive. A more adequate self permits attention to wander far afield from self while the inadequate person, desperately seeking maintenance and enhancement of self, must, of necessity, focus most of his perceptions on events contributing directly to such feelings. Failure of need satisfaction produces narrowness and rigidity of perceptual organization. The adequate individual, on the other hand, with a secure self, has a more fluid, open field of perceptions. It follows, then, that the production of a more available field requires the development of a positive view of self, and a positive self, we have already seen, is a function of the kinds of experiences provided in the course of a child's maturing.

In this paper I have attempted to describe the truly adequate, healthy person in terms of four characteristics of the perceptual field: a positive view of self, identification with others, acceptance of and openness to experience, and the richness and availability of the perceptual field. Since all of these ways of perceiving are learned, they can also be taught if we can but find ways to provide the necessary kinds of experiences. No other agency in our society is in a more crucial position to bring about these necessary conditions than are the public schools. Indeed, the production of such people must be the primary goal of education.

To contribute effectively to the production of such persons, however, is not as much a question of revolution as it is of evolution. To produce adequate persons requires not that we do something entirely new and different, but that we all do more efficiently and effectively what some of us now do only sometimes and haphazardly. Educators have been in the business of effecting changes in perception since teaching was invented. No one knows better than they how to bring such changes about. Our new understandings of the truly healthy personality provide us with new and important objectives toward which to direct our efforts. Who can say what kind of world we might create if we could learn to increase our production of adequate people?

4

EDUCATIONAL OBJECTIVES

BEHAVIORAL OBJECTIVES AND
THE INSTRUCTIONAL PROCESS

Robert J. Kibler, Larry L. Barker, David T. Miles

Behavioral objectives are statements which describe what students will be able to do after completing a prescribed unit of instruction. For example, a behavioral objective for a unit in history might be: "The student will be able to list three major factors which gave rise to the Industrial Revolution."

Behavioral objectives serve two major functions. First, they are used by instructors to design and evaluate their instruction. Second, they are used to communicate the goals of instructional units to such interested persons as (1) students planning to complete the unit; (2) instructors who teach preceding and following units; and (3) persons responsible for planning and evaluating curricula. Each of these functions requires a different type of behavioral objective.

The function of behavioral objectives as a prerequisite for planning and evaluating instruction can best be shown by presenting a breakdown of the major steps involved in planning and carrying out instruction. On the following pages a "General Model of Instruction" is presented.

You may attempt to achieve some specific instructional objectives for the model or just read through it to see what it says. If you choose the first option, you should (1) read the objectives for the model; (2) read the material and complete the practice exercises on the pages to follow; (3) engage in further practice to the extent necessary to be able to demonstrate mastery of the objectives; and (4) complete the test at the end. If you choose the other option, you can ignore the practice exercises and test.

*From Kibler, Barker and Miles, *Behavioral Objectives and Instruction,* Boston: Allyn & Bacon, Inc., 1970, pp. 1-27. Reprinted by permission.

Instructional Objectives for the General Model of Instruction

Upon completing this unit you should be able to:

1. Draw a diagram of the General Model of Instruction (GMI).
2. Briefly describe the premise underlying the GMI and its two major functions.
3. List the major factors to consider in each component of the GMI.

The General Model of Instruction

The General Model of Instruction (GMI) is a procedural guide for designing and conducting instruction. The model is applicable to all levels of education (*e.g.*, elementary, secondary, higher), all subject matters (*e.g.*, English, science, art, vocational), and any length of instructional unit (*e.g.*, one hour, one week, one semester).

The major philosophical *premise* underlying the model is that *the goal of instruction is to maximize the efficiency with which all students achieve specified objectives.* The model is based on a technology of instruction which has developed in the past several years from the research and development work in three areas—experimental psychology, military training, and programed instruction. The three individuals who have contributed most to the specific model presented in this document are Robert Gagné (1965a, 1965b and 1965c), Robert Glaser (1965) and James Popham (1965).

The two major *functions* of the model are (1) to *guide instructional designers and teachers* through the major steps in designing and carrying out instruction; and (2) to *provide* an overall *structure* with which to view and study the instructional process. Although the model itself has not been validated experimentally for instructional efficiency, several of the prescriptive principles contained in it are derived from empirical research.

A flow diagram of the model is shown below. Each step in the model actually composes a body of knowledge with which anyone concerned with instruction should be intimately familiar.

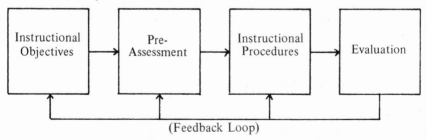

(Feedback Loop)

On the following pages each step is explained briefly and several of the major factors to consider in completing each step are presented. The material is designed to provide an overview of the instructional process and to expose the important relationship between the "objectives" component of the model and the other three components.

INSTRUCTIONAL OBJECTIVES

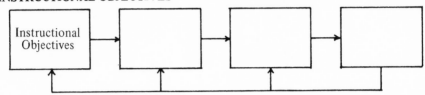

Preparing instructional objectives is probably the most important test in the entire model, for the instructor must decide what he wants to teach. The four major factors involved in preparing objectives—selection, classification, analysis, and specification—are discussed briefly below.

Selection. The selection of appropriate objectives usually is based on the following factors: (1) what the students are able to do before beginning the unit; (2) what the students should be able to do in instructional units that follow the unit of concern, and what they should be able to do after completing their education; and (3) the available instructional resources, including the instructor's capabilities with his subject matter.

Classification. The taxonomies, by Bloom and others (1956) and Krathwohl and others (1964), are useful in making sure that the objectives selected are of the level or type actually desired. For example, by classifying objectives in the cognitive domain into taxonomic categories, the instructor can determine whether the desired behaviors are knowledge, comprehension, application, analysis, synthesis, or evaluation. Gagné (1965c) and Guilford (1967) also have produced systems for classifying human performance that are useful for this purpose.

Analysis. Once a set of objectives has been selected, the instructor should perform a behavioral analysis in which he demonstrates what a student will be expected to *do* to demonstrate achievement of the objective. The actual components to be examined in a behavioral analysis are (1) the important stimuli to which a student responds; (2) the important responses made; and (3) the criteria which the responses must meet to be considered successful.

Such an analysis can be performed by observing students who have already achieved the objective as they exhibit the desired behavior. Previous students can be interviewed, and the products (tests, papers, etc.) they produced can be examined. No matter how the behavioral analysis is conducted, a list of instructional objectives should be defined which clearly and completely prescribe the behaviors students are to acquire as a result of completing the instruction.

Specification. Behavioral objectives will be most valuable if they contain the following three elements recommended by Robert Mager in *Preparing Instructional Objectives (1962).*

1. A description of the type of *observable behavior* which the student will be asked to employ in demonstrating mastery of the objective (*e.g.,* "to write," "to solve," "to identify," "to orally describe"). Terms such as "to know," "to understand," and "to appreciate" must be avoided since they do not refer to observable behavior.
2. A description of the important *conditions* under which the student will be expected to demonstrate achievement of the objective (*e.g.,* time limits, materials or equipment that will be available, or special instructions).
3. The *criterion* which will be used to evaluate the success of the student's performance (*e.g.,* must get 70 percent correct, correctly apply three principles, complete the task in 15 minutes, or correctly identify eight out of ten).

Prior to moving on, it should be emphasized that the function of these behavioral objectives is for *planning* instruction, not for *informing* others of instructional intentions. These objectives are more detailed than the behavioral objectives used typically for the purpose of communicating goals to others. Several types of extremely important objectives are difficult to measure and, thus, difficult to specify in behavioral terms. As a matter of fact, it seems that the more significant an objective is, the more difficult it is to measure. Examples of objectives which fall into the difficult-to-specify-and-measure category are those in the areas of problem solving, creativity, attitudes and values. The only solution we see to this problem is for such objectives to be specified as clearly as possible and for the instructor to be as resourceful as he can in developing evaluative measures, including attitude inventories and creativity tests.

Such objectives (*e.g.,* "to shape favorable attitudes toward your subject matter and toward learning") should *not* be eliminated because they are difficult to measure; they should be included and the instructor should work toward improving his measures.

Practice Exercises

At this stage it may be a good idea to be sure you are learning what is intended in this unit. By now, you should be able to fill in the first component in the model. If you also can complete the others, do it.

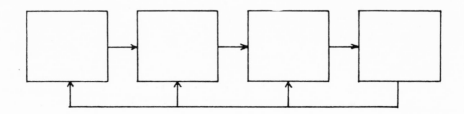

In addition, identify the premise underlying the model and the two major functions of the model. If you cannot remember the premise or the functions, take a quick look back and then write them below.

Premise: _____

_____

Functions: 1. _____

_____

2. _____

_____

Now, list the four factors or substeps in the first component of the model. Peek if you must.

1. _____
2. _____
3. _____
4. _____

You should check on the accuracy of your responses by referring back to the preceding pages before proceeding.

PRE-ASSESSMENT

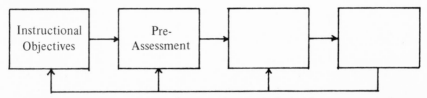

Prior to beginning a unit of instruction, it is desirable to assess students to determine (1) how much of what is to be learned in the unit they already know; (2) whether they have the necessary behavioral capabilities for the instruction to follow; and (3) the instructional activities that should be prescribed for each student.

Of course, the assessment should be based on the specific instructional objectives specified for the unit. The results of this assessment should indicate (1) whether any students may *omit* any of the objectives in the unit; (2) whether any students should be required to master *prerequisite* skills before beginning the unit; and (3) what specific *instructional activities* should be provided for specific students. The above alternative courses imply that individualized instruction or tracking procedures are available for the instructional event. However, it is frequently possible to require prerequisite behavioral competencies and omit objectives for individual students in group-paced instruction.

You will be asked to recall the three courses of action which can be taken as a result of pre-assessment (1. omit objectives; 2. require prerequisites; 3. prescribe instruction) upon completing this unit so you may wish to rehearse them a few times before proceeding.

INSTRUCTIONAL PROCEDURES

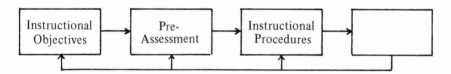

After students are pre-assessed and adjustments are made, such as adding or eliminating objectives or requiring prerequisite learning, the instructional procedures are implemented. The design of the instructional procedures involves (1) selection of available instructional materials (*e.g.,* books, films, or lesson plan); (2) preparing new instructional materials when necessary; and (3) developing a sequential plan which appears to be the most efficient for achieving the stated objectives. Decisions should be based upon research evidence when it is available.

The ten generalizations specified below are, to a large extent, based upon research evidence and are examples of principles which should be consulted in designing instructional activities. It should be noted that every application of these principles will not apply automatically to all students and all subject matters. Students vary in the way they learn, subject matters vary in their structures, and teachers vary in the way they interpret and apply principles of instruction. Thus, applications of these principles in each situation and with each student must be tested continually.

1. Pre-Learning Preparation. Learners must master the prerequisite behaviors to succeed in new learning experiences. Instructors should prepare students for new learning experiences by warming them up, telling them what previously learned behaviors will be helpful or harmful, and helping them to acquire an appropriate "set" (predisposition to respond in a particular way) for what is to follow. For example, a preview at the beginning of a chapter or film can increase learning efficiency. Providing students with the behavioral objectives for a unit has also been found to facilitate learning.

2. Motivation. Students are more efficient if they want to learn what is being taught. This desire can be promoted by convincing learners of the value of mastering the subject matter and by offering rewards (*e.g.,* social approval or grades) for accomplishing learning objectives. Selecting subject matter that interests students and permits them to participate in planning their educational activities can increase their incentive to learn. Shaping favorable attitudes toward the subject matter, the instructor, learning, and education in general can have positive long-range consequences for student motivation.

3. Providing a Model of Terminal Performance (Mastery). When possible, learners should be shown examples of what they are to produce or to do at the end of a learning experience. Imitative learning is one of the most effective procedures by which humans acquire new behaviors. Showing students sample term papers, completed projects, or final exam papers or demonstrating a desired performance can facilitate learning dramatically.

4. Active Responding. At the outset of training, learners can profit from watching or listening to someone else perform the acts to be learned, but most learners will become proficient only if they perform the acts themselves. Thus, it is what the learner does—not what the teacher does—that determines learning. In learning verbal material from a textbook, most students can profit by overtly reviewing what they have read while not looking at the material.

5. Guidance. When attempting to demonstrate new behaviors to be learned, instructors should guide and prompt the students. For example, they could give verbal guidance for each step in carrying out long division problems. Such prompts should be eliminated gradually until the learner is able to perform the task without them.

6. Practice. Opportunities should be provided for learners to use newly learned behaviors repeatedly. Practice will be effective to the extent that the behaviors practiced are similar to behaviors to be performed in the future (the terminal objectives). For example, after learning initially to subtract, students should practice with a variety of number combinations.

7. Knowledge of Results. A learner should have prompt and frequent knowledge of the success of his responses. He must find his success rewarding in order for the behavior to be reinforced. Ideally, he should know an instant after he makes a response whether it is appropriate or not. When he is personally confident of the correctness of his response, external confirmation may be unnecessary, but when he is unsure, such feedback is generally desirable.

8. Graduated Sequence. Subject matter should be organized in a hierarchical form from the simple to the complex—from the familiar to the unfamiliar. The steps should be paced so that the learner succeeds in each step but does not become bored. It has been found that permitting students to follow their own sequence in achieving well-defined objectives yields better results than insisting upon teacher-designed learning sequences (Mager and McCann, 1961).

9. Individual Differences. People learn at different speeds; therefore, learning experiences should be designed so that each student may proceed at his own pace. Some students will require considerable practice to master a concept while others may acquire the same concept upon first encounter.

10. Classroom Teaching Performance. Skills in stimulating interest, explaining, guiding, identifying and administering reinforcers, and managing classroom behavior can make an enormous difference in instructional effectiveness. Unfortunately, such social skills are often the most difficult to learn, but some current work on the analysis of social and personality factors in teaching shows promise of reducing the difficulty. The changing role of the teacher from information-dispenser to manager of instructional experiences is also an encouraging development.

Practice Exercises

Although it would be desirable for you to learn all of the information within the ten factors, for the present goal (obtaining an overview of the model) you are only asked to be able to list the ten topic headings. The ten topics are:

1. *Pre-Learning Preparation*
2. *Motivation*
3. *Providing a Model of Terminal Performance*
4. *Active Responding*

5. *Guidance*
6. *Practice*
7. *Knowledge of Results*
8. *Graduated Sequence*
9. *Individual Differences*
10. *Classroom Teaching Performance*

One way to memorize this list is to view the first seven items as a chronological sequence of events which should happen in a learning sequence. The other three are more general and apply to the entire instructional process.

After reading the list a couple of times, try to write all the factors down.

EVALUATION

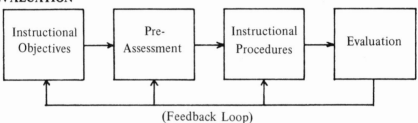

(Feedback Loop)

When students complete an instructional unit, they are evaluated to determine whether the instruction was successful in achieving the unit's objectives. Typically, evaluation involves using tests and instruments to measure the acquisition of knowledge, skills and attitudes. Fr equently, it is necessary to specify or describe student achievement. This is usually a difficult task.

If the objectives have been specified clearly, test preparation is quite simple. An important consideration in designing evaluative measures is that the instrument measure the identical behavior specified in the objectives. It also is important to note that the success of the instruction is being evaluated, not the success of the pupils.

In most instances in formal education, it is both desirable and feasible for all students to master all objectives. If all students do not perform acceptably on all objectives, an explanation must be sought from among the following three reasons:

1. The unsuccessful students were prepared inadequately for the unit, which could mean that the objectives were unrealistic or that the students should not have begun the unit without prior training.
2. The unsuccessful students were not motivated properly to master the material.
3. The instruction was not designed properly or insufficient time was provided for the students to master the objectives.

Changes in the objectives, the pre-instruction evaluation procedures, the instruction, or the post-instruction evaluation are to be made on the basis of the evaluational results (note the *feedback loop* on the flow chart). In addition to making changes based on observed results, instructors should make modifications on the basis of new developments in materials and techniques, new research findings, and changing values.

The results of evaluation can also be used to inform students and other interested parties regarding the degree of success each student achieved in the unit. However, since all students may be required to master all objectives, this information may consist of only an indication of the different lengths of time each student took to complete the unit.

The most important factors you should remember about evaluation are:

1. It is the success of the *instruction* which is being evaluated.
2. Unsuccessful instruction is probably a result of one of the following:
   a. Students did not have the *prerequisites* necessary to begin the unit.
   b. The students were *motivated inadequately* before or during the unit.
   c. The *instructional* activities were designed *inadequately*.
3. Changes in objectives, pre-assessment, and instructional procedures should be made, if necessary, so that all students achieve all required objectives.

Different Types of Educational Objectives

Instructional objectives are written at various levels of specificity. We already have introduced two of the most important types of objectives for instruction: *planning* and *informational* objectives. Most readers will have been exposed to a third, more general type of objective: *general educational objectives.* A discussion of general educational objectives is included in *The Cardinal Principles of Secondary Education* (1937) and, more recently, in *The Central Purposes of American Education* (1961), published by the Educational Policies Commission of the National Education Association.

Figure 2 shows how the three types of objectives differ with respect to specificity.

GENERAL, NONSPECIFIC OBJECTIVES   HIGHLY SPECIFIC OBJECTIVES

General
Educational
Objectives

Informational
Objectives

Objectives
Planning

SPECIFICITY CONTINUUM OF OBJECTIVES

At the extreme end of nonspecificity are the very general objectives of educational institutions and broad educational programs (for example, "to make better citizens," "to advance humanity," and "to promote our cultural ideals"). At the other end of the continuum are the highly specific objectives recommended by Mager (1962), which are invaluable for designing instruction. Somewhere in the middle are the objectives written for a curriculum, a course, a weekly unit, or a daily lesson plan.

Some educational objectives do not fit neatly into any of the three categories described above. For example, outlines of objectives for elementary (Kearney, 1953) and secondary (French, 1957) educational levels have been published. These objectives would be placed between general educational objectives and informational objectives. A recently developed set of objectives for the language arts would be placed in a similar position (Lazarus and Knudson, 1967). The types of objectives included in the two volumes of the *Taxonomy of Educational Objectives* (Bloom, *et al.,* 1956, and Krathwohl, *et al.,* 1964) would probably be placed slightly to the left of informational objectives. A more extensive examination of the implication of different kinds of objectives is discussed by Lindvall (1964).

Informational objectives are used by instructional designers to communicate their intentions to others. These behavioral objectives, important in education, are abbreviations of the planning objectives. They are typically written after the planning objectives have been specified. Note the relationship between the following planning objective and informational objective.

> *Planning Objective:*
> In a half-hour test at the end of the week, the student will be able to list the steps a bill follows through Congress, specifying the requirements for passage at each step. All steps must be included in the correct order, and the passage requirements must match the ones in the textbook.
> *Informational Objective:*
> The student will be able to list, in correct order, the steps a bill follows through Congress, specifying the requirements for passage in each step.

The informational objective omits the conditions under which the behavior was to be performed ("in a half-hour test at the end of the week") and the criteria to be used in judging acceptable performance ("all steps must be in the correct order, and the passage requirements must match the ones in the textbook"). It contains a reference to the type of behavior expected of the student ("to list") and a description of the product he is to produce ("a listing of the steps a bill follows. . ."). This example should provide a rough idea of the distinction between planning objectives and informational objectives.

The Value of Planning Objectives

Teachers or instructional designers benefit in three ways from defining planning objectives.

1. Given clearly defined goals to work toward, teachers can design instructional experiences to achieve them and can evaluate the effectiveness of such experiences according to whether the goals are achieved.
2. Students can be examined prior to beginning instruction to determine whether they have already mastered any of the objectives. Information regarding their preparedness for the instruction to follow can also be obtained.
3. Each student can be evaluated on mastery of the unit's objectives. In this way every student can be required to master all objectives. This is in contrast to grading students on how well they performed in comparison with the rest of the class (grading on the curve) or in achievement of a certain percentage of the objectives of the unit.

The Value of Informational Objectives

Students, curriculum planners, student advisors, teachers and administrators benefit from the use of informational objectives.

1. Several studies have demonstrated that students can be more efficient learners if they are provided with objectives (Mager and McCann, 1961; McNeil, 1966; Miles, Kibler, and Pettigrew, 1967). Perhaps one of the reasons students do better when given copies of the objectives of a unit of instruction is that they are spared the frustration and time-consuming effort of trying to guess what the teacher expects of them.
2. Given such clearly specified objectives, curriculum planners are better able to

arrange sequences of courses or units of instruction. Knowing what students (hopefully all students) are able to do at the end of courses and what students are able to do at the beginning of courses (prerequisites), it should be possible to eliminate unnecessary overlap of courses and to identify and fill in gaps between courses.

3. Students and their advisors are able to plan their course programs better when they can read course descriptions which include informational objectives.

4. Through clear behavioral objectives, teachers are able to tell other teachers what they teach. Stating that "students learn to name each state and its capital in the United States" tells considerably more than stating "United States geography is taught."

5. Teachers and administrators can determine the level of objectives students will be able to achieve in terms of taxonomic classifications. For example, in the cognitive domain, objectives can be classified as knowledge, comprehension, application, analysis, and evaluation, thereby avoiding undue emphasis on a certain level of objectives.

Controversial Issues Regarding Behavioral Objectives

Even though the authors take the position that behavioral objectives are an extremely important part of the educational process, it must be clear that all educators do not share this point of view. Some heated discussions have taken place among educators regarding whether or not behavioral objectives are either important or useful. Therefore, there is merit in examining some of the controversial issues associated with such objectives.

1. Can all important outcomes of education be defined and measured behaviorally?

2. Can prespecification of objectives prevent teachers from achieving objectives which might arise unexpectedly during a course of instruction?

3. Will more trivial learner behaviors, which are the easiest to operationalize, receive a greater emphasis than more important educational outcomes?

James Popham has written an insightful paper which deals with these and several other arguments that have been presented in opposition to behavioral objectives.

Three issues with which Dr. Popham does not deal are given brief consideration here.

1. Pre-Specifying the Objectives for a Unit of Instruction Which a Teacher Has Not Previously Taught

This is indeed a complex task. But it has been our experience that a procedure such as the following can reduce some of the complexity and result in a fairly complete set of objectives for the succeeding times the course is taught.

A.   Specify a set of objectives, stating them in general terms. These objectives should be based on an analysis of post-instructional performance expectancies and pre-instructional performance capability.
B.   Specify more precise objectives for each unit as it occurs.
C.   Evaluate the results of each unit and base the objectives for the following units on these results.
D.   Identify and record objectives which are achieved in addition to those prespecified for each unit.

This procedure is essentially a crude technique for testing hypotheses regarding objectives, identifying unpredicted objectives, and determining criteria for appropriate levels of performance. Thus, experience with the first attempt at a course is used to develop a set of precise objectives for succeeding presentations of the course.

2. Deciding Whether All Students Should be Required to Achieve the Same Objectives

With the increasing emphasis on individualized instruction, this decision is indeed relevant. Our viewpoint is that for most courses in public school, industrial, and undergraduate education, all students should achieve a common set of goals. This does not, however, preclude the possibility of specification of behavioral objectives for *individual* student achievement. Opportunities should be available for students in many of these courses to go beyond the basic requirements to pursue individual areas of interest. One technique which has been employed frequently involves each student's stating his specific objectives. Such a procedure seems quite appropriate when one of the teacher's objectives is for students to be able to identify and acquire behavioral competencies of personal concern.

3. Deciding Whether All Students Should Be Required to Achieve the Same Level of Mastery for Each Objective

This issue is related to the previous one. Brought into question here is the value of using the norm-referenced evaluation and grading system, in which students are assessed on the basis of their performance relative to the group, instead of the criterion-referenced system, in which students are evaluated according to their achievement of specified criteria—irrespective of how the group performs. The norm-referenced system is presently the most widely-used system, although the criterion-referenced system is growing in popularity.

Without clearly defined objectives and performance criteria for measuring attainment of the objectives, the norm-referenced system is probably the most reasonable method available for assessing student achievement. However, given specific objectives and evaluation criteria, the practice of measuring the relative achievement of the objective may be open to question. Much has been written on this issue recently, and very likely the increased use of behavioral objectives is to a great extent responsible for the dialogue.

Some educators feel that the purpose of education is not to determine who learns more and less of a given subject matter, but rather to see to it that all students learn what is considered necessary. From this viewpoint, the criterion-referenced system would be the desirable choice, and all students could be required to achieve the same level of mastery on each objective. This approach does not negate the possibility of providing the opportunity for students to go beyond the basic required objectives. The latter possibility may be extremely important to a more widespread acceptance of criterion-referenced evaluation, since the relative achievement information (presently provided by norm-referenced evaluation and grading) is employed for a large variety of seemingly vital functions. School grades are used as a basis for selecting students for college, major areas of study, graduate school, honors programs, scholarships, and post-school employment; for retaining students in school; for influencing students' occupational choices; and for recording progress toward certificates and degrees. They also are used as incentives and rewards. Thus, it appears that some kind of information regarding a student's academic performance relative to other students is needed. Possibly standardized academic ability or achievement tests eventually can provide such information and the results of instructional evaluation could be used only for determining the effectiveness of instruction when students have achieved specified objectives.

Two generalizations regarding this issue seem appropriate. When mastery of an objective is vital to the achievement of subsequent objectives (for example, some language and computational skills are essential to much of what follows in and comes after school), then all students should be required to fully master the objective. When subsequent performance demands are not so clear-cut, it may be appropriate to permit students to achieve varying levels of mastery of an objective—above some minimum criterion.

The other generalization involves the domain of evaluation in education. The three primary functions of evaluation in instruction are to provide information regarding (1) student achievement of instructional objectives; (2) the success of instruction in getting students to achieve objectives; and (3) student achievement and ability which can be used for academic and occupational selection. Although both the norm-referenced and criterion-referenced systems can provide information for the three functions, the criterion-referenced system probably is a more desirable procedure for accomplishing the first and second functions, and the norm-referenced system is more appropriate for meeting the third function. The different amounts of time students spend in reaching criteria could provide information for Function 3 within a criterion-referenced system, but such a practice may tend to result in an over-emphasis on speed of acquisition and an under-emphasis on retention and transfer.

Thus, it is our position that a criterion-referenced system should be employed for the basic fundamentals of instruction, and all students should be required to meet the standards considered necessary for post-instruction performance. In addition, opportunities for students to go beyond the required standards should be provided, and the results of students' performance in these areas, plus the results of standardized achievement and ability tests, should be used to satisfy the functions for which grades are used presently.

5

PLANNING FOR INSTRUCTION

POSITIVES AND AVERSIVES

Robert F. Mager

To help you apply the conditions and consequences principles more effectively, we'll examine positive and aversive events in more detail. Although it isn't always possible to know whether an event is positive or aversive for a given individual, some conditions and consequences are universal enough in their effect to provide considerable guidance. So that we can end this chapter on a positive note, let's consider conditions and consequences that are aversive first.

> An *aversive condition or consequence* is any event that causes physical or mental discomfort. It is any event that causes a person to think less highly of himself, that leads to a loss of self-respect or dignity, or that results in a strong anticipation of any of these. In general, any condition or consequence may be considered aversive if it causes a person to feel smaller or makes his world dimmer.

There are several conditions and consequences that are avoided by enough people to warrant their being referred to as *universal aversives.* When these conditions or consequences are associated with the subjects we teach or appear as a result of subject matter contact, then the subject matter, learning, or even school itself may take on a less desirable hue . . . and no amount of righteous indignation on our part will alter this effect, no declaiming of how the student "ought" to be more interested will have nearly as much effect toward that end as reducing the aversive characteristics of the learning situation.

On the pages that follow, some universal aversives will be described and illustrated with examples of school practices.

*From Robert F. Mager, *Developing Attitude Toward Learning,* pp. 49-60. Copyright 1968 Fearon Publishers/Lear Siegler, Inc., Education Division. All rights reserved.

Pain is an acute physical discomfort, as you very well know. Though there are probably no longer many teacher-provoked occasions where a student is in pain when in the presence of subject matter or as a consequence of approaching subject matter, the event is by no means unheard of.

I know a violin instructor who, in an angry attempt to get his student's fingers properly positioned, makes those fingers hurt. He makes his students cry with pain and tremble with fear. His claim that this is "good" for his student is nothing more than justification for his uncommon version of educational malpractice.

Perhaps the only remaining instance of the pain universal aversive in schools, though almost extinct, is that of hitting a student as a response to something he has or has not done. Understand that the concern here is not with whether punishment should or should not be allowed, but with the effects of conditions and consequences on the subject matter approach behavior of the student. In this case, if the student is to be bashed because of something he has done or not done, see to it that the bashing is done someplace where the student is not in the presence of the subject matter, and see to it that the bashing is done with something *other than* the subject matter.

There are instances of the pain universal aversive that do not directly involve the instructor or school. Sometimes, for example, a student is in pain when he is trying to read; if a student has an uncorrected eye condition, trying to read can actually hurt.

Fear and anxiety are distress or uneasiness of the mind: apprehension of danger, misfortune, or pain; tension, foreboding, worry, or disquiet; anticipation of the unpleasant.

Procedures leading to fear and anxiety are those that threaten various forms of unpleasantness. They include:

- Telling the student by word or deed that nothing he can do will lead to success, or that contact with the subject will lead to undesirable consequences.
- Telling the student, "You won't understand this, but . . . ."
- Telling the student, "It ought to be perfectly obvious that . . . ."
- Threatening the exposure of "ignorance" by forcing the student to solve problems at the chalkboard in front of the class.
- Basing an attrition rate on administrative fiat rather than on student performance ("Half of you won't be here a month from now," or "I don't believe in giving high grades").

- Threatening failure by telling the student, "If you aren't motivated enough, you shouldn't be here." (*Translation:* "If you aren't motivated enough to learn in spite of my poor teaching, you certainly aren't going to get any help from me.")
- Being unpredictable about the standard of acceptable performance. (For example, a sixth grade teacher recently told his students that they didn't have to listen to his discussion if they were having no difficulty with its topic. Five minutes later he berated half the class for "not paying attention.")
- A common form of punishment in some schools is "going to see the principal." Because of some real or imagined infraction, the student is sent to the principal's office, where vengeance is expected to be wreaked upon the student by the principal. How many times have I seen a poor young student sitting there waiting for the verbal lash—small, frightened, and bewildered— starting in fright at the smallest movement. *This is education?*

Frustration is a condition or consequence that occurs when goal-directed activities are blocked, when purposeful or motivated activity is interfered with. To frustrate is to thwart, to foil, to circumvent, to interfere with, to check, to make an effort come to no avail, to defeat. Practices that can generate frustration include:

- Presenting information in larger units, or at a faster pace, than the student can assimilate. (The more motivated the student is, the greater the frustration when his efforts are blocked.) Jack Vaughn describes this as the situation where the student came to drink from the fountain of knowledge and somebody turned on a fire hose.
- Speaking too softly to be heard easily (blocking the student's effort to come into contact with the subject).
- Keeping secret the intent of the instruction, or the way in which performance will be evaluated.
- Providing unreadable print; type too small or too ornate, reading level too high.
- Providing obscure text, or implying more profundity than actually exists, as in, "When two parallel lines are cut by a transversal, the alternate interior angles are equal."
- Teaching one set of skills, and then testing for another.
- Testing for skills other than those stated in announced objectives.
- Refusing to answer student questions.
- Using test items with obscure meanings.
- Forcing all students to proceed at the same pace, thus frustrating the slow and boring the quick.

- Calling a halt when a student is absorbed with his instruction or attempting to complete a project (ringing a school bell, for example).
- When a well-meaning teacher trying to get his material across doesn't set up adequate feedback or consequences, or if the consequences are so remote in time that the student doesn't associate them with the learning activity, a frustration situation exists. The student is trying to do well, but his efforts simply go unrecognized (for example, delaying the return of test results).

Humiliation and embarrassment are caused by lowering a person's pride or self-respect, by making him uncomfortably self-conscious; by shaming, debasing, or degrading him; or by causing him a painful loss of dignity. Procedures that lead to these conditions include:

- Publicly comparing a student unfavorably with others.
- Laughing at a student's efforts. When Dr. David Cram returned his comments on the original draft of this book, he included the following:
  "My own pappy relates his music career thusly: 'We had a singing session and the teacher asked me to sing alone. When I did, all the kids laughed. The next day he asked me to do it again. Well, sir, I wouldn't do it. So the teacher made me come to the front of the class, but I still wouldn't do it. So he hit my hand with a ruler. But he could have cut off my fingers and I *still* wouldn't have done it. I didn't, either. Ever!' "
- Spotlighting a student's weaknesses by bringing them to the attention of the class.
- Making a student wear a badge of his "stupidity" (putting him in a special seat or section, for example).
- Belittling a student's attempt to approach the subject by such replies to his questions as, "Stop trying to show off."
- Insulting a student for his attempt to approach the subject by such comments as, "You couldn't possibly understand the answer to that question," or otherwise telling him by word or deed that his questions are considered stupid.
- Repeated failure. It is perfectly appropriate to challenge students enough to cause them to fail on occasion, provided that the consequence of failure is not an avoidable aversive situation. Repeated failure, however, is sure to lead a student to think less highly of himself and to try to avoid the situation that has come to signify such a shrinkage of self-esteem. Repeated failure is often engineered into our educational system. One practice is that of grading on a curve. Whenever performance is evaluated by comparing it with what a group of chance neighbors happens to do, a person with the below-average aptitude will almost always come out on the lower half of the curve. He may have

achieved all the objectives set out for him; he may have learned to work faster or more effectively; he may be exceeding the standard set out by the instructor. No matter. When his performance is compared with that of more talented neighbors, he will always be the loser. This use of the curve is only slightly less reprehensible than the instructor who brags that he has a "tough" course because 40 per cent of his class "failed." (Has it ever occured to him that he is only 60 per cent successful?)

- The "special class" set up for students the teacher is not competent enough to cope with. Students are singled out and sent to another place for a variety of remedial treatment. They are branded as "different" and somehow inadequate. (In one state, first and second graders with minor speech deficiencies are sent to a special class and taught that they are *handicapped* persons. They are taught stories about Helen Keller and others who have had severe handicaps. They are taught that they, too, must overcome their special "burden" if they are to succeed. Such a practice can only be labeled "Crimes We Commit in the Name of Education.")

- A common elementary school practice leading to humiliation and embarrassment frequently occurs after a teacher has asked the class a question. In almost every class there seems to be at least one student who is so anxious to come into contact with the subject, so eager to demonstrate his competence, that while frantically waving his hand in the air the answer slips out from between his lips. What is the consequence of this behavior on the part of the student? Does his world become a little brighter, is he encouraged to think more highly of himself as a result of his action? Sometimes. Often, however, the consequenc is a finger pointed sternly in his direction followed by, "I . . . didn't . . . call . . . on . . . you!" And what the student is learning is that it doesn't pay to get very excited about the things that happen in school, that showing too much interest can lead to embarrassment; to humiliation. Oh, I know. Students must be taught discipline (and discipline *will* be a problem as long as students are forced to sit in neat little rows listening to lectures). But there are better ways of handling discipline problems, ways that do not embarrass the student while in the presence of the subject matter.

Boredom is caused by a situation in which the stimuli impinging on the student are weak, repetitive, or infrequent. Typical avoidance responses are those of leaving the situation and of falling asleep. Procedures leading to boredom include:

- Presenting information in a monotone.
- Rocking rhythmically back and forth while speaking.
- Insisting the student sit through instruction covering something that he al-

ready knows.

- Using impersonal, passive language.
- Providing information in increments so small that they provide no challenge or require no effort.
- Allowing lethargy-inducing temperatures to exist.
- Using only a single mode of presentation (no variety).
- Reading the textbook aloud. Consider for a moment the effect on a student of the instructor whose principal technique is to read aloud from the textbook. If a student has prepared himself for the class by studying the assignment in the textbook, he is punished for his effort in the classroom through the boredom of repetition. How can the student avoid some of the boredom of this situation? Very simply. He can stop doing his textbook assignments before coming to class. In this way, although he may suffer through a dull reading of the textbook during the class hour, at least the material read will not be familiar. This is one situation where the student is rewarded for being less, rather than more, diligent. He is reinforced for disregarding the assignments of his instructor. Since this situation is one in which the student's act of entering the classroom is followed by an unpleasant event (boredom), and since people tend to avoid unpleasant events, the student will simply try to avoid attending class whenever possible. And why not? Are *you* eager to place yourself in a boring situation? (Wake up there!)

Physical discomfort is an uneasiness, a hardship, mild pain. Though there are several ways of inducing physical discomfort while the student is in the presence of a subject, most of them are not under the direct control of the instructor. A partial list would include:

- Allowing excessive noise or other distractions.
- Insisting the student be physically passive for longer periods of time than his state of development can tolerate. (Here is an example of how discomfort, combined with reward, led to a most unexpected result. A woman had a ten-year-old son who attended Sunday school with some reluctance. She wanted him to feel more positively toward church. The technique she selected for achieving this goal was to make the boy attend the *regular* service that followed the Sunday school session. The boy found the regular service a very uncomfortable affair indeed. He had to sit in a hard pew . . . he had to be quiet . . . he had to restrain himself from fidgeting. In addition, he was expected to listen to something he didn't understand at all. Since "sitting in church" was aversive, it was rewarding to leave church, because church-leaving led to a turning off of the discomfort. Result: Church became a

symbol of discomfort and boredom, and was avoided whenever possible.)
- Insisting that the student pay close attention immediately after a meal.
- Making the student travel farther between classrooms than can easily be accomplished in the time allotted.
- Making the classroom too hot or too cold.

One school practice that produces aversive conditions and consequences appears to be so common that I want to comment on it separately. This is the practice of using subject matter as an instrument of punishment. You know how it goes: "All right, because you were unruly you can just stay after school and work twenty-five arithmetic problems"; or "For that you can just read four chapters tonight instead of the one chapter I was going to assign." Again, the issue has nothing to do with the appropriateness or inappropriateness of punishment. It concerns only the *instrument* of punishment. People tend to avoid the things they are hit with, whether it be a club, a stick, or a subject matter assignment.

You might think, after reading the section on universal aversives, that I regard school as nothing but a big bag of aversive conditions and that I think teachers do little else than dispense aversive consequences. Nothing could be farther from the truth. Although there is no shortage of aversive conditions and consequences, the balance is in favor of the positive. It's just that the aversives are so easy to spot; they stand out like blackbirds in a cherry pie.

A *positive condition or consequence* is any pleasant event that exists during the time the student is in the presence of the subject matter, or that follows his approach to the subject matter. In the way that an aversive condition or consequence causes the student's world to become dimmer or causes him to think less highly of himself, a positive condition or consequence causes the student to think a little more highly of himself, causes his world to become a little brighter.

Conditions and consequences that are *universal positives* are just the opposite of the universal aversives. They are the events that lead to success experiences and acknowledge that success, insure a variety of stimulation, lead to an increase of self-esteem or improved self-image, and lead to an increase in confidence. Positive practices include:

- Acknowledging students' responses, whether correct or incorrect, as attempts to learn, and following them with accepting rather than rejecting comments ("No, you'll have to try again," rather than "How could you make such a stupid error!").
- Reinforcing or rewarding subject approach responses.

- Providing instruction in increments that will allow success most of the time.
- Eliciting learning responses in private rather than in public.
- Providing enough signposts so that the student always knows where he is and where he is expected to go.
- Providing the student with statements of your instructional objectives that *he* can understand when he first sees them.
- Detecting what the student already knows and dropping that from his curriculum (thus not boring him by teaching him what he already knows).
- Providing feedback that is immediate and specific to the student's response.
- Giving the student some choice in selecting and sequencing subject matter (especially where you maintain rigid control over the goals of the instruction), thus making positive involvement possible.
- Providing the student with some control over the length of the instructional session.
- Relating new information to old, within the experience of the student.
- Treating the student as a person rather than as a number in a faceless mass.
- Using active rather than passive words during presentations.
- Making use of those variables known to be successful in attracting and holding human attention, such as motion, color, contrast, variety, and personal reference.
- For administrators only: Allowing only those instructors who like and are enthusiastic about their subjects (and students) to teach.
- Making sure that the student can perform with ease, not just barely, so that confidence can be developed.
- Expressing genuine delight at seeing the student (*Delighted* to see you again!).
- Expressing genuine delight at seeing the student succeed.
- Providing instructional tasks that are relevant to your objectives.
- Using only those test items relevant to your objectives.
- Allowing students to move about as freely as their physiology and their curiosity demand.

Here are some of the comments interviewees made about teacher practices they believed to have a positive influence on their interest in the subject under discussion:

He taught us how to approach a problem so we could solve it for ourselves. He gave us the tools for learning.

He broke the subject matter down into pieces we could understand. When we couldn't understand something, he tried to find another way of approaching it.

He made books available at our level. That is, these were books that answered questions we had about the subject at that particular time.

He led discussions, but did not dominate them.

He had a magnificent manner of presentation; he taught history as though it were a news analysis course, tying current happenings to historical happenings.

He was always able to make the student understand what was expected of him and where he stood.

She used a lot of variety; she brought in other instructors, used films and demonstrations rather than pure lecture.

He asked, and respected, the opinion of students . . . even though he didn't always agree with them.

He knew his subject and always appeared to have time.

There is nothing revolutionary about the procedures listed in this chapter. Every instructor who is interested in increasing the capabilities of his students uses many or all of them, and quite a few others as well.

Then why go into such detail? Simply because *good intentions are not enough.* Though we are generally in favor of sending students away at least as interested in our subject as they were when they arrived, we do little or nothing to *insure* that this is the case. Such apathy is frightening if one considers that the continuing use of factors leading to subject avoidance represents an enormous loss of potential skills. Those lost skills may well be one of the greatest burdens our economy will have to carry as we move into an age where a man without skills is virtually unemployable.

IMPROVING RESULTS

Robert F. Mager

A poker player down to his last coins was asked, "How're ya doin'?"
"I dunno," he replied.
"What? You don't know how you're making out?"
"Oh, sure," said the player. "I know how I'm making out, but I don't know
how I'm doing it."

Sometimes we know how well we are doing, but we don't know exactly how
we are doing it. If we knew what we were doing that was contributing to success,
and if we knew what we were doing that was contributing to failure, we could do
more of the one and less of the other.

There are factors other than the instructor that influence student behavior.
There are peers, parents, relatives, and the mass media. This being the case, it isn't
realistic to expect that all students will leave your influence anxious to learn more
about your subject or to behave enthusiastically at the mention of it. It isn't
realistic to feel responsible for all of the negative affect with which your students
leave. But should you feel responsible for any of it? How can you find out whether
you are among the sources of negative influence?

The object of this chapter is to suggest ways to assess the approach-avoidance
characteristics of instructional activities, to detect whether avoidance-producing
influences may have sneaked onto the scene without your knowing it, and to
identify the positive influences that might be strengthened.

The method suggested consists of identifying discrepancies between *principles*
of good practice and *actual* practice. This is done by asking a series of questions of
your instruction and your instructional environment (1) to determine whether
practices that produce aversive conditions and consequences may have inadvertent-
ly crept into the classroom and (2) to determine ways in which practices that lead

*From Robert F. Mager, *Developing Attitude Toward Learning*, pp. 83-98. Copyright 1968
Fearon Publishers/Lear Siegler, Inc., Education Division. All rights reserved.

to positive conditions and consequences may be strengthened or emphasized.

This procedure, called an *affect analysis,* for want of a better name, has been developed with the help of some very tolerant teachers. Originally, the procedure was designed to be used while working as a private consultant to teachers interested in achieving the affect objective as well as they might. It has been modified somewhat so that a do-it-yourself version could be offered for your consideration.[1]

The affect analysis, as originally conducted, consists of two or three periods of classroom observation, interviews of several students who are enrolled in the target course and several who are not, and a review of instructional materials, the immediate environment, and administrative practices. The object of the analysis is to identify conditions and consequences experienced by students when they approach and contact the target subject. This is no less and no more than the practice of diagnosis. When the physician looks at a person to identify ways his health can be improved, the physician first makes an examination . . . collecting information through which he can spot discrepancies between what is and what ought to be. The patient's comments tell him that something is awry (such as "Oh, Doctor, my stomach is awry"), and his analysis of conditions is intended to tell him just what may be causing the difficulty.

The results of the analysis are given to the teacher who asked for it, *and to no one else.* The discussion with the teacher is designed to point out favorable and unfavorable practices, and to discover ways in which the teacher might work around any aversive conditions not under his control.

An example may serve to illustrate the usefulness of this procedure. A fourth grade art teacher was very successful in motivating an interest in art activities. She was liked by her students, and they wanted to be able to do the things she could do. But by mid-semester it became clear that interest in art was declining. Many of the children demonstrated increasing apathy toward art, and began expressing antagonism toward art class (not toward the teacher, but toward "art *class"*). An affect analysis for this teacher revealed the somewhat subtle cause of this situation. In explaining the project for the day, the teacher used between one-fourth and one-half of the class period. Then, just as the children had organized their materials and were hard at work, the bell rang and they had to stop and go on to another classroom.

There was good motivation in this case, and an enthusiastic and skillful teacher. But there was also an event that successfully blocked the motivated activity of the students . . . and frustration resulted. Since frustration is one of the conditions people try to avoid, these students came to associate art class with something unpleasant. Aggravating the situation still further was the fact that the teacher knew time was short, and this caused her to hover over the students while they worked and urge them to work faster.

Once this state of affairs was pointed out to the teacher, there was no need to suggest a solution; making her aware of it was enough. Although she had no control over the length of the period and could not change the administrative rules, she was able to get around the restrictive time allocation by reorganizing her activities so more work time would be available to the students.

The pages that follow will describe a procedure by which you can observe and analyze your own instruction. It isn't possible to be completely objective about ourselves, so you may miss an item or two that might be spotted by a more objective observer. Moreover, some of the conditions that effect approach behavior are a little too subtle to spot singlehandedly, and one or two others may be a little too embarrassing to be visible. That really doesn't matter, however, because the procedure described will allow you to be at least partially able to stand beside yourself or behind yourself (which is a neat trick) and attain a reasonable amount of objectivity.

What to Observe

Observations are confined to school-related conditions that may exist while the student is in the presence of the subject matter, because it is these over which we have most control. Record all conditions you suspect might contribute to the increase or decrease of the student's interest in the subject he is studying. Record all conditions that are themselves aversive or that might cause an aversive condition to appear.

There are thousands of acts, conditions, and processes that might influence approach and avoidance behaviors, and it would be impossible to list them all here. Some of these conditions and events have a minor effect, and some have major effects. Record those that stand out and those you suspect of being strong enough to have an influence.

There are five areas for observation, but only these four will be considered here:[2]

The instructor.
Instructional materials and devices.
The physical environment.
Administrative rules or policies.

There are three categories of questions to answer for each of the areas for observation.

Contact Difficulty. How difficult is it for the student to make contact with the subject? How difficult is it for the student to experience the subject?

Contact Conditions. How difficult is it for the student to stay in the presence of, or in contact with, the subject? What conditions associated with subject matter manipulation make it easy or difficult for the student to continue the activity?

Contact Consequences. What are the consequences of working with the subject? What are the results of the student's attempts to learn and produce in relation to the subject?

On the pages that follow, suggested items for observation are offered in all four observation areas. It is fully recognized, however, that not all of the aversive conditions discovered in the analysis are under the control of the instructor . . . not all can be eliminated or modified by the instructor. Some aversive conditions may be beyond everyone's control. But you can't fix it if you can't find it. To eliminate or alleviate problems, it is first necessary to identify and define them. Once that is accomplished, decision about appropriate action may be made.

The Instructor

Contact Difficulty. What does the instructor do that makes it easy or difficult for the students to experience the subject?

Does he speak loud enough for all to hear easily?

Does he speak clearly?

Is his vocabulary level consistent with the subject level? (Does he use a freshman vocabulary for freshman subjects, or a senior vocabulary for freshman subjects?)

Does he continually orient students so that they always know where they are and where they are going?

Does he specify his objectives clearly? Does he give students written copies of the objectives?

Does he allow or encourage questions?

Does he allow or encourage discussion? Does he allow the student to express and develop his own ideas?

Are students allowed or encouraged to pursue some special interest they may have developed in the subject, or must they all follow the instructor?

Contact Conditions. What does the instructor do to make it easy or difficult to stay in contact with the subject?

Does he put students to sleep with a monotone?

Does he read the textbook aloud?

Does he do little else than lecture?

Does he ramble?

How interested or enthused does he appear to be about the subject?

Must students remain inactive for long periods of time?

Is he interested in teaching students, or is he more interested in keeping order?

What happens while students are taking exams? Are they eager to demonstrate their achievement, or are they frightened and anxious?

Does *he* behave as he wants his students to behave?

Does he generate discomfort while talking about or presenting the subject? (One college instructor drops cigarette ashes on the students who are forced to sit in the front row. All eyes are on his ash, and it is very difficult to pay attention to the subject.)

Contact Consequences. What happens to the students when they do work with, or manipulate, the target subject?

How are their questions answered? With interest? With hostility? With insult, ridicule, or disdain? Are they ignored?

How are student comments or attempts to discuss the subject responded to? Is the student made to feel stupid? Is he encouraged or discouraged by the instructor's responses?

What happens when a student completes a project? Turns in an assignment? Are exam results returned promptly?

Is student work treated with respect or held up to ridicule?

Are projects or assignments evaluated promptly? By whom?

Does the instructor use subject matter as an instrument of punishment?

Does the instructor insist that assignments be turned in promptly, and then ignore them?

Does the instructor do anything that convinces the student he could never be competent in the subject? That his best efforts aren't good enough?

Instructional Materials and Devices

Contact Difficulty. Do the materials facilitate or inhibit student contact with the subject?

Are there materials that help the student work with the subject, or is there nothing more than the instructor's words *about* the subject?

Do type size and style make it difficult to read the material? (Ask a student.)

Is the sound quality of audio materials good enough so that students can hear with ease?

Is the material organized so that the student can easily find what he is looking for? Is it clearly indexed?

Are the materials easy to get at?

Can the projectors be operated easily? Extension cord available? Threading easy? Screen handy? Material clearly visible on screen without extensive room-darkening efforts?

Contact Conditions. How easy or difficult is it to continue to use the materials?

Are the models in good shape, or do they require pampering to be used?

Are the films deadly dull?

Are the texts boring?

Are the materials relevant?

Is it easy to see the place or importance of the materials, or do students consider them nuisances?

What is the reading difficulty? (An introductory text was once prepared by a corporation for use in courses attended by men with a high school education. The text was well illustrated, comprehensive, and attractively bound. Some time after it had been distributed, however, it was found to be far too difficult for the students; the students couldn't get next to the ideas because of the vocabulary. Here was a case of freshman subject matter being taught with graduate school vocabulary. The discrepancy between subject matter level and vocabulary level was "discovered" when it was found that at least one group of instructors had written *another* text designed to teach the students to understand the *introductory* text.)

What is the viewing difficulty?

What is the hearing difficulty?

Contact Consequences. What is the result of using the course materials?

Do students have eyestrain or headaches after difficult reading or viewing?

Do students suffer from "relevance confusion"? Do they come away wondering why the materials are used?

Are they exasperated or frustrated because of equipment malfunction?

Are they frustrated because they had to watch while other students performed the experiments, made the adjustments, or took the measurements?

The Physical Environment

Contact Conditions. How does the physical environment make it difficult or easy for the student to experience the subject?

> Is the room too large for students in the back to see well?
> Does room shape make it difficult for some to see over the heads of others?
> Does lack of wall space minimize subject matter displays?
> How are the acoustics?
> How good is the lighting?
> Does the student have adequate work space?
> Is student work space relatively comfortable? Or uncomfortable enough to prove distracting?
> Does the seating arrangement facilitate distraction?
> Is the noise level reasonable?
> Is the environment generally too cold? Too hot? Too stuffy?

Contact Consequences. Would the student's work *improve* as a result of *leaving* the environment in which he was closeted with the subject?

> Is the student anxious to get away from the environment?
> Is the student relieved when he leaves the environment? Why?

Administrative Rules or Policies

Contact Difficulty. Are there rules that make it difficult for the student to approach the subject?

> Is the instructor accessible to the students when needed?
> Does distance get between the student and the subject? How far does he have to travel between classroom and laboratory? Between classrooms?
> Are materials accessible to the student when he needs them?
> Is the library open when the student is free to use it?
> Ar e library books easily accessible to the student, or does the librarian stand between the student and the books?
> How much paper work (form-filling) stands between the student and library books?
> How much administrative procedure stands between the instructor and course materials?
> Are projectors permanently available where the student can use them?
> Are films and filmstrips permanently available where the student can use

them?

Are students allowed to operate equipment?

Are visuals permanently available where the instructor uses them?

What proportion of a laboratory period does the student spend in setting up and taking down experiments? In signing out and signing in?

What proportion of the laboratory period does the student spend making calculations, or doing other things that could as easily be done elsewhere?

Does the instructor insist on checking every step of the student's work before he is allowed to proceed?

What conditions exist that might discourage students from operating equipment and using materials?

Contact Conditions. Do the rules make it difficult for the student to stay in contact with the subject?

Are all students made to proceed at the same rate?

Are brighter students prevented from "getting ahead" of slower students?

Are slower students given more time to understand the subject and to achieve than other students?

Are students to turn off their interest in one subject when a rigid time block ends (the bell rings) and turn on their interest in another subject? In other words, must student interest conform to administrative policy, or does policy encourage students to work with a subject until *they* reach a stopping point?

Are classes frequently interrupted by announcements over a PA system or by other intrusions?

Are students of considerably differing abilities paired, causing boredom to the faster and frustration or embarrassment to the slower?

What conditions exist that make it difficult for the instructor to maintain interest in his students and in his subject?

Is the instructor overloaded with busywork?

Does the instructor have to give the same presentation more than twice?

Contact Consequences. Does administrative policy reward or punish the student for his efforts?

If a student finishes his work earlier than the others, is he made to sit still until others finish or until the period is over? Is his diligence followed by some other form of unpleasant consequence, such as cleaning chores or "make work" assignments?

Are grades related to student achievement in relation to course objectives, or to how well the student's peers happen to have performed? In other words, is evaluation based on objective-related performance?

What kinds of recognition or privileges are there for student achievement?

Do administrators hand out as many rewards as they do punishments? (Does the principal call as many students to his office for *good* performance as he does for *poor* performance?)

For what kind of performance does the administrator reward the instructors? Are instructors rewarded on the basis of their interest in, and efforts on behalf of, students? Are instructors rewarded on the basis of the amount of student behavior they have changed? Or are they rewarded mostly for committee work, publications, and PTA attendance?

Does administrative policy *allow* successful teachers to be rewarded more than unsuccessful teachers?

Does administrative policy reward unsuccessful teaching by taking from the classroom those students with whom the teacher has failed and giving them to specialists to work with in special rooms?

What do administrators *do* to identify how well each instructor is performing?

Each of the questions posed will provide a clue to one or more conditions possibly operating to depress subject-matter interest. They are by no means all the questions to ask, and do not identify all the things to look for. They provide a guide to get you started, and will, hopefully, remind you of other factors to check on.

While reading through the questions you may have had your doubts about the way they were organized . . . you may feel that one or more items should come under a different heading. Put them there. The object of the checklist is not to provide a neat classification system . . . the object is to provide an aid to the analysis of instructional effects.

How to Observe

1. Record one or two of your class sessions. Though videotaping is preferable because it provides more information, an audio recording is better than nothing. If your course has lab sessions, record one or two of them, too.

2. Play back the recordings in private, while considering the questions listed. Try to assume you are looking or listening to recordings taken in someone else's class. There is no need to get elaborate about the notes you take. After all, you are looking for clues to ways of increasing the percentage of approach responses, not in collecting data for a journal article. So keep it simple.

3. Spend some time looking over the materials used in the course. Inspect the

texts, films, project materials, and anything else that is used during instruction. If the student is expected to operate such equipment as slide projectors, tape recorders, etc., operate them yourself while asking the suggested questions.

4. Consider administrative policies in relation to their effect on the student. Consider the time of day that students study the subject, the length of the period, the difficulty of getting to the class from the previous one, administrative interruptions, and administrative rules that may affect approach.

5. Talk with a few of your students with a view toward checking the observations you have made during the previous steps. The students are the ones being influenced and, although their self-knowledge isn't perfect, their comments about their reactions are better than your guesses. If it is at all possible, talk with a few of the students who have completed the course under consideration. They may have a better idea about the durability of the effect of conditions that influence their interest.

Acting on Observations

What is the most aversive condition or consequence you have discovered? Is it under your direct control? If it is under your control, try to reduce or eliminate it. If it isn't under your control, it might be useful to bring the condition to the attention of the appropriate person. If the condition is not under your control and you judge it to be so much a part of the current system that you would have no chance of influencing it, it probably wouldn't help to mention it to anyone. Instead, try to find a way of working around it or minimizing it. For example, the aversive effects of an uncomfortable physical environment can be reduced by allowing students more freedom of movement.

Imagine that the notes you have taken are the result of an analysis of someone else's course and that you are going to summarize for him the best and worst of his instructional situation. Check those items in your notes. They are the items with which you should concern yourself. Ignore the rest. It is not easy to change, even for good causes; you are more likely to succeed if you concentrate on one item at a time.

It may come to pass that a colleague will ask you to help him with an affect analysis of his instruction and instructional environment. If this happens, and you accept, you have an obligation to report to him, *and to no one else.* You should consider that you have contracted a client-counselor relationship; keep all results in the deepest confidence. If the person for whom you have made the observations wants to tell others about them . . . that is his prerogative . . . but it is not yours. In accepting a request to make observations and collect information, you agree to do just that—to make observations and collect information. It is highly inappropriate to pass judgment on your results by communicating it to others. Remember the wisdom that stems from the comment about casting the first stone, and about glass houses. Discretion is essential.

If you have never performed as a consultant before, one further word of caution is in order. Though your observations will be aimed at conditions relating to approach or avoidance, you will observe other things as well. You may very well observe events, procedures, or content not consistent with your own notions of effective instruction. Although it is inevitable that you *will* make such observations . . . *leave them alone.* Do not record them, do not talk about them, and do not report them to the person for whom you are observing. Even though this person has asked you to tell him about anything you think may be improved, it is unwise to take him at his word. He is no more exempt from the laws of behavior than you or I, and one of the best ways of turning yourself into an aversive stimulus that he will tend to avoid is to inundate him with criticism. Tell him only about the conditions that may be affecting approach and avoidance behavior toward the subject. None of us likes to hear about our weaknesses . . . so be objective . . . and above all, be gentle. Do unto others . . . .

Summing Up

Our success in influencing future performance is in part a function of our success at sending students away with tendencies to approach, rather than avoid, the things we want them to think about, feel about, and do about.

How can we improve our chances of strengthening approach?

By making sure there are as few aversive conditions present as possible while the student is in the presence of the subject we are teaching him.
By making sure that the student's contact with the subject is followed by positive, rather than aversive, consequences.
By modeling the very kind of behavior we would like to see exhibited by our students.

How can we identify conditions and consequences that are attractive or aversive?

By learning what we can about principles of behavior and about how to recognize their application in the world around us.

By conducting an affect analysis to find ways of improving the match between what we do and what these principles suggest that we do.

How can we measure our success at strengthening approach?

By identifying as many observable behaviors as possible that we would accept as evidence of approach tendency.

By comparing the percentage, or frequency, of approach responses to our subject when the student arrives with that recorded when he leaves.

FOOTNOTES

[1]Interaction analysis is a more sophisticated procedure for looking at effects produced by teachers. An excellent reference is E. J. Amidon and J. B. Hough (eds.), *Interaction Analysis: Theory, Research and Application,* Reading, Mass.: Addison-Wesley Publishing Co., Inc., 1967.

[2]The fifth area is that of social environment. It includes those attitude-related conditions generated by students themselves, such as: disrupting or assisting others, ridiculing or applauding the work of others, and demonstrating that contact with the subject is either an "in" or "out" thing to do. This area can have serious positive or negative influence, and it is excluded from the affect analysis outline only because I cannot talk about social environment analysis from firsthand experience.

6

TEACHING THE INDIVIDUAL

THE INTERPERSONAL RELATIONSHIP
IN THE FACILITATION OF LEARNING

Carl R. Rogers

. . . It is in fact nothing short of a miracle that the modern methods of instruction have not entirely strangled the holy curiosity of inquiry; for this delicate little plant, aside from stimulation, stands mainly in need of freedom; without this it goes to wrack and ruin without fail.

Albert Einstein

I wish to begin this paper with a statement which may seem surprising to some and perhaps offensive to others. It is simply this: Teaching, in my estimation, is a vastly overrated function.

Having made such a statement, I scurry to the dictionary to see if I really mean what I say. Teaching means "to instruct." Personally I am not much interested in instructing another. "To impart knowledge or skill." My reaction is, why not be more efficient, using a book or programmed learning? "To make to know." Here my hackles rise. I have no wish to *make* anyone know something. "To show, guide, direct." As I see it, too many people have been shown, guided, directed. So I come to the conclusion that I *do* mean what I said. Teaching is, for me, a relatively unimportant and vastly overvalued activity.

But there is more in my attitude than this. I have a negative reaction to teaching. Why? I think it is because it raises all the wrong questions. As soon as we focus on teaching, the question arises, what shall we teach? What, from our superior vantage point, does the other person need to know? This raises the ridiculous question of coverage. What shall the course cover? (Here I am acutely aware of the fact that "to cover" means both "to take in" and "to conceal from view," and I believe that most courses admirably achieve both these aims.) This notion of coverage is based on the assumption that what is taught is what is learned; what is presented is what is assimilated. I know of no assumption so obviously untrue. One does not need research to provide evidence that this is false. One needs only to talk with a few students.

But I ask myself, "Am I so prejudiced against teaching that I find no situation in which it is worthwhile?" I immediately think of my experience in Australia only a few months ago. I became much interested in the Australian aborigine. Here is a group which for more than 20,000 years has managed to live and exist in a desolate environment in which a modern man would perish within a few days. The secret of his survival has been teaching. He has passed on to the young every shred of knowledge about how to find water, about how to track game, about how to kill the kangaroo, about how to find his way through the trackless desert. Such knowledge is conveyed to the young as being *the* way to behave, and any innovation is frowned upon. It is clear that teaching has provided him the way to survive in a hostile and relatively unchanging environment.

How I am closer to the nub of the question which excites me. Teaching and the imparting of knowledge make sense in an unchanging environment. That is why it has been an unquestioned function for centuries. But if there is one truth about modern man, it is that he lives in an environment which is *continually changing.* The one thing I can be sure of is that the physics which is taught to the present day student will be outdated in a decade. The teaching in psychology will certainly be out of date in 20 years. The so-called "facts of history" depend very largely upon the current mood and temper of the culture. Chemistry, biology, genetics, sociology, are in such flux that a firm statement made today will almost certainly be modified by the time the student gets around to using the knowledge.

We are, in my view, faced with an entirely new situation in education where the goal of education, if we are to survive, is the *facilitation of change and learning.* The only man who is educated is the man who has learned how to learn; the man who has learned how to adapt and change; the man who has realized that no knowledge is secure, that only the process of *seeking* knowledge gives a basis for security. Changingness, a reliance on *process* rather than upon static knowledge, is the only thing that makes any sense as a goal for education in the modern world.

So now with some relief I turn to an activity, a purpose, which really warms me—the *facilitation of learning.* When I have been able to transform a group—and here I mean all the members of a group, myself included—into a community of *learners,* then the excitement has been almost beyond belief. To free curiosity; to permit individuals to go charging off in new directions dictated by their own interests; to unleash curiosity; to open everything to questioning and exploration; to recognize that everything is in process of change—here is an experience I can never forget. I cannot always achieve it in groups with which I am associated but when it is partially or largely achieved then it becomes a never-to-be-forgotten group experience. Out of such a context arise true students, real learners, creative scientists and scholars and practitioners, the kind of individuals who can live in a delicate but ever-changing balance between what is presently known and the flowing, moving, altering, problems and facts of the future.

Here then is a goal to which I can give myself wholeheartedly. I see the facilitation of learning as the goal of education, the way in which we might develop the learning man, the way in which we can learn to live as individuals in process. I see the facilitation of learning as the function which may hold constructive, tentative, changing, process answers to some of the deepest perplexities which beset man today.

But do we know how to achieve this new goal in education, or is it a will-of-the-wisp which sometimes occurs, sometimes fails to occur, and thus offers little real hope? My answer is that we possess a very considerable knowledge of the conditions which encourage self-initiated, significant, experiential, "gut-level" learning by the whole person. We do not frequently see these conditions put into effect because they mean a real revolution in our approach to education and revolutions are not for the timid. But we do find examples of this revolution in action.

We know—and I will briefly describe some of the evidence—that the initiation of such learning rests not upon the teaching skills of the leader, not upon his scholarly knowledge of the field, not upon his curricular planning, not upon his use of audio-visual aids, not upon the programmed learning he utilizes, not upon his lectures and presentations, though each of these might at one time or another be utilized as an important resource. No, the facilitation of significant learning rests upon certain attitudinal qualities which exist in the personal *relationship* between the facilitator and the learner.

We came upon such findings first in the field of psychotherapy, but increasingly there is evidence which shows that these findings apply in the classroom as well. We find it easier to think that the intensive relationship between therapist and client might possess these qualities, but we are also finding that they may exist in the countless interpersonal interactions (as many as 1,000 per day, as Jackson [1966] has shown) between the teacher and his pupils.

What are these qualities, these attitudes, which facilitate learning? Let me describe them very briefly, drawing illustrations from the teaching field.

Realness in the Facilitator of Learning

Perhaps the most basic of these essential attitudes is realness or genuineness. When the facilitator is a real person, being what he is, entering into a relationship with the learner without presenting a front or a facade, he is much more likely to be effective. This means that the feelings which he is experiencing are available to him, available to his awareness, that he is able to live these feelings, be them, and able to communicate them if appropriate. It means that he comes into a direct personal encounter with the learner, meeting him on a person-to-person basis. It means that he is *being* himself, not denying himself.

Seen from this point of view it is suggested that the teacher can be a real person in his relationship with his students. He can be enthusiastic, he can be bored, he can be interested in students, he can be angry, he can be sensitive and sympathetic. Because he accepts these feelings as his own he has no need to impose them on his students. He can like or dislike a student product without implying that it is objectively good or bad or that the student is good or bad. He is simply expressing a feeling for the product, a feeling which exists within himself. Thus, he is a person to his students, not a faceless embodiment of a curricular requirement nor a sterile tube through which knowledge is passed from one generation to the next.

It is obvious that this attitudinal set, found to be effective in psychotherapy, is sharply in contrast with the tendency of most teachers to show themselves to their pupils simply as roles. It is quite customary for teachers rather consciously to put on the mask, the role, the facade, of being a teacher, and to wear this facade all day removing it only when they have left the school at night.

But not all teachers are like this. Take Sylvia Ashton-Warner, who took resistant, supposedly slow-learning primary school Maori children in New Zealand, and let them develop their own reading vocabulary. Each child could request one word—whatever word he wished—each day, and she would print it on a card and give it to him. "Kiss," "ghost," "bomb," "tiger," "fight," "love," "daddy"—these are samples. Soon they were building sentences, which they could also keep. "He'll get a licking." "Pussy's frightened." The children simply never forgot these self-initiated learnings. Yet it is not my purpose to tell you of her methods. I want instead to give you a glimpse of her attitude, of the passionate realness which must have been as evident to her tiny pupils as to her readers. An editor asked her some questions and she responded: " 'A few cool facts' you asked me for. . . . I don't know that there's a cool fact in me, or anything else cool for that matter, on this particular subject. I've got only hot long facts on the matter of Creative Teaching, scorching both the page and me."

Here is no sterile facade. Here is a vital *person* with convictions, with feelings. It is her transparent realness which was, I am sure, one of the elements that made her an exciting facilitator of learning. She does not fit into some neat educational formula. She *is,* and students grow by being in contact with someone who really *is.*

Take another very different person, Barbara Shiel, also doing exciting work facilitating learning in sixth graders. She gave them a great deal of responsible freedom, and I will mention some of the reactions of her students later. But here is an example of the way she shared herself with her pupils—not just sharing feelings of sweetness and light, but anger and frustration. She had made art materials freely available, and students often used these in creative ways, but the room frequently looked like a picture of chaos. Here is her report of her feelings and what she did with them.

> I find it (still) maddening to live with the mess—with a capital M!
> No one seems to care except me. Finally, one day I told the
> children . . . that I am a neat, orderly person by nature and that
> the mess was driving me to distraction. Did they have a solution?
> It was suggested they could have volunteers to clean up. . . . I said
> it didn't seem fair to me to have the same people clean up all the
> time for others—but it *would* solve it for me. "Well, some people
> *like* to clean," they replied. So that's the way it is.

I hope this example puts some lively meaning into the phrases I used earlier,
that the facilitator "is able to live these feelings, be them, and able to communicate
them if appropriate." I have chosen an example of negative feelings, because I think
it is more difficult for most of us to visualize what this would mean. In this
instance, Miss Shiel is taking the risk of being transparent in her angry frustrations
about the mess. And what happens? The same thing which, in my experience,
nearly always happens. These young people accept and respect her feelings, take
them into account, and work out a novel solution which none of us, I believe,
would have suggested in advance. Miss Shiel wisely comments, "I used to get upset
and feel guilty when I became angry—I finally realized the children could accept *my*
feelings, too. And it is important for them to know when they've 'pushed me.' I
have limits, too."

Just to show that positive feelings, when they are real, are equally effective,
let me quote briefly a college student's reaction, in a different course. ". . . Your
sense of humor in the class was cheering: we all felt relaxed because you showed us
your human self, not a mechanical teacher image. I feel as if I have more understanding and faith in my teachers now. . . . I feel closer to the students too."
Another says, ". . . You conducted the class on a personal level and therefore in my
mind I was able to formulate a picture of you as a person and not merely as a
walking textbook." Or another student in the same course,

> . . . It wasn't as if there was a teacher in the class, but rather
> someone whom we could trust and identify as a "sharer." You
> were so perceptive and sensitive to our thoughts, and this made it
> all the more "authentic" for me. It was an "authentic" *experi-
> ence,* not just a class.

I trust I am making it clear that to be real is not always easy, nor is it
achieved all at once, but it is basic to the person who wants to become that
revolutionary individual, a facilitator of learning.

Prizing, Acceptance, Trust

There is another attitude which stands out in those who are successful in facilitating learning. I have observed this attitude. I have experienced it. Yet, it is hard to know what term to put to it so I shall use several. I think of it as prizing the learner, prizing his feelings, his opinions, his person. It is a caring for the learner, but a non-possessive caring. It is an acceptance of this other individual as a separate person, having worth in his own right. It is a basic trust—a belief that this other person is somehow fundamentally trustworthy.

Whether we call it prizing, acceptance, trust, or by some other term, it shows up in a variety of observable ways. The facilitator who has a considerable degree of this attitude can be fully acceptant of the fear and hesitation of the student as he approaches a new problem as well as acceptant of the pupil's satisfaction in achievement. Such a teacher can accept the student's occasional apathy, his erratic desires to explore byroads of knowledge, as well as his disciplined efforts to achieve major goals. He can accept personal feelings which both disturb and promote learning—rivalry with a sibling, hatred of authority, concern about personal adequacy. What we are describing is a prizing of the learner as an imperfect human being with many feelings, many potentialities. The facilitator's prizing or acceptance of the learner is an operational expression of his essential confidence and trust in the capacity of the human organism.

I would like to give some examples of this attitude from the classroom situation. Here any teacher statements would be properly suspect, since many of us would like to feel we hold such attitudes, and might have a biased perception of our qualities. But let me indicate how this attitude of prizing, of accepting, of trusting, appears to the student who is fortunate enough to experience it.

Here is a statement from a college student in a class with Morey Appell.

> Your way of being with us is a revelation to me. In your class I
> feel important, mature, and capable of doing things on my own. I
> want to think for myself and this need cannot be accomplished
> through textbooks and lectures alone, but through living. I think
> you see me as a person with real feelings and needs, an individual.
> What I say and do are significant expressions from me, and you
> recognize this.

One of Miss Shiel's sixth graders expresses much more briefly her misspelled appreciation of this attitude, "You are a wounderful teacher period!!!"

College students in a class with Dr. Patricia Bull describe not only these prizing, trusting attitudes, but the effect these have had on their other interactions.

> ... I feel that I can say things to you that I can't say to other professors ... Never before have I been so aware of the other students or their personalities. I have never had so much inter-action in a college classroom with my classmates. The climate of the classroom has had a very profound effect on me ... the free atmosphere for discussion affected me ... the general atmosphere of a particular session affected me. There have been many times when I have carried the discussion out of the class with me and thought about it for a long time.
>
> ... I still feel close to you, as though there were some tacit understanding between us, almost a conspiracy. This adds to the in-class participation on my part because I feel that at least one person in the group will react, even when I am not sure of the others. It does not matter really whether your reaction is positive or negative, it just *is*. Thank you.
>
> ... I appreciate the respect and concern you have for others, including myself. ... As a result of my experience in class, plus the influence of my readings, I sincerely believe that the student-centered teaching method does provide an ideal frame-work for learning; not just for the accumulation of facts, but more important, for learning about ourselves in relation to others. ... When I think back to my shallow awareness in September compared to the depth of my insights now, I know that this course has offered me a learning experience of great value which I couldn't have acquired in any other way.
>
> ... Very few teachers would attempt this method because they would feel that they would lose the students' respect. On the contrary. You gained our respect, through your ability to speak to us on our level, instead of ten miles above us. With the complete lack of communication we see in this school, it was a wonderful experience to see people listening to each other and really communicating on an adult, intelligent level. More classes should afford us this experience.

As you might expect, college students are often suspicious that these seeming attitudes are phony. One of Dr. Bull's students writes:

> ... Rather than observe my classmates for the first few weeks, I concentrated my observations on you, Dr. Bull. I tried to figure

out your motivations and purposes. I was convinced that you were a hypocrite. . . .I did change my opinion, however. You are not a hypocrite, by any means. . . . I do wish the course could continue. "Let each become all he is capable of being." . . . Perhaps my most disturbing question, which relates to this course is: When will we stop hiding things from ourselves and our contemporaries?

I am sure these examples are more than enough to show that the facilitator who cares, who prizes, who trusts the learner, creates a climate for learning so different from the ordinary classroom that any resemblance is, as they say, "purely coincidental."

Empathic Understanding

A further element which establishes a climate for self-initiated, experiental learning is empathic understanding. When the teacher has the ability to understand the student's reactions from the inside, has a sensitive awareness of the way the process of education and learning seems *to the student,* then again the likelihood of significant learning is increased.

This kind of understanding is sharply different from the usual evaluative understanding, which follows the pattern of, "I understand what is wrong with you." When there is a sensitive empathy, however, the reaction in the learner follows something of this pattern, "At last someone understands how it feels and seems to be *me* without wanting to analyze me or judge me. Now I can grow and blossom and learn."

This attitude of standing in the other's shoes, of viewing the world through the student's eyes, is almost unheard of in the classroom. One could listen to thousands of ordinary classroom interactions without coming across one instance of clearly communicated, sensitively accurate, empathic understanding. But it has a tremendously releasing effect when it occurs.

Let me take an illustration from Virginia Axline, dealing with a second grade boy. Jay, age 7, has been aggressive, a trouble maker, slow of speech and learning. Because of his "cussing" he was taken to the principal, who paddled him, unknown to Miss Axline. During a free work period, he fashioned a man of clay, very carefully, down to a hat and a handkerchief in his pocket. "Who is that?" asked Miss Axline. "Dunno," replied Jay. "Maybe it is the principal. He has a handkerchief in his pocket like that." Jay glared at the clay figure. "Yes," he said. Then he began to tear the head off and looked up and smiled. Miss Axline said, "You sometimes feel like twisting his head off, don't you? You get so mad at him." Jay tore off one arm, another, then beat the figure to a pulp with his fists. Another boy, with the perception of the young, explained, "Jay is mad at Mr. X because he licked him this noon." "Then you must feel lots better now," Miss Axline commented. Jay grinned and began to rebuild Mr. X.

The other examples I have cited also indicate how deeply appreciative students feel when they are simply *understood*—not evaluated, not judged, simply understood from their *own* point of view. If any teacher set herself the task of endeavoring to make one non-evaluative, acceptant, empathic response per day to a pupil's demonstrated or verbalized feeling, I believe he would discover the potency of this currently almost nonexistent kind of understanding.

Let me wind up this portion of my remarks by saying that when a facilitator creates, even to a modest degree, a classroom climate characterized by such realness, prizing, and empathy, he discovers that he has inaugurated an educational revolution. Learning of a different quality, proceeding at a different pace, with a greater degree of pervasiveness, occurs. Feelings—positive and negative, confused—become a part of the classroom experience. Learning becomes life, and a very vital life at that. The student is on his way, sometimes excitedly, sometimes reluctantly, to becoming a learning, changing being.

The Evidence

Already I can hear the mutterings of some of my so-called "hard-headed" colleagues. "A very pretty picture—very touching. But these are all self reports." (As if there were any other type of expression! But that's another issue.) They ask, "Where is the evidence? How do you know?" I would like to turn to this evidence. It is not overwhelming, but it is consistent. It is not perfect, but it is suggestive.

First of all, in the field of psychotherapy, Barrett-Lennard developed an instrument whereby he could measure these attitudinal qualities: genuineness or congruence, prizing or positive regard, empathy or understanding. This instrument was given to both client and therapist, so that we have the perception of the relationship both by the therapist and by the client whom he is trying to help. To state some of the findings very briefly it may be said that those clients who eventually showed more therapeutic change as measured by various instruments, perceived *more* of these qualities in their relationship with the therapist than did those who eventually showed less change. It is also significant that this difference in perceived relationships was evident as early as the fifth interview, and predicted later change or lack of change in therapy. Furthermore, it was found that the *client's* perception of the relationship, his experience of it, was a better predictor of ultimate outcome than was the perception of the relationship by the therapist. Barrett-Lennard's original study has been amplified and generally confirmed by other studies.

So we may say, cautiously, and with qualifications which would be too cumbersome for the present paper, that if, in therapy, the client perceives his therapist as real and genuine, as one who likes, prizes, and empathically understands him, self-learning and therapeutic change are facilitated.

Now another thread of evidence, this time related more closely to education. Emmerling found that when high school teachers were asked to identify the problems they regarded as most urgent, they could be divided into two groups. Those who regarded their most serious problems, for example, as "Helping children think for themselves and be independent"; "Getting students to participate"; "Learning new ways of helping students develop their maximum potential"; "Helping students express individual needs and interests"; fell into what he called the "open" or "positively oriented" group. When Barrett-Lennard's Relationship Inventory was administered to the students of these teachers, it was found that they were perceived as significantly more real, more acceptant, more empathic than the other group of teachers whom I shall now describe.

The second category of teachers were those who tended to see their most urgent problems in negative terms, and in terms of student deficiencies and inabilities. For them the urgent problems were such as these: "Trying to teach children who don't even have the ability to follow directions"; "Teaching children who lack a desire to learn"; "Students who are not able to do the work required for their grade"; "Getting the children to listen." It probably will be no surprise that when the students of these teachers filled out the Relationship Inventory they saw their teachers as exhibiting relatively little of genuineness, of acceptance and trust, or of empathic understanding.

Hence we may say that the teacher whose orientation is toward releasing the student's potential exhibits a high degree of these attitudinal qualities which facilitate learning. The teacher whose orientation is toward the shortcomings of his students exhibits much less of these qualities.

A small pilot study by Bills extends the significance of these findings. A group of eight teachers was selected, four of them rated as adequate and effective by their superiors, and also showing this more positive orientation to their problems. The other four were rated as inadequate teachers and also had a more negative orientation to their problems, as described above. The students of these teachers were then asked to fill out the Barrett-Lennard Relationship Inventory, giving their perception of their teacher's relationship to them. This made the students very happy. Those who saw their relationship with the teacher as good were happy to describe this relationship. Those who had an unfavorable relationship were pleased to have, for the first time, an opportunity to specify the ways in which the relationship was unsatisfactory.

The more effective teachers were rated higher in every attitude measured by the Inventory: they were seen as more real, as having a higher level of regard for their students, were less conditional or judgmental in their attitudes, showed more empathic understanding. Without going into the details of the study it may be illuminating to mention that the total scores summing these attitudes vary sharply. For example, the relationships of a group of clients with their therapists, as perceived by the clients, received an average score of 108. The four most adequate high school teachers received a score of 34. The lowest rated teacher received an average score of 2 from her students on the Relationship Inventory.

This small study certainly suggests that the teacher regarded as effective displays in her attitudes those qualities I have described as facilitative of learning, while the inadequate teacher shows little of these qualities.

Approaching the problem from a different angle, Schmuck has shown that in classrooms where pupils perceive their teachers as understanding them, there is likely to be a more diffuse liking structure among the pupils. This means that where the teacher is empathic, there are not a few students strongly liked and a few strongly disliked, but liking and affection are more evenly fused throughout the group. In a later study he has shown that among students who are highly involved in their classroom peer group, "significant relationships exist between actual liking status on the one hand and utilization of abilities, attitude toward self, and attitude toward school on the other hand." This seems to lend confirmation to the other evidence by indicating that in an understanding classroom climate every student tends to feel liked by all the others, to have a more positive attitude toward himself and toward school. If he is highly involved with his peer group (and this appears probable in such a classroom climate), he also tends to utilize his abilities more fully in his school achievement.

But, you may still ask, does the student actually *learn* more where these attitudes are present? Here an interesting study of third graders by Aspy helps to round out the suggestive evidence. He worked in six third-grade classes. The teachers tape-recorded two full weeks of their interaction with their students in the periods devoted to the teaching of reading. These recordings were done two months apart so as to obtain an adequate sampling of the teacher's interactions with her pupils. Four-minute segments of these recordings were randomly selected for rating. Three raters, working independently and "blind," rated each segment for the degree of congruence or genuineness shown by the teacher, the degree of her prizing or unconditional positive regard, and the degree of her empathic understanding.

The Reading Achievement Tests (Stanford Achievement) were used as the criterion. Again, omitting some of the details of a carefully and rigorously controlled study, it may be said that the children in the three classes with the highest degree of the attitudes described above showed a significantly greater gain in reading achievement than those students in the three classes with a lesser degree of these qualities.

So we may say, with a certain degree of assurance, that the attitudes I have endeavored to describe are not only effective in facilitating a deeper learning and understanding of self in a relationship such as psychotherapy, but that these attitudes characterize teachers who are regarded as effective teachers, and that the students of these teachers learn more, even of a conventional curriculum, than do students of teachers who are lacking in these attitudes.

I am pleased that such evidence is accumulating. It may help to justify the revolution in education for which I am obviously hoping. But the the most striking learnings of students exposed to such a climate are by no means restricted to greater achievement in the three R's. The significant learnings are the more personal ones—independence, self-initiated and responsible learning; release of creativity, a tendency to become more of a person. I can only illustrate this by picking, almost at random, statements of students whose teachers have endeavored to create a climate of trust, of prizing, of realness, of understanding, and above all, of freedom.

Again I must quote from Sylvia Ashton-Warner one of the central effects of such a climate.

> ... The drive is no longer the teacher's, but the children's own. ... The teacher is at last with the stream and not against it, the stream of children's inexorable creativeness.

If you need verification of this, listen to a few of Dr. Bull's sophomore students. The first two are mid-semester comments.

> ... This course is proving to be a vital and profound experience for me. ... This unique learning situation is giving me a whole new conception of just what learning is. ... I am experiencing a real growth in this atmosphere of constructive freedom. ... The whole experience is very challenging. ...
>
> ... I feel that the course has been of great value to me. ... I'm glad to have had this experience because it has made me think. ... I've never been so personally involved with a course before, especially *outside* the classroom. It's been frustrating, rewarding, enjoyable and tiring!

The other comments are from the end of the course.

> ... This course is not ending with the close of the semester for me, but continuing. ... I don't know of any greater benefit which can be gained from a course than this desire for further knowledge. ...

...I feel as though this type of class situation has stimulated me more in making me realize where my responsibilities lie, especially as far as doing required work on my own. I no longer feel as though a test date is the criterion for reading a book. I feel as though my future work will be done for what *I* will get out of it, not just for a test mark.

...I have enjoyed the experience of being in this course. I guess that any dissatisfaction I feel at this point is a disappointment in myself, for not having taken full advantage of the opportunities the course offered.

...I think that now I am acutely aware of the breakdown in communications that does exist in our society from seeing what happened in our class.... I've grown immensely. I know that I am a different person than I was when I came into that class.... It has done a great deal in helping me understand myself better.... Thank you for contributing to my growth.

...My idea of education has been to gain information from the teacher by attending lectures. The emphasis and focus were on the teacher.... One of the biggest changes that I experienced in this class was my outlook on education. Learning is something more than a grade on a report card. No one can measure what you have learned because it's a personal thing. I was very confused between learning and memorization. I could memorize very well, but I doubt if I ever learned as much as I could have. I believe my attitude toward learning has changed from a grade-centered outlook to a more personal one.

...I have learned a lot more about myself and adolescents in general.... I also gained more confidence in myself and my study habits by realizing that I could learn by myself without a teacher leading me by the hand. I have also learned a lot by listening to my classmates and evaluating their opinions and thoughts.... This course has proved to be a most meaningful and worthwhile experience....

If you wish to know what this type of course seems like to a sixth grader, let me give you a sample of the reactions of Miss Shiel's youngsters, misspellings and all.

...I feel that I am learning self ability. I am learning not only school work but I am learning that you can learn on your own as well as someone can teach you.

... I have a little trouble in Social Studies finding things to do. I have a hard time working the exact amount of time. Sometimes I talk to much.

... My parents don't understand the program. My mother say's it will give me a responsibility and it will let me go at my own speed.

... I like this plan because thire is a lot of freedom. I also learn more this way than the other way you don't have to wate for others you can go at your on speed rate it also takes a lot of responsibility.

Or let me take two more, from Dr. Appell's graduate class.

... I have been thinking about what happened through this experience. The only conclusion I come to is that if I try to measure what is going on, or what I was at the beginning, I have got to know what I was what I started—and I don't. . . . So many things I did and feel are just lost . . . scrambled up inside. . . . They don't seem to come out in a nice little pattern or organization I can say or write. . . . There are so many things left unsaid. I know I have only scratched the surface, I guess. I can feel so many things almost ready to come out . . . maybe that's enough. *It seems all kinds of things have so much more meaning now than ever before.* . . . This experience has had meaning, has done things to me and I am not sure how much or how far just yet. I think I am going to be a better me in the fall. *That's one thing I think I am sure of.*

... You follow no plan, yet I'm learning. Since the term began I seem to feel more alive, more real to myself. I enjoy being alone as well as with other people. My relationships with children and other adults are becoming more emotional and involved. Eating an orange last week, I peeled the skin off each separate orange section and liked it better with the transparent shell off. It was jucier and fresher tasting that way. I began to think, that's how I feel sometimes, without a transparent wall around me, really communicating my feelings. I feel that I'm growing, how much, I don't know. I'm thinking, considering, pondering and learning.

I can't read these student statements—6th grade, college, graduate level—without my eyes growing moist. Here are teachers, risking themselves, *being* themselves, *trusting* their students, adventuring into the existential unknown, taking the subjective leap. And what happens? Exciting, incredible *human* events. You can sense persons being created, learnings being initiated, future citizens rising to meet the challenge of unknown worlds. If only one teacher out of one hundred dared to risk, dared to be, dared to trust, dared to understand, we would have an infusion of a living spirit into education which would, in my estimation, be priceless.

I have heard scientists at leading schools of science, and scholars in leading universities, arguing that it is absurd to try to encourage all students to be creative—we need hosts of mediocre technicians and workers and if a few creative scientists and artists and leaders emerge, that will be enough. That may be enough for them. It may be enough to suit you. I want to go on record as saying it is *not* enough to suit me. When I realize the incredible potential in the ordinary student, I want to try to release it. We are working hard to release the incredible energy in the atom and the nucleus of the atom. If we do not devote equal energy—yes, and equal money—to the release of the potential of the individual person, then the enormous discrepancy between our level of physical energy resources and human energy resources will doom us to a deserved and universal destruction.

I'm sorry I can't be coolly scientific about this. The issue is too urgent. I can only be passionate in my statement that people count, that interpersonal relationships *are* important, that we know something about releasing human potential, that we could learn much more, and that unless we give strong positive attention to the human interpersonal side of our educational dilemma, our civilization is on its way down the drain. Better courses, better curricula, better coverage, better teaching machines, will never resolve our dilemma in a basic way. Only persons, acting like persons in their relationships with their students can even begin to make a dent on this most urgent problem of modern education.

I cannot, of course, stop here in a professional lecture. An academic lecture should be calm, factual, scholarly, critical, preferably devoid of any personal beliefs, completely devoid of passion. (This is one of the reasons I left university life, but that is a completely different story.) I cannot fully fulfill these requirements for a professional lecture, but let me at least try to state, somewhat more calmly and soberly, what I have said with such feeling and passion.

I have said that it is most unfortunate that educators and the public think about, and focus on, *teaching*. It leads them into a host of questions which are either irrelevant or absurd so far as real education is concerned.

I have said that if we focused on the facilitation of *learning*—how, why, and when the student learns, and how learning seems and feels from the inside, we might be on a much more profitable track.

I have said that we have some knowledge, and could gain more, about the conditions which facilitate learning, and that one of the most important of these conditions is the attitudinal quality of the interpersonal relationship between facilitator and learner. (There are other conditions, too, which I have tried to spell out elsewhere.)

Those attitudes which appear effective in promoting learning can be described. First of all is a transparent realness in the facilitator, a willingness to be a person, to be and to live the feelings and thoughts of the moment. When this realness includes a prizing, a caring, a trust and respect for the learner, the climate for learning is enhanced. When it includes a sensitive and accurate empathic listening, then indeed a freeing climate, stimulative of self-initiated learning and growth, exists.

I have tried to make plain that individuals who hold such attitudes, and are bold enough to act on them, do not simply modify classroom methods—they revolutionize them. They perform almost none of the functions of teachers. It is no longer accurate to call them teachers. They are catalyzers, facilitators, giving freedom and life and the opportunity to learn, to students.

I have brought in the cumulating research evidence which suggests that individuals who hold such attitudes are regarded as effective in the classroom; that the problems which concern them have to do with the release of potential, not the deficiencies of their students; that they seem to create classroom situations in which there are not admired children and disliked children, but in which affection and liking are a part of the life of every child; that in classrooms approaching such a psychological climate, children learn more of the conventional subjects.

But I have intentionally gone beyond the empirical findings to try to take you into the inner life of the student—elementary, college, and graduate—who is fortunate enough to live and learn in such an interpersonal relationship with a facilitator, in order to let you see what learning feels like when it is free, self-initiated and spontaneous. I have tried to indicate how it even changes the student-student relationship—making it more aware, more caring, more sensitive, as well as increasing the self-related learning of significant material.

Throughout my paper I have tried to indicate that if we are to have citizens who can live constructively in this kaleidoscopically changing world, we can *only* have them if we are willing for them to become self-starting, self-initiating learners. Finally, it has been my purpose to show that this kind of learner develops best, so far as we now know, in a growth-promoting, facilitative, relationship with a *person*.

ANGELS ON A PIN

Alexander Calandra

Some time ago, I received a call from a colleague who asked if I would be the referee on the grading of an examination question. He was about to give a student a zero for his answer to a physics question, while the student claimed he should receive a perfect score and would if the system were not set up against the student. The instructor and the student agreed to submit this to an impartial arbiter, and I was selected.

I went to my colleague's office and read the examination question: "Show how it is possible to determine the height of a tall building with the aid of a barometer."

The student had answered, "Take the barometer to the top of the building, attach a long rope to it, lower the barometer to the street, and then bring it up, measuring the length of the rope. The length of the rope is the height of the building."

I pointed out that the student really had a strong case for full credit, since he had answered the question completely and correctly. On the other hand, if full credit were given, it could well contribute to a high grade for the student in his physics course. A high grade is supposed to certify competence in physics, but the answer did not confirm this. I suggested that the student have another try at answering the question. I was not surprised that my colleague agreed, but I was surprised that the student did.

I gave the student six minutes to answer the question, with the warning that his answer should show some knowledge of physics. At the end of five minutes, he had not written anything. I asked if he wished to give up, but he said no. He had many answers to this problem; he was just thinking of the best one. I excused myself for interrupting him, and asked him to please go on. In the next minute, he dashed off his answer which read:

"Take the barometer to the top of the building and lean over the edge of the

*Alexander Calandra, "Angels on a Pin," from *Saturday Review,* December 21, 1968, p. 60. Copyright 1968 Saturday Review, Inc. Reprinted by permission of *Saturday Review* and the author.

roof. Drop the barometer, timing its fall with a stopwatch. Then, using the formula $S=1/2at^2$, calculate the height of the building."

At this point, I asked my colleague if *he* would give up. He conceded, and I gave the student almost full credit.

In leaving my colleague's office, I recalled that the student had said he had other answers to the problem, so I asked him what they were. "Oh, yes," said the student. "There are many ways of getting the height of a tall building with the aid of a barometer. For example, you could take the barometer out on a sunny day and measure the height of the barometer, the length of its shadow, and the length of the shadow of the building, and by the use of a simple proportion, determine the height of the building."

"Fine," I said. "And the others?"

"Yes," said the student. "There is a very basic measurement method that you will like. In this method, you take the barometer and begin to walk up the stairs. As you climb the stairs, you mark off the length of the barometer along the wall. You then count the number of marks, and this will give you the height of the building in barometer units. A very direct method.

"Of course, if you want a more sophisticated method, you can tie the barometer to the end of a string, swing it as a pendulum, and determine the value of 'g' at the street level and at the top of the building. From the difference between the two values of 'g,' the height of the building can, in principle, be calculated."

Finally he concluded, there are many other ways of solving the problem. "Probably the best," he said, "is to take the barometer to the basement and knock on the superintendent's door. When the superintendent answers, you speak to him as follows: 'Mr. Superintendent, here I have a fine barometer. If you will tell me the height of this building, I will give you this barometer.'"

At this point I asked the student if he really did not know the conventional answer to this question. He admitted that he did, but said that he was fed up with high school and college instructors trying to teach him how to think, to use the "scientific methods," and to explore the deep inner logic of the subject in a pedantic way, as is often done in the new mathematics, rather than teaching him the structure of the subject. With this in mind, he decided to revive scholasticism as an academic lark to challenge the Sputnik-panicked classrooms of America.

7

TEACHING THE GROUP

LEARNING IN THE SMALL GROUP

Allan A. Glatthorn

Let me begin by stating flatly that the small group is one of the most important educational innovations to be discussed at this conference. We could survive without the large group. We could manage without the complexities of the flexible schedule. But without the small group we would inevitably fail in our educational task. The reason is simple: it is only through the small group that we can multiply the opportunities for pupil-teacher interaction. And very significant kinds of learning take place only through such interaction.

This interaction becomes of prime importance for the student. He learns best when he is involved actively in the learning process, and the small group most effectively provides for such involvement. In the small group the student is seen as the individual learner—he cannot be ignored, he cannot get lost as a passive listener. The shy student finds himself more at ease and gradually begins to speak up and opens to the few who are with him. The talkative student who enjoys impressing a large class feels a bit different when five or six are sitting with him in the quiet of a seminar room, and he begins to listen. And the students are perceptive of the value of the small group. Most surveys of student opinion reveal overwhelming approval of the small group as a learning environment.

The teacher also benefits in very obvious ways. He finds himself functioning in a different kind of role—because the setting demands such a change. We have frequently heard the educational platitude that "changing a schedule won't change the teacher." Don't believe it. We have found that scheduling the teacher for a small group does change teacher behavior. Even the most dogmatic and didactically oriented teacher finds that he just can't lecture to five or six students. Our experience has been that once teachers have been successfully introduced to a small group, they want more and more time for it.

These benefits for the students and the teacher apply in all subjects. It is a mistake to think that small groups are useful only in English and social studies:

*From Allan A. Glatthorn, *Learning in the Small Group,* published by the Institute for Development of Educational Activities, August 1969, pp. 3-16. Reprinted by permission of the author.

they have proved to be effective in mathematics, science, and foreign language. Incidentally, we have found small groups very effective as a way of working with problem students in guidance oriented seminars. Use this as a general maxim: if you can teach it in a group of 27, you can teach it better in a group of 10.

Given its basic importance, how do we schedule for the small group? There are those who say it should not be scheduled. Let the teacher divide his class group when he sees the need for it, the argument goes; he will thus achieve greater flexibility. Unfortunately, the average teacher does not operate this way. Given the option, most teachers would be so obsessed with their need to dominate instruction that they would only very reluctantly and only very occasionally divide their classes into small groups.

We begin then by arguing that the small group is such a vital component of learning that it must be a scheduled activity—and scheduled as often as possible. Given this basic premise let's turn our attention to other specific matters dealing with the small group.

First, what physical arrangements would make for the best small-group performance? We should not make the mistake of assuming that the small group can function effectively in any kind of environment. Adequate ventilation, proper seating, good acoustics, and attractive environment all produce better discussion. While there has been much well deserved kidding about the teacher who always wants to "put our chairs in a circle and begin to discuss," such scorn should not make us forget that for most small group purposes, the arrangement whereby people who are speaking to each other can also face each other is the best arrangement. Very careful research has documented the fact that such an arrangement produces the most productive exchange of ideas. One interesting sidelight: even in a circular arrangement, members tend to address more communications to the person opposite them, not to the person on their right or on their left.

How small should the small group be? Possibly no other aspect of small-group learning has been so diligently researched. The research suggests that, first of all, there is no single ideal size for all groups. The best size depends on the nature of the task and the skills available in the members of the group. It has been suggested by Thelen that for any task-oriented group the ideal size is the smallest number that represents all the required skills necessary for the accomplishment of the task. In a group that is essentially discussion oriented the evidence seems quite clear that five or six represents the optimum number. With a group fewer than five, the individual members feel threatened; they know clearly they are on the spot. Such a threatening situation tends to inhibit free response.

On the other hand, in a group larger than five the amount of participation by the individual members can fall off sharply. The bigger the group, the greater the gap there is between the most frequent contributor and the rest of the group. In a t ypical class group of thirty, it usually happens that no more than one-third participate actively in a forty-five minute period. Even in the group of twelve or fifteen you will probably notice that only the most forceful individuals are expressing their ideas. My hunch—and it is only a hunch—is that the small group starts to look like a class when it gets to be about 14 or 15.

Does this mean that if teachers have been scheduled with a group of fifteen they must conduct the discussion with such a number? Not necessarily. They should experiment with group size, find to what extent all can be actively involved and, if necessary, subdivide the seminar of fifteen into two groups of seven or eight. One note about the composition of a small group. One study has indicated, perhaps surprisingly, that heterogeneous groups are superior to homogeneous groups in finding inventive solutions.

So much for the matters of physical arrangement, size, and composition. Let us next turn our attention to the nature of leadership in the small group. Here again there is much confused thinking. There are those who contend that only the teacher can direct the small group—and only the teacher who also teaches these same students in class. Others insist so strongly on the importance of a student-centered situation that they assert that only the student can lead. Both positions ignore the very simple point that leadership is a function of task. Later we shall attempt to point out more specifically how this is so. Even when student leadership is used, however, merely appointing the student leader does not end the teacher's responsibility. He must work with the leader, prepare him, help him see the kinds of questions that must be asked, help him evaluate the discussion. It is usually wise to rotate student leadership. Also, it is considered desirable to use the student observer in the group. The observer can serve as a summarizer, evaluate progress and, most importantly, can keep track of participation. Most teachers are blind to the extent to which students do not participate in most discussions.

We have heard much talk and have read much about the importance of democratic leadership in a group. A few points perhaps need to be made here. Democratic leadership does not mean laissez faire leadership. It means, first, the active participation by the teacher as a guide who has respect for student opinions. It means the teacher must listen to student ideas, must give students a chance to express their feelings, and should within reason permit student preferences to determine the nature of the group task and the methods for group attack. In the long run, democratic leadership may be preferred by the group; initially, however, students resent it and prefer the most directive kind of approach. One study showed that in a group with an active leader as opposed to a group with only an observer, the leader-group more frequently arrived at the correct answer, since the leader was able to secure a hearing for the minority viewpoint.

Just as leadership will vary with the nature of the group task, so will the optimum length of time for any single meeting of the small group. As we discuss below the special types of small groups, it will probably be possible for you to make some inferences about the time needed. I would, however, like to make some general observations based on our experiences with two years of small group work. First, we have found that our single module of twenty-three minutes can be effective for some types of discussion. While some teachers complain that it seems a bit too short, I personally have found that it is desirable not to reach closure with the small group—but to have students leave with the issues still unresolved, with questions turning over in their minds. Also, some teachers report that our double module of forty-six minutes is just a bit too long for the low ability student to keep a good discussion going. But these judgments are probably best arrived at through your own experience, not by listening to ours. As a very general rule, let me suggest that a thirty-minute period might work well for most small group activities.

What of these small group tasks to which we have alluded? What can the small group do in the educational setting? Here again there has been a too narrow view of the small group. Some teachers think that the small group must be tied in closely with the content of the curriculum, and they get much upset if each of their small groups does not follow a given large-group presentation. Such teachers are too much concerned with covering the curriculum where they should be concerned with *uncovering* and *discovering* with students a world of exciting knowledge. And it is in the small group that uncovering and discovering best take place. Actually, of course, the small group has numerous roles and functions which can be identified simply by asking, "What can I do with a group of ten that I cannot do just as effectively with a larger group?" I would like to discuss with you several different types of instructional groups.

The first might be called the task group. In our "life adjustment" days we called it committee work. But it is not to be sneered at. The small task group can be an effective way of involving students in many types of meaningful work in which each member can make a significant contribution. The rules for the successful task group are known to all of us who have worked unproductively on committees: be sure the task is clearly defined and understood by all; be certain that roles and individual assignments are sharply delineated; provide the necessary resources or indicate where they might be obtained; check closely on the progress of the group and hold them to a realistic schedule; provide for some type of feedback to the larger group through oral, written, and/or audio-visual reports. This diagram perhaps illustrates the nature of the task group:

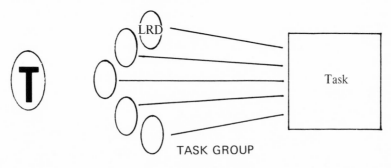

TASK GROUP

The second type of small group I would designate as the didactic group. In the didactic small group the teacher—or a student leader—presents material with the purpose of informing. At times we hear educational dogmatists state that the teacher should never teach in a small group. I always suspect such dogmatic generalizations. There is justification, I think, for the teacher occasionally to use the small group to review, to clarify, to instruct, permitting the students to interact with questions and comments. I think there are certain things a teacher can teach in a small group—and I mean teach—that can not be taught as well in a class of twenty-seven. I would diagram the didactic group like this:

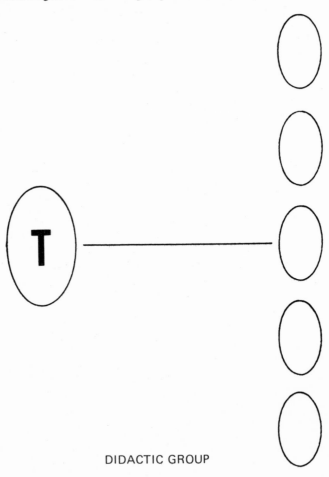

DIDACTIC GROUP

The third type might best be called the tutorial. Here the emphasis is on individual instruction, usually of a remedial nature, although it may well be individual instruction, motivation, or evaluation for an independent study project of an advanced nature. The teacher—or again an able student—merely uses the small group sessions to deal in turn with the individual members. A good teacher can probably give effective individual attention to seven or eight students in a half-hour period and accomplish much real benefit for the learner. The small group tutorial might look like this:

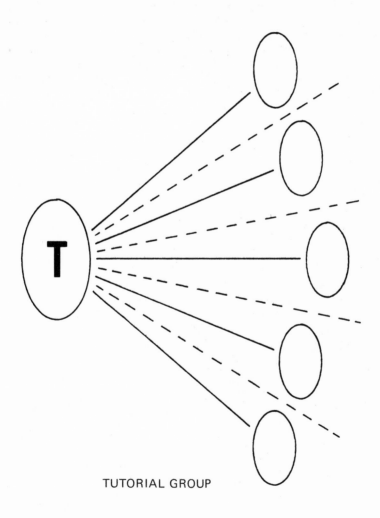

TUTORIAL GROUP

The fourth type is one which we term the discursive group. This is the free and uninhibited discussion by students of a topic of prime importance to them. It would be a mistake for teachers to exclude completely the discursive discussion or to indulge in it too much. It can make a very valid contribution to any class where the subject matter involves controversy or issues of significant interest to students. No preparation is, of course, needed by the teacher except to find the topic of sufficient interest for the class. And the teacher's role is merely one of an interested observer. All he needs to do is stay out of the way. He should listen attentively to student opinion, notice carefully who is taking part, watch closely for student reaction. Teachers, of course, need to be admonished about overusing the discursive approach. It can be a great waste of time and often is productive of nothing except the exchange of prejudices, serving merely to reinforce erroneous ideas. Teachers who boast again and again, "We have the greatest discussions in my class," often are deluding themselves if these so called "great discussions" are only bull-sessions. The discursive group might look like this:

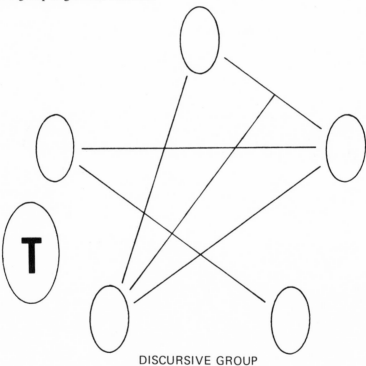

DISCURSIVE GROUP

The fifth type of small group is perhaps best characterized by the term "brain storming" coined by Alex Osborn, the originator of the technique. "Brain storming," like the bull-session, is free and uninhibited. It tends, however, to be problem centered, or solution centered. The teacher's role in the "brain storming" discussion is merely to motivate, to get the ball rolling, and then to stay out. The teacher should not criticize, evaluate, or react negatively to any idea advanced in the "brain storming" session.

Here are a few suggestions culled from Osborn's books: 1. The ideal number for a brainstorming group is about twelve. 2. Choose a subject that is simple, familiar, and talkable. When a problem calls for use of paper and pencil, it usually fails to produce a good session. 3. Criticism is ruled out; adverse judgments of ideas must be withheld until later. 4. "Free-wheeling" is welcomed; the wilder the idea, the better. 5. Quantity is wanted. 6. Combination and improvement are sought. In addition to contributing ideas of their own, participants should suggest how ideas of others can be turned into better ideas, or how two or more ideas can be joined into still another idea.

Those who are interested in more information about "brain storming" are referred, of course, to Osborn's own works.

The diagram below shows the problem-centered concern of the brain-storming group.

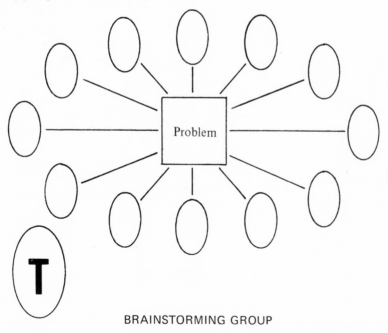

BRAINSTORMING GROUP

The sixth type of small group might best be termed heuristic. Here the emphasis is on inquiry and discovery, and the teacher becomes what Suchman calls a responsive environment. Briefly, the emphasis on the Suchman inquiry training is to develop the skills of scientific inquiry—to make students skillful askers of questions. As you know, with Suchman's approach the students are first presented with a concrete problem to serve as a focal point for their investigations: in his particular use of inquiry the concrete problem is a film of a physical event. The second condition he establishes is a responsive environment: we make it possible for the children to gather whatever additional data they need by asking specific questions which are restricted to the "yes-or-no" format. Third, we provide guidance in the process of inquiry. He sees three stages emerging here: the first is episode analysis asking questions that make sure you have an accurate picture of what it is you are trying to explain. Stage two is called the determination of relevance, asking yes-no questions to determine which facts are relevant to the explanation and which are not, which conditions are necessary to the outcome of the filmed demonstration.

The third stage he calls the induction of relational constructs. This is where hypotheses are formulated and tested. The children construct an hypothesis based on relational constructs, test their hypothesis and find it tenable or untenable. The Suchman approach provides finally for critiques of past inquiries, using tape recordings of previous sessions.

While some of us have reservations about a possible over-emphasis on process in the Suchman inquiry training, all of us can learn much from the general approach of making students the question-askers and teaching them the skill of scientific question asking. A diagram of the heuristic small group might look like this:

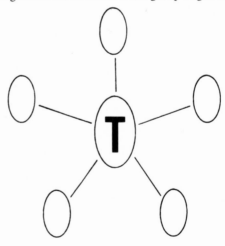

HEURISTIC GROUP

The final type of small group we would call maieutic or Socratic. Here the teacher becomes the Socratic questioner and responder. He begins by posing a problem for the group: "Is *Death of a Salesman* a great tragedy?" Note that the problem posed should be one in which the answer can best be determined through the open and honest exchange of informed opinion—through the dialog of searching minds. If the problem can be answered by consulting a reference book, it is not a suitable problem for the maieutic discussion. Having posed the problem and defined it clearly, the teacher does not retire to the rear; instead, he continues throughout the discussion to have a very active role and the good maieutic discussion can be led only by a highly trained teacher. It is the most taxing and demanding of all his tasks.

The maieutic discussion probably begins with the teacher challenging, disturbing, demanding definitions, driving the discussants back into a corner to examine their prejudices, to defend their position, to analyze their biases and preconceived notions. At times during the preliminary stage the teacher will play the devil's advocate, seeming to assume positions he really doesn't hold. The teacher's responses during this stage would probably sound negative to those committed to the dogma of interaction analysis—"Prove it. Define it. Why do you think that? Where is your evidence? Had you considered this possibility? Do you really mean that? What do you mean?" The first stage probably ends with the students confused, upset, and dismayed to see their prejudices demolished. But this is only a first stage. Unfortunately, some teachers—usually very young ones—leave them there. The first stage is destructive, and destruction should be only a necessary preliminary to reconstruction, the second stage.

At the conclusion of this first stage, it might be wise for the teacher to do a bit of constructive summarizing. "Now look, we have made some false starts but we also have come to some tentative agreements. We have defined tragedy as the fall of a great man through some external or internal force, a fall which leads to some greater reconstruction. Now let's take that definition and apply it to Miller's play."

During the second stage the teacher must do a lot of good hard listening. (And did you ever notice what poor listeners we really are? We really don't hear what students are saying—with their words and their non-verbal communication.) We must listen then very carefully to every student answer and we make a split-second judgment about how to respond to it. Is the comment totally irrelevant and should I very gently get him back to the subject? Is his comment totally unproductive and should I give him a bit of encouragement but try subtly to get another answer from someone else? Does this answer contain a piece of the truth which can be related to what has been said before by someone else? Does this response contain some glaring fallacy which should be challenged by some other student? Does this response contain a really fresh insight which should become the focus for a new line of thinking?

It is evident that during this stage the teacher becomes more than a challenger and more than a listener. He becomes a leader and a participant in the search for truth. Suddenly he finds himself caught up in an exciting dialog of searching minds. He probes, directs, stimulates, entices, responds, channels, synthesizes. And he learns. Any teacher who doesn't learn from every discussion he conducts just hasn't listened.

I might make this other point about the small group maieutic discussion. Be sure that the students develop the art and skill of listening and responding to each other. With the unskilled teacher the small group discussion too readily becomes teacher centered, with all questions and answers aimed unilaterally at the teacher.

Note, as this diagram shows, the role of the teacher is the unique one of participant-leader, with the students responding to each other and to him. As I indicated this participant-leader role in the *maieutic* discussion is the most challenging kind of teaching. And anyone who says airily, "My students can lead a discussion just as well as I" is talking through his modular hat.

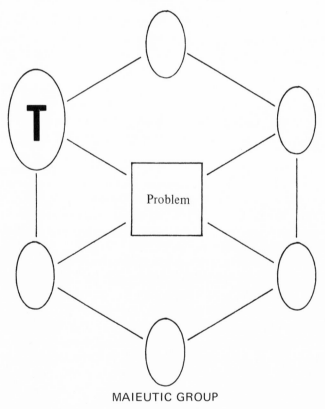

MAIEUTIC GROUP

With these major types established, let us conclude with some final general matters.

First, can the small group be evaluated? Obviously it can be and it must be. Some suggestions follow: First, there is need for group evaluation which says in effect, "How did we do today?" "Did we reach our goal?" "How many of us participated?" As mentioned before, an observer is of much help here. Second, there is obviously a need for teacher evaluation. But such evaluation should not be purely quantitative. The teacher is unwise who says in effect, "The one who talked the most gets the best grade." The teacher should learn to distinguish between meaningless verbalism and thoughtful analysis: he should learn to treasure the student who makes a few insightful comments and to chasten the garrulous dominator of discussion who really contributes nothing of substance. Finally, there is the need for individual student evaluation. In some cases it might be wise for students to keep a log of the discussions in which they participate.

Since in the small-group discussion teacher-student relationships are of key importance, it might be helpful at this stage to turn our attention to this crucial nature of teacher-student relationship. Again, there is no easy answer. The teacher must learn to play it by ear and must respond to individuals. While it is difficult to generalize, perhaps we can be of help by making some suggestions about handling certain typical small-group types. First, what do you do about the hand-waver; the student who constantly thrusts his hand in your face and almost demands your attention? To begin with, you cannot ignore him completely. This would only tend to make him resentful or else intensify his demands. Neither should you take the easy way out and call on him any time he has his hand waving. The best answer is to make him see that you value his participation, but you don't want others to be excluded. Second, what about the student who is the constant butt of class ridicule? To begin with, he needs your support. The class needs to learn that each of us has a right to be heard and that no student or teacher deserves ridicule. No matter how outrageous his questions or answers may be, find something in them to support. Make him see that your class is an open forum for the exchange of ideas, not merely a place where the sycophant can perform.

What about the shy type, the student who rarely answers just because he lacks security? Sometimes it helps, if the problem is especially acute, to talk to the student, to encourage him to participate and to prepare him for the discussion to come. You might say, for example, "John, tomorrow I'd like to discuss the garden symbolism in 'Rappaccini's Daughter.' Will you give this your careful attention tonight and be prepared to make some comments tomorrow." Also, it is helpful with this kind of student to ignore the oft-repeated warning about not mentioning a student's name first when asking a question; give the shy student some warning that he has to answer. Don't confront him abruptly with a difficult question. Say something to this effect, "John, I'd like you to give thought to this. The garden in

'Rappacini's Daughter' has a symbolic significance. What do you think the garden really stands for?" Then pause. Don't be afraid of silence, but give him a chance to think by amplifying the question. "Of course, it may not have any symbolic significance at all, but most who have read the story generally are convinced that it does have. Do you have any notion, John, as to what the symbolism may be?"

So much for the shy type. Now let us say something about the diversionist, the student who purposely or unintentionally sidetracks discussion. He must be dealt with firmly. You can answer his question of a diversionary nature briefly and then say, "That's not really the substance of our discussion. Let's get back to the point." At times, of course, the sidetrack can be illuminating and provocative, but for the most part the problem-centered discussion should stay on the track.

Finally, what of the shocker—usually a gifted student who tries to shock you and his classmates by giving some outrageous answer. The obvious answer is not to be shocked, since that is the effect he wants. Deal with his ridiculous answer calmly and quietly but deal with it effectively. Do not permit nonsense (from any source) to go unchallenged in the classroom.

It is evident that the teacher needs much training to function effectively in all small groups, regardless of the type. What type of training is most effective? He should be knowledgeable about the findings of the specialists in group dynamics and sociometry; Shepherd's *Small Groups* is a good source here. He should explore the use of one of the more promising types of methods for analyzing student-teacher interaction in the small group. The work of Flanders and Amidon looks most helpful here; and Olmsted's *The Small Group* provides a good summary of other interaction analyses methods. But most of all the teacher needs some in-service training in the school on the spot. We at North Campus have effectively devoted entire faculty meetings to the matter of the small group and have used small group demonstration lessons with good effect. I think also the teacher needs much feed-back through observer reports, pupil rating sheets, and audio and video tape. The last, I think, has much promise for improving the teacher's performance in the small group.

But we must also help the student grow in his skills with the small group, and these skills can be presented in a large-group lecture. A few suggestions for teachers might be appropriate here: 1. Stress the importance of the small group sessions. Some compulsive students will feel that they are a waste of time and demand that you get on with the "business" of teaching; other students will be tempted to waste the time with frivolous talk. 2. Use the procedures suggested in selecting and training student leaders and observers; have them use an observer evaluation check list. 3. Help the students develop goals and objectives for each discussion: what should we try to accomplish in this session? 4. Stress the importance of listening skills in the small group. Critical listening is especially important here: they need to develop the ability to listen objectively to contrary points of view, to weigh arguments critically, to detect fallacies in thinking, to recognize prejudices. 5. Help them develop the skills of responding—knowing how to differ without animus and rancor, how to take a point made by another and use it as grist for one's own intellectual mill, how to advance discussion, how to get discussion back on the track. 6. Help students evaluate their discussions. From time to time tape a discussion and play it back for critical evaluation. Take a few minutes at the conclusion of each discussion to ask, "How did we do?"

I hope it is evident from this discussion that the small group serves so many vital functions that all schools regardless of their commitment to modules or to classes should find more and more time for small group activities.

THE TEACHER'S PURPOSES

Arthur W. Combs

Two Kinds of Teachers for Professional Education

To assist students in discovering their own and society's purposes through the problems approach, we must have one of the following:

1. Professors who are highly competent in all the social, philosophical, psychological disciplines and also highly skilled in discussion approaches to teaching through which students can be helped to explore and discover personal meaning. If such people are to be found in the same skin, they must surely be very rare. It seems unlikely that we shall be able to find many in the near future.

2. The alternative seems to call for some kind of team operation which would bring together resource persons from the various foundations disciplines with persons skilled in discussion leadership and the curricular aspects of teaching. The specific combinations of such persons would depend on the peculiar staff talents available in a given college and the degree of flexibility of operations possible.

To implement such a program will not be easy in most colleges because it runs head-on into rigid job descriptions by which most faculties are chosen. Once established, these job descriptions are jealously guarded even when they no longer have relevance or meaning. Job descriptions assume that human talent is entirely organized around content or "knowledge of the subject." One finds everywhere hundreds of articles written on the role of the teacher, or counselor, or principal, or visiting teacher, or school psychologist, and so on, as though these roles could really be defined by prescriptions instead of by people and their behavior. The assumption that beginning teachers can only be taught philosophy, psychology, sociology, aesthetics, or curriculum by experts in these fields is simply not true without reference to the level at which the problems are to be confronted. Roles defined in terms of content are only valid if content is the only question with which we are concerned.

Beginning students need to get acquainted with problems and to explore where these problems may take them. This calls for a kind of instructor who may not be a content specialist but, like the elementary teacher, an expert in encouraging and assisting the processes of learning. Teaming such persons with the content experts would provide both information and exploration aspects needed for the problems approach. A number of colleges have already been experimenting with procedures of this sort with excellent results. Among these are the University of Florida, San Francisco State College, the Project I studies at Rochester, Cornell,

*From Arthur W. Combs, *The Professional Education of Teachers: A Perceptual View of Teacher Preparation,* Boston: Allyn & Bacon, Inc., 1965, pp. 91-97. Reprinted by permission.

Buffalo, and Syracuse University, and Florida Atlantic University. All of them attempt to involve students deeply in professional matters and each has experimented with various ways of providing students with rich experiences in content as well as opportunities to explore and discover its meaning in seminars or discussion groups under the supervision of trained leaders.

The Use of Discussion Groups for Exploration Purposes

The use of discussion groups has become an increasingly popular method of instruction in many teacher-preparation programs. In some it is even used almost exclusively while other methods are regarded with much disdain by the faculty. There is no doubt that well-run discussion groups can provide valuable experiences for students. The interaction involved in such groups lends itself especially well to the exploration and clarification of personal purposes. Like any other method of teaching, however, groups are no panacea. What students get out of them varies greatly. They can be exciting and fruitful or downright dull and banal, depending very largely upon the skill of the leaders.

Some of the failures of discussion groups to live up to expectations seem to be due to a confusion between two quite different kinds of discussion groups. Each of these has important values, which unfortunately are often dissipated or destroyed by otherwise skillful instructors who are not aware of the differences between these two kinds of groups and so use them inappropriately.

The Decision Group

One approach to group discussion might be called the "decision group." Here the purpose is to explore a problem and arrive at some kind of decision about it. In the course of acting in the decision group, members may learn a great deal about the problem under observation. This group is also a kind of small scale model of what our democratic government is like. As a consequence, such groups are popular with instructors concerned about "educating for democracy."

As a means of helping members discuss issues and arrive at group decisions, the decision group has immense value. As a technique for inducing learning and the exploration of purposes, however, it has some serious limitations. The decision group is focused on group action and its goal is arriving at a decision. But learning is an individual matter, and this objective may actually impede effective learning.

The moment a group is required to come to some kind of decision, it begins to operate in ways that coerce its members. It tends, therefore, to cut short individual exploration and discovery in favor of arriving at a group decision. In a decision group there inevitably comes a time when the members who have arrived at a decision begin to put pressure on those who have not. This coercion may be applied with great gentleness so that people are not even conscious of what is happening to them. One way to clothe the iron hand with a velvet glove is to call for a vote. Despite the general acceptance of the vote as a veritable symbol of democracy, it is nevertheless a coercive device of great power, especially on those in the minority. As one of my students expressed it, "A vote is only a means of stopping a discussion." People can be forced to participate, but involvement is another matter requiring an act of will on the part of the person. There is an important place for the decision group in education, but as a technique for inducing effective learning it leaves something to be desired.

The Learning Group

The second type of group I have called the "learning group." Its purpose is to allow members to explore and discover ideas and their personal meanings. Since the exploration and discovery of meaning is a purely personal goal, there is no need in such a group for a group decision and, hence, no coercion of individual members. It is even conceivable that there might be less agreement at the end of the discussion than at the beginning. The atmosphere in a learning group is one of mutual assistance and interaction in a setting which respects the dignity and integrity of individuals.

To help students in my classes at the University of Florida use such groups more effectively, we have devised a set of suggestions describing learning groups and how to get the most out of them. I include it here as a thumbnail description of learning groups for interested readers.

Group Discussion Suggestions

What Is a Group Discussion?

It is easy for a group of people to engage in talk but this does not mean that they are having a group discussion. A group discussion is not a debate. Neither is it a bull session. The purpose of a debate is to convince other people of the rightness of one's own position. "Convincing" may even proceed without any real regard for accuracy, but only with a desire to win the argument irrespective of the merits of the position. A bull session, on the other hand, is a pleasant sort of pastime in which one seeks to regale others by descriptions or stories of things he knows or events which have happened to him. Bull sessions are a kind of friendly game of "one-upmanship" in which one person tells a story and the next seeks to top it with still another. Good group discussions are neither of these. The purpose of group discussion is neither to win an argument nor to amuse oneself. Its purpose is to explore and discover personal meanings.

There are two kinds of group discussions in general use in teaching. One of these is the decision group, in which the primary purpose is to arrive at a consensus or decision on some matter. Almost everyone is familiar with such groups and has participated in them at one time or another. Decision groups can be very helpful in bringing about an agreement on a plan of action. Unfortunately, they may also interfere with the freedom of the individual to explore and move in directions unique to his own needs, for decision groups have the unhappy effect of coercing their members to arrive at the approved solutions.

A second type of discussion is the "exploratory" or "learning" group. In these sessions the purpose is not to arrive at decisions, but to help each member explore ideas and discover meanings through interaction with other people. Much of our everyday talk is made up of description in which we seek in one way or another to convey ideas to other people. It is usually concerned with what we know. It proceeds with such expressions as "I saw," "I said," "He told me," "There was," etc. A learning group discussion is far more tentative, even halting, in its progress, for it deals not with certainty but with search. It is an exploration of feelings, beliefs, doubts, fears, and concerns. Listening to a group discussion, one is likely to hear such expressions as "It seems to me," "I'm not sure about this but," "Sometimes I wonder if," "What do you think about?," "I think," "I believe," "I wish," and even sometimes if a group feels very safe with each other, "I'm afraid," "I'm angry about" or "I love." Group discussion does not seek to convince. Rather, it deals with matters unsolved and seeks to help each member find meanings not existing before.

A good group discussion is not brought about simply by bringing a group of people together to talk. Good groups take time to form and it is only as the members of a group discover each other as warm, friendly people over a period of time that good group discussion can come about. The following are some suggestions which may help you make your group a more profitable one for all concerned.

General Considerations

1. For good thinking there must be a sense of relaxation. Group discussion should always be leisurely, not desultory or wandering, but also not hastened or tense. It is more important to think slowly and thoroughly than to cover any prearranged amount of material.

2. Although we hope that all members of our groups will feel free to contribute to the discussion and will want to share their thinking with others, we also recognize that for some people this is a difficult and trying thing to do. No one in our groups is under compulsion to speak. Participation is not measured by words spoken and a silent person may be participating more than his more verbal colleagues.

3. The purpose of the group discussion is the discovery of personal meaning. This calls for "kicking ideas around," testing them, "trying them on for size," examining, comparing, thinking about and talking about ideas until they fit the particular needs and being of each person. This is best accomplished when group members are willing to express their own thinking, beliefs, and feelings freely on the one hand and to listen receptively and sympathetically to other people's ideas.

4. Sometimes in a group discussion there may be periods of silence. These need not cause concern. They are a normal function of group discussion which occur at points when a group is thinking deeply, is in process of shifting gears or has exhausted a particular question.

5. Group discussion proceeds best in an atmosphere of warmth and friendliness. Nothing causes people to clam up quicker than being threatened, ridiculed or humiliated. An atmosphere of acceptance and an honest seeking for understanding is most conducive to good group operation. The more quickly you can get to know and appreciate your fellow group members as individual people, the more quickly your group will begin to pay dividends in growth and development of its members.

Some Specific Suggestions to Group Members

1. Maintain an attitude of searching for a solution. You are trying to find the best answer, not trying to convince other people. Try not to let your previously held ideas interfere with your freedom of thinking. Be on guard against the effect of your own prejudices. You will find this difficult but highly rewarding.

2. Speak whenever you feel moved to do so (and have the right of way, of course) even though your idea may seem incomplete. If the answers were all known, there would be no point in exploring.

3. Cultivate the art of careful listening. You can practice this by trying to formulate in your own mind the gist of what a previous speaker has been saying before adding your own contribution.

4. Try to stay with the group. Discussion which strays too far afield may kill the topic at hand. Avoid introducing new issues until the decks are clean of the business under discussion.

5. Talk briefly. Saying too much may cause people's minds to wander so that they miss the value of what you wish to express.

6. Avoid long stories, anecdotes, or case studies which only illustrate a point. It is ideas, beliefs, implications, and understandings which are the meat of a discussion. Listening to one person after another tell long tales of "what happened to me" can quickly destroy a good discussion.

7. Be as sympathetic and understanding of other people's views as you can. If you disagree, say so, but avoid the appearance of being belligerent or threatening other people.

Ground Rules for Our Discussions

1. Cross examination of other speakers is not permitted. Remember that a group discussion is neither a debate nor a trial. The object is to explore one's own thinking in interaction with others, so we have made it a rule that group members may not ask questions of other group members which smack of cross questioning or which might prove embarrassing. When you feel the urge to cross question another, try instead expressing what you believe and inviting comment and criticism about that.

2. Traffic rules. Speak whenever you feel moved to do so without seeking recognition so long as the track is clear. However, whenever the traffic gets heavy and more than one person seeks to speak at once, then look to the leader to direct the traffic and seek recognition before speaking.

3. A group discussion can only operate well when all members are concerned with the issues before the house. We have therefore made a rule to restrict side conversations to a minimum. Do not hold lengthy conversations with your neighbors, as this forms new groups and destroys the cohesiveness of the total group. Besides, it isn't very well mannered.

8

CLASSROOM MANAGEMENT

THE CLASSROOM SCENE

Raymond S. Adams and Bruce J. Biddle

Which Way the View?

A number of questions might be asked about classrooms.

As *parents* we might ask, "How often does my child get individual attention from the teacher?" Or, "Does the teacher really *understand* junior's special problem?" Or, "Are they teaching him to *Think?*" Or, "How much work do the kids really have to do?" Or, "Surely his teacher doesn't put up with that sort of nonsense?"

As *employers* we might ask, "Why don't they teach kids to spell, or write legibly, or type without errors, or defer to superiors, or strive harder?"

As *citizens* we might ask, "How do children learn loyalty, morality, responsibility, and respect these days?"

As *college faculty* we might ask, "Where has intellectual ingenuity gone? What has happened to the inquiring mind? Why don't high school graduates *know* their history, literature, mathematics, chemistry, and so on?"

However, in our study we did not ask questions like these. Such questions prejudge the outcomes of classroom instructions and, more disastrously, focus on only select parts of the educational enterprise. Our question was much more basic. It asked simply, "What goes on in classrooms?"

However, the simplicity of this question is deceptive. In fact, any question that asks for an objective description must be more complicated than it first seems. Consider for a moment one fist-sized stone. It is "seen" very differently by the geologist, the road mender, the small boy bent on mischief, and the novitiate balanced precariously on his bicycle.

In the same way, any scientist setting out to describe reality is contaminated by the way he habitually looks at things. For instance, the psychologist watching a protest rally "sees" individuals who are aggressive, individuals who are anxious, and others who are conformist. The sociologist "sees" the whole gathering as perhaps symptomatic of general social ferment. Similarly, the sanitary inspector whose usual frame of reference is hygiene, notes the cleanliness of the group; the moralist sees "evidence" of corruption or nobility; the racist discerns discrimination; and so on.

An educationist then, who goes to look at classrooms and who wishes to describe what is there, has similar problems. Habitually, he starts to think of discipline, control, motivation, application, alertness, warmth, participation, and other approved educational concepts. Reinforcing his perceptions are the years of exposure he has had to the philosophical and psychological doctrines that permeate education. He will undoubtedly have firm convictions about what *ought* to go on in the classroom. He will undoubtedly have some well-grounded beliefs about what kind of conditions promote learning. (It does not matter that many educationists disagree fervently on both of these issues, that evaluators of teacher efficiency are consistently inconsistent, and that connections between teacher activities and learning outcomes have not been established.) As a result, he too tends to see what he expects to see or, even worse, what he *wants* to see. Each one of us is a prisoner of our perceptual habits. Consequently, there is an advantage in occasionally stepping aside from a conventional interpretation—seeing life as it were through new eyes.

As Viewed from Above

Imagine an everyday classroom situation. Pedagogy tells us that in it we shall see a teacher teaching. Psychology tells us that in it we shall see children learning. When, however, pedagogical and psychological prejudgments are put aside and unsophisticated eyes are used, then the scene appears differently. To that grossly overworked and accommodating man from Mars, the classroom might be appreciated in quite another way.

In the interests of the illustration, let our man from Mars have grown up in a society to all intents and purposes like our own but lacking one particular ingredient—schools. Due to means unknown to us as mortals, he and his kind come intuitively to the knowledge and experience we strive to gain through our school system. Consequently, teaching is unknown to him and learning as a process carries no meaning either. What does he see in a classroom? First he sees people occupied variously. Some sit, some stand, some move about, some talk, some keep silent, some write, draw, point, prod, sing, fidget, cry, laugh, whisper, some even sleep. Among these people, one appears to dominate. This one, apparently, exerts a controlling influence, gives directions which are usually carried out, and makes condemnatory and approving comments. Others may do this also, but one person seems to do it most.

There is a great deal of communication in this classroom. Some of it is surreptitious, but most of it is public. It takes the form of talking primarily, although much writing is done. It is possible, too, that a peculiar mannerism of the inhabitants, the raising of one arm and agitating it fiercely in the air, is also a means of communication. Messages may be conveyed in other ways in the setting. The individual who dominates the situation may, for instance, frown, raise an admonitory finger, or crash a leather strap on a desk or upon a reluctant hand whereupon the other members become silent. Communication in its many forms appears to be of considerable importance.

Not all of the communication is devoted to exchanges like the last one illustrated however. There are many occasions on which information in one form or another is placed before the members. Then the main preoccupation appears to be with the accuracy of its detail. There are, as well, occasions when the members (or some of them) show a measure of mutual concern over intellectual processes. This is when the focus is placed on reasons rather than facts, systems of logic rather than events. It seems, too, that every so often these humans engage simultaneously in individual activities which involve no apparent communication and which presumably give the members opportunity to repeat or practice earlier experiences.

Perhaps, with our Martian's indulgence, he may be pressed to observe a number of classrooms seeing these behaviors again but in various forms and combinations. Perhaps he will come to discern in this variety certain characteristic kinds of behavior that he can use to point out critical differences between the classrooms. Perhaps, too, as he becomes more experienced, he may be able to predict that where he sees certain behaviors (for instance, emphasis on free discussion) certain other behaviors are also likely to occur (perhaps a greater zest for learning). Finally, assuming that he comes to wear a normative disposition as easily as do others long exposed to educative systems, he may even judge one classroom setting as "better" than another.

The conclusion that follows from the kind of conjecturing exhibited above is that even before attempting to describe the character of classroom interaction it is necessary to recognize what aspects are being *selected* for description and what aspects are not. In other words, prior to observation, a conceptual map must be constructed which shows the extent and character of the behavior under consideration.

Other Views

To a limited extent earlier research has already made some attempt at preparing such a conceptual map. For example, Harrington in 1955 was content with a very restricted frame of reference; he sought only to identify smiles. Urban (1943) also confined his attention rigorously—to sneezes. However, Flanders in 1960 defined a broader range of activity. He selected ten kinds of behavior which he thought would give him insight into the nature of teaching. Of his ten categories, seven were concerned with teacher behavior. They were: accepts feelings; praises or encourages; accepts or uses ideas; ask questions; lectures; gives directions; criticizes or justifies authority. Two other categories were concerned with student behavior: student response; student initiation. The final category, a residual one, provided for moments of silence or confusion. Making ingenious use of these categories, Flanders classified teachers as direct or indirect (loosely interpretable as "authoritarian" and "democratic," respectively).

At about the same time Medley and Mitzel (1958) were developing a more comprehensive scale which had some seventy categories that included such diverse activities as "teacher illustrates at blackboard," "teacher talks to visitor," and "pupils shuffle feet." The categories were grouped, so that Medley and Mitzel could be regarded as interpreting the classroom as a place where (1) the teacher under-takes certain activities; (2) the pupils undertake certain activities; (3) certain kinds of group structures occur; (4) there is some emotional interplay; and (5) certain "props" or teaching aids are used.

Finally, in 1953 Cornell, Lindvall, and Saupe (who had the largest number of categories—102) saw the classroom as a place where behavior would be classified according to its "differentiation," "social organization," "initiative," "content," "variety," "competency," and "manifested classroom climate."

In contrast with these earlier research projects, the kind of interpretation used in the current study had few of the characteristics of conventional interpreta-tions of classroom behavior. We did not even start from the assumption that the classroom *had* to be either a place where teaching *or* learning goals were being ful-filled. Instead, we took a position similar to that taken by anthropologists when they look at group behavior and seek to determine how people interact. Taking such a position forced us to develop new terms to describe aspects of the situation. These terms are best understood once a broad general description has been given.

Our General View

At the outset we accepted the idea that the classroom is a *behavior setting*. As such, the classroom has many unique qualities that distinguish it clearly from other social groups. The members of its "society" live only part of their lives there, and within it they neither seek nor get full and complete satisfaction of all their spiri-tual and temporal needs. Teachers are members of this society because they achieve a limited fulfillment, mostly vocational or economic; pupils are constrained to be members because forces more powerful than they decree it.

Once within the boundaries of the classroom, the "unnaturalness" of the social situation is apparent. For here, in unbalanced distribution, are a number of children often neatly confined within a limited age range, and one adult, probably female, who asserts power far beyond the limits that reason might (democratically) lead one to expect. We have here a system—characterized by some confusion—which tries bravely to be "all things to all pupils" but which often only succeeds in stressing examinable results that are subsequently, and sometimes naively, equated with "education."

The classroom has a number of artifacts. These may vary from chalk to cheese. However, most of them are thought to be relevant to a task or process that is peculiar to educational settings in general. This process involves interaction among the individuals who comprise the personnel. The stated purpose of the process is to change the behavior of the individuals who constitute the majority group (students), especially in the areas of meanings (knowledge), norms (socially sanctioned behavior), and values (general concepts of good and bad, right and wrong).

In its personnel, then, the manner in which they are constrained, the idealistic nature of its task objectives, and the procedures by which attempts are made to achieve the objectives, the classroom is manifestly different from other social groups.

A Closer Look

What is it then that makes classrooms similar from a behavioral point of view? As we see it, similarity resides in the nature of the interaction process that occurs between the members. However, interactions can occur in a variety of ways. Some are short, others are drawn out. Some are concerned with weighty issues, some with trivia. More importantly, sometimes a series of interactions may be seen as fulfilling a discernible and perhaps unique function. For example, the full exposition of a Pythagorean theorem may entail quite a number of interactions, one after another. Such sequences are, educationally, more significant than the single interaction. To recognize their distinctive character, we called these educationally significant combinations of interactions, *transactions,* and the process (reasonably enough) the *transactional process.*

In order that transactions may occur, communication among the personnel or between the personnel and the artifacts, must occur. Without communication (defined in its broadest terms), transactions would be impossible. This assumption leads automatically to a number of questions. For example: If there is communication, what is is about? In what manner is it undertaken? Who is involved in the communication process? To what extent? Are there distinctive communication networks? What patterns do they exhibit? What effect does the distribution of members have on the pattern of communication? At a more practical level there are other questions. For example: How much subject matter is being presented? How much time is being spent on organization and control? Are the children being challenged to think? How much does the teacher dominate the situation? Do children participate equally in the interaction?

Up to this point the transactional process has been defined somewhat loosely as *what conventionally goes on in classrooms* or, more precisely *what kind of behavior is common to most classrooms.* The term then is strictly behavioral. It is still imprecise, however, because we have yet to specify what does happen in classrooms. So far we have provided a blanket term so that we have a name by which to call it. But this blanket term covers a number of more specific behaviors. These specific behaviors now need to be described in detail and some definition of other terms also is necessary.

Words and Our Meanings

Transactions have both *functional* and *structural* characteristcs. At the risk of grossly oversimplifying a complex process, function is taken here to mean how communications are given and what they are about. Structure means who gives the communication, to what extent, and under what conditions.

FUNCTION. The functions of transactions can be examined from two points of view: their *content* and their *mode* or manner. Each will be dealt with in turn.

There are three basic kinds of content: subject-matter content, sociation content, and organization content.

Subject-Matter Content. Two kinds of subject matter are taken into account in this section of the conceptual map: scheduled subject matter and nonscheduled matter. *Scheduled subject matter* refers to contents of communications that directly relate to the kind of lesson specified at the time. For example, in an "arithmetic lesson" scheduled subject matter means communications about arithmetic. However, many communications in classrooms do not bear on the subject ostensibly being taught. Thus, even an arithmetic lesson can be punctuated by excursions into social studies, biology, literature, and the like. Such subject-matter digressions are classified as *nonscheduled subject matter.*

Sociation content. In this study "sociation" applies to the transaction where content either focuses on the process of being sociable or clearly represents recognized social conventions. "Good morning class," "how do you do," are communications of the latter kind. In the case of the former, exhortations to "be good citizens," "be tidy workers," "stop fighting," "be well mannered," "be nice," are all appropriate examples. Such communications are concerned with aspects of behavior that psychologists recognize as affective.

Organization Content. Whenever the content of any communication is devoted to matters that directly involve the administration of the classroom, the appropriate content category is "organization." Under this heading fall communications that are concerned with controlling and directing personnel or property in the setting. It covers the numerous teacher directives that help (or hinder) the functioning of the classroom.

Given information on the extent to which attention is devoted to the three different contents, it would be possible to make statements like this one: "In this classroom fifteen percent of the total time is devoted to organizational procedures, two percent to matters concerned with interpersonal behavior, seventy percent to scheduled subject matter, and thirteen percent to nonscheduled subject matter." This kind of information has two principal uses. First, once enough classrooms are sampled we will know how classroom time conventionally is spent. Second, the discovery of marked differences between classrooms may lead to an explanation of the reasons for many educational outcomes. For instance, presumably children who are engaged in a greater amount of scheduled subject matter should be better informed. Those whose attention is directed toward sociation should be more socially sensitive and better adjusted, and so on.

However, content is only one of a number of aspects that have been conceptualized. Mode is the next. The mode concept is less easy than content to illustrate in that it represents a relatively novel interpretation. Again there are three kinds: information dissemination, intellectualization, and operation.

Information Dissemination Mode. Information dissemination refers to all communications devoted to the conveying of information. Statements concerned with providing facts, clarifying facts, demonstrating facts, exhibiting evidence, and the like, all fall under this heading.

Some of our reasons for isolating information dissemination may be gleaned by reflecting briefly on the nature of examination scripts and upon the average textbook. They demonstrate the fact (if it needed demonstration) that acquiring information is of prime importance in education. Factual knowledge is regarded highly. Necessarily then, factual information features prominently in the teaching-learning intercourse. Facts are presented, interpreted, explained, elaborated, illustrated, and repeated with monotonous inevitability. This is what information dissemination is about.

Intellectualization Mode. Intellectualization refers to all communications devoted expressly to the procedures involved in considering, in reasoning, and in indulging in deductive and inductive thought. It also includes those nonlogical procedures such as expressing attitude, opinion giving, judgment making, interpretation making, assessing, and evaluating. It should be noted that *the focus is on the procedure itself* and not on what the individuals concerned might be presumed to be thinking. As such intellectualization is quite distinct from the "intellectualizing" that is usually (sometimes optimistically) inferred as lying behind communications made by individuals.

We fixed on the idea of intellectualization because it seems apparent that one of the conceits that many teachers at all levels permit themselves is that they teach their students "to think." Furthermore, whether it is due to their efforts or not, children *do* learn how to think, at least in some fashion. We assume therefore a proportion of the communications occurring in classrooms must focus on the actual procedure by which the members become familiar with the processes of thinking, reasoning, forming opinions, and so on. Intellectualization *statements* are characterized by the use of phrases such as "the reason for," "it follows from this," "because of," and so on. Intellectualization *questions* tend to be of the "why" and "by what means" kind. Intellectualization also includes those untidy, illogical, and frequently unsystematic but nonetheless intellectual communications which give evidence of opinions, prejudices, judgments, and interpretations. This is *irrespective of the quality* of the opinion, judgment, or evaluation itself.

Again, this component of intellectualization is distinguished from information dissemination by its emphasis on the nature of the procedure rather than the "facts" that might confirm or deny the judgment.

Operation Mode. The third subcategory refers to those classroom processes which cannot be classified under the other two headings and which appear to exist merely for the sake of the experience itself. Group singing is classified under this heading. Any practice activities (reciting arithmetic tables, practicing a motor skill, doing writing drills) also are included. So too are creative activities such as painting (without instruction) and dancing. Group quizzes, tests, and examinations also are located under this heading. Such activities often are ritualized in classrooms. They persist over time often with little variation. They carry their own momentum in that they circumscribe and prescribe behavior. At such times, group behavior becomes more overtly homogeneous. These are the occasions when uniformity reigns and conformity is the norm.

In a somewhat limited sense, the three mode concepts represent "knowing," "understanding," and "doing." To have on record the extent to which "knowing," "understanding," and "doing" feature in classrooms seems potentially useful. The prospect of differentiating classrooms on this basis also looks promising because it offers the opportunity for comparing the educational outcomes of classes which stress practice, those which stress understanding, and those which stress organization.

STRUCTURE. The structure of transactions is viewed a little differently from its function. Structure refers to an order that persists among the parts of a system, hence to ordered features of the transaction. There are four different kinds of structure. They will be dealt with in turn.

Communication Structure. Theoretically, the number of classroom members involved in any one communication exchange could range from two to everybody in the group. During certain kinds of exchanges, however, some members may not be involved in the communication network at all; these are the *disengaged.* At other times no communication of any kind may be in evidence. These different states of affairs have been accommodated by identifying different communication groups. These groups are differentiated on the basis of the extent to which they command the attention of class members. When more than fifty percent of the class are attending to a single communication, this is called a *central group.* Any member who is *not involved* actively in any of these groups is recognized as belonging to a *residue.* Taken together, the various groups within a classroom form a communication structure, a pattern that may give evidence of considerable change and variation over time.

The selection of communication structure can be justified on a priori grounds. For example, since Dewey and Kilpatrick, the idea of the classroom as a stage upon which the virtuoso teacher gives a continuing performance has undergone reform. Numerous teaching methods have relegated lecturing to a subservient position. Yet controlling some thirty children poses its own problems and, it must be admitted, children are not always the best agents to convey an educational message. Consequently, lecturing to the "whole class" is still a recognizable teaching activity. Nevertheless, the degree to which "whole class" activities occur, and the extent to which they dominate the situation is unknown. To contrast classrooms where lecturing is infrequent with others where it is not holds potential interest. Here again it would be intriguing to compare educational outcomes in classrooms where, say, a great deal of (unofficial) peripheral group activity occurs, with others where it does not.

Communication structure patterns occur over time. They also occur through the individuals who are in the classroom setting. In our research, personnel involved in communication groups have been identified in two ways: according to the *positions* they hold, and according to the *roles* they play.

Positions. Only two *"positions"* have been specified. They are, obviously enough, (1) *teacher* and (2) *students.* This rather gross categorization was sufficient for the purposes of this study. In future studies it should be possible to identify a number of other positions that differentiate one student from another so that we become concerned with discussion-leaders, monitors, errand boys, and so on.

Roles. Three different *communicating roles* were also specified for communication groups. They are respectively *emitter, target,* and *audience.* An *emitter* is the person who speaks first when a communication group is set up. The *target* is a person or group to whom the emitter addresses himself. The *audience* consists of those members who are attending to the communication.

Role and position are complementary. Any role can be identified according to whether a teacher or student is performing it, and teachers and students may be identified according to the roles that they play.

The use of these positions and role concepts claims legitimacy from sociological convention. A number of researchers[1] have noted that the teacher dominates the classroom. Consequently, to discover the extent to which he undertakes an emitter role as distinct from an audience or target role has many implications for modern educational development. For instance, if the teacher is characteristically the *deus ex machina,* when the machines themselves—teaching machines—begin to take over, what effect will this have on the whole configuration of classroom interaction? If the teacher as principal emitter organizes his ideas on the basis of adult logical systems which, as Piaget suggests, children are incapable of comprehending, what are the consequences in terms of developing patterns of thinking?

In contrast with the teacher-dominated classroom, schools like Summerhill have long advocated a truly child-centered classroom education. But what does this mean in patterns of interaction? Are pupils continuously independent? Is there no group-structured activity? Are there no lectures? Once again, to determine the operating characteristics of different kinds of classrooms—the different ways they run the show—opens up the possibility of relating educational outcomes with what actually occurs.

Location. Finally, at any point in time each person in the classroom occupies a particular location. Structure, therefore, can also be regarded as a geographical distribution of the members. By plotting where the actors are, it is possible to arrive at a clear picture of where the action occurs in each classroom. Is it, for instance, distributed (democratically) throughout the room? Is it confined to a few select locations? To what extent do the "props" in the situation (blackboard, bookcase, teacher's desk) determine where the action is? Plotting locations makes answers to such questions possible. Oddly enough, social science has not been particularly concerned with the demography of small groups. Hall (1959) has made some provocative comments about the significance of nonverbal (demographic) aspects of interaction but, by and large, demography has been left to those who are interested in large societies.

Panorama

In brief review of the discussion so far, the structural aspects of the classroom may perhaps be regarded as the web on which the tapestry of the transactional picture is to be woven. It limits the extent of the picture, dictates the degree of fineness of work, and provides the foundation framework that will determine the durability of the finished product. Nonetheless, the appeal and beauty of the work will owe little to it. Elegance will derive mainly from the functional character of the classroom. Function will constitute the woven pattern, the blending of forms, the balance of color, the over-all design.

There is one final definitional act that has to be undertaken. The foregoing discussion lists a number of different kinds of individual and collective behaviors. Because we will refer to such behavior-states repeatedly from here on, they need a generic designation. It is at this point that we run up against one of social science's problems. The kind of term needed has to cover both individual behaviors and behaviors engaged in by a number of people at once. Unfortunately, there are few terms in the English language that refer unequivocally to collective behavior. (Cohesiveness is an excellent one in that it has no equivalent for individuals—it is impossible for one person to cohere.) The solution offered for the particular problem here is to call all these kinds of behaviors whether collective (for instance, communication structure, role allocation) or individual (teacher location, teacher role assignment, and so on), by the term *activities.* However, this term should not be thought to have any overtones of value. One "activity" is not thought to be better than another. One "activity structure" is similarly no better than its brethren. In fact the existence of "activities" is not even regarded as essentially better than the complete nonexistence of activity of any sort. Activity, as it is used here then, is not to be mistaken for "self-directed activity," "activity-period," or "activity-corner" or any other pedagogically approved activity term.

The ideas that were contained in the conceptual framework just discussed have been represented in the figure as a model or paradigm. The model starts at the top with "communication" which is then broken down into its functional and structural parts. The functional part comprises the three contents (subject matter, sociation, and organization) and the three modes (information dissemination, intellectualization, and operation). The structural part consists of the kinds of group structures (central, peripheral, and residual); positions (teacher and student); roles (emitter, target, and audience); and location.

It was with the intention of discovering the extent to which the different functional and structural activities could be shown to exist in classrooms that the actual field work was undertaken.

FOOTNOTE

[1]Flanders (1960), Bellack (1967), and Jackson (1968).

DISCIPLINE IN PUBLIC SCHOOLS

Helen B. Shaffer

The nation's public schools are about to open their doors to what is likely to be their most critical year for disciplinary management since the schoolmaster put away the birch rod. The private schools will have their troubles, too, but they are still in position to pick and choose, to suspend and expel, as they see fit, and they are not so hemmed in by bureaucratic controls nor so harassed by conflicting pressures. The public schools, holding a mandate for mass education but possessed of inadequate resources and involved in social crises beyond their control, are in for a rough time, and most of their teachers and administrators know it. The trouble is complex, pervasive, many-faceted; the most immediate problem before the educators can be summed up in two words: student unrest.

Student disorders during the 1968-69 school year gave warning of what to expect in the year ahead. Trouble was not confined to crowded and decaying schools of the inner city; it struck repeatedly at country and suburban schools as well. Long before the term ended in June, it had become clear that the crack in the authority structure of American education, first opened on college campuses, had spread down into senior and junior high schools and even reached into elementary schools. Concern over the situation currently centers on the secondary schools. A high-ranking official of the Department of Health, Education and Welfare told newsmen, Aug. 20, that a diminution of disorder on college campuses was expected this autumn but that the prospect of rising violence in senior and junior high schools remained.

A new assertiveness, incredibly brazen by standards of the past, has obviously taken hold of the adolescent captives of the compulsory education system. Some adults cheer it, many deplore it; the consensus seems to be that it has aspects both good and bad. Youth's concern for the quality of education and for peace and justice raises few complaints. But its contempt for authority and its roughshod

*Copyrighted *Editorial Research Reports,* Vol. II, No. 8, August 27, 1969, pp. 635-52.

manner of expressing grievances are unsettling, almost frightening to the elders of school and community. Even when motivated by youthful idealism, the challenge to authority thrown down by young militants has helped to create an atmosphere in many schools conducive to the release of aggressive impulses of less benign origin.

Violence in the schools has been a particularly ominous development. Vandalism, assaults on teachers, and warfare between student factions have increased. The principal of a high school in the Bronx section of New York City told an educators' meeting in March 1969 that "my faculty are fearful of actual physical violence" and "parents call almost daily, reporting attacks on their children."[1] The High School Principals Association of that city had appealed to the Mayor and the Board of Education in January for help to meet a crisis; "disorders and fears of new and frightening dimensions stalk the corridors of our schools," the association said. ". . . The hour is late, our schools are in peril." New York City School Superintendent Bernard E. Donovan on March 16 directed every junior and senior high school to name a security official, and he stationed trained security aides in the troubled schools.

School authorities in other large cities have likewise taken emergency action to curb outbreaks of student violence. Police or armed guards have been placed in schools in many cities—Chicago, Flint, Mich., Harrisburg, Pa., Kansas City, Newark, Oakland, Philadelphia, and others. The Toledo City Council on April 21 adopted an ordinance, described as an "emergency measure," prescribing special penalties for persons convicted of assaulting teachers or students, of disrupting or interfering with educational activities, or of using "improper, indecent or profane" language to a teacher.[2]

Teachers in big-city schools may well remember 1968-69 as the year when hazards of the profession became serious enough to inject the question of "combat pay" into discussions of public school salaries. The American Federation of Teachers rejected "the ugly concept of combat pay" when it was suggested in congressional debate that federal funds might properly be made available for that purpose. An editorial in the union newspaper asserted that such payments would be equivalent to "a bribe to teach in a ghetto school," and that they would stigmatize the school in the minds of students and parents. But a Brooklyn teacher retorted that "combat pay . . . [was] justified" by conditions in the "ghetto school."[3]

It may not be coincidental that in the autumn of 1969 members of the leading national high school principals' association will be offered coverage under a new "Educators' Professional Liability Policy" that will provide benefits of up to $300,000 for personal injury, and similar protection against liability for injury to others, as well as $500 for bail bond and $2,000 for legal expenses. This development and a trend toward extending similar insurance coverage to teachers under statewide plans reflect the increase in litigation over school issues, which is another facet of the upheaval in the schools and the challenge to traditional authority in the disciplining of students.

Student Activism as Major Source of Disorder

The active concern of students over school questions, or about public issues of the day, has led in many cases to school disorders and a challenging of disciplinary procedures. "To ignore student activism in 1970," the principal of a Wilmington, Del., high school said at a recent seminar for school administrators, "is to invite total chaos in a school."[4] Another big-city high school principal observed that "To be a principal in times like these is not for the faint-hearted and we're just getting started on this protest business." According to the National Association of Secondary Principals, to whom the latter remark was addressed, such statements are echoes of "what principals are saying across the nation, in the poverty-ridden cities or prosperous suburbs—and even in rural communities."

This assessment was based on the returns from a questionnaire sent in January 1969 to a national sample of high school principals. Of 1,026 who replied, 606 or 59 per cent reported that there had been some kind of student activism in their schools, and many who had not yet experienced it said they expected it in the near future. Urban and suburban schools showed no difference in the prevalence of activism; in each group the incidence was 67 per cent as against 53 per cent in large and small rural schools taken as a single group. Large suburban schools (more than 2,000 students) were the most affected; 81 per cent of them reported student activism, as did 74 per cent of the large urban schools. Even among the least affected, the small rural schools, fully 50 per cent reported activism of some kind.[5]

"One of the surprises of the survey," N.A.S.S.P.'s researchers reported, "was the fact that protest is almost as likely to occur in junior . . . as in senior high schools." Three-fifths of the urban and suburban junior high schools reported protest activity. "Student activism is the subject of the hour," the report stated. ". . . Everyone has an opinion on it." Targets of the protests were numerous: a large number concerned dress and grooming rules, but approximately one-fourth of the total involved race relations, the peace movement, or the draft. Significantly, 45 per cent of the schools with activist experience reported attacks on the character of the educational program; more than four-fifths of the large urban senior high school protests were in that area.

Student activism gained momentum during the school year. A monitoring of 1,800 daily newspapers by the Center for Research and Education at Columbia University showed a tripling of the frequency of disturbances over a four-month period, November 1968 - February 1969. This study, which was carried out under contract with the U.S. Office of Education, showed that 348 schools in 38 states experienced disruptions in the four-month period and that 239 of the disruptions were "serious episodes" like strikes, sit-ins, riots, or other forms of violence.

The onset of spring brought a seasonal rise. Dr. Alan F. Westin, director of the Center survey, estimated in May that at least 2,000 high schools in the nation had suffered disruptions. In some of the larger cities, a majority of high schools had serious outbreaks at some time during the school year. *The Urban Crisis Monitor,* put out by the Urban Research Council in Chicago, said in May 1969 that any survey made at that time "would show a sharp increase in protests in high schools."

Influence of New Left in Secondary Schools

The mood in the high schools has encouraged a growth of juvenile radicalism of the New Left variety. The Students for a Democratic Society, which started on college campuses, has been trying to recruit members in the high schools. They have had the greatest success in high schools located near college campuses, which supply many of the organizers for the movement. Michael Klonsky, S.D.S. national secretary, said recently that the average age of S.D.S. members was getting lower. "Our biggest growth," he said, "has been among high school and junior high school students."[6]

The S.D.S. published in 1967 a treatise on how to "take over" a high school. This document, *High School Reform: Toward a Student Movement,* was written in 1965 by a Los Angeles high school student and has served to guide organizers of radical movements in the schools. It suggests ways in which minor student grievances can be escalated into major protest demonstrations. One of its recommendations is to establish an underground newspaper in which students can freely express gripes against the "system."

Whether or not the adolescent Machiavellis of the S.D.S. were influential in the matter, the 1968-69 school year was marked by an unprecedented growth of juvenile journalism, carried on without the guiding hand of a faculty adviser and aping the style, content and format of underground papers put out by older anti-establishment youths. Estimates of the number of underground high school papers rose from 500 early in the year to around 1,000 by the time the spring semester was drawing to a close. The papers were serviced by their own national news service, known as HIPS (High School Independent Press Service), with headquarters in New York.

The underground papers tend to sustain the mood of warfare between the school as authority ("jail-keepers") and the victim-students ("prisoners"). "The papers attack the despotism of the principal, the dullness and incompetence of teachers by name, and the irrelevance and the reactionary nature of the curriculum," the principal of a high school in the Bronx said in an address to his colleagues. "They extol the glories of 'pot,' . . . give advice on sex and birth-control, . . . [and] recruit for demonstrations."[7] A somewhat more sympathetic account of the high school underground papers describes them as "fresh, crazy, biased, irreverent, . . . and often unexpectedly inventive." The papers "talk with the authority of the insider about the follies of the institution and the ways it might be undermined or openly confronted." The more "seasoned" papers "operate confidently on the understanding that change in the schools is their first order of business."[8]

One of the ways in which the underground paper serves the radical movement is to provide the occasion for a confrontation and for escalation of conflict. This occurs when a school disciplines a student for selling a paper on school premises without authorization. A large number of students may then be moved to protest the disciplinary action as a violation of the students' right of access to the paper. Punitive action has been taken by a number of schools against underground paper sellers who have refused to desist when so ordered. In some cases the action was taken in response to pressure by conservative elements in the community.

Damage to Buildings and Equipment by Vandals

Perhaps the most difficult aspect of the disciplinary problem is the general feeling of hostility toward school and the "system" which apparently underlies much of the disorderly and disruptive behavior of today's students. Such hostility appears among bright students as well as slow learners, among children from comfortable homes who have "everything going for them" as well as children who live in the most deprived circumstances; among students in new, well-equipped, relatively uncrowded schools and students in derelict, overcrowded, understaffed schools in poor districts.

Anger at the school or indifference to its welfare accounts for the rising toll of vandalism. The U.S. Office of Education has estimated that damage done by vandals to public schools across the country adds up to as much as $100 million a year. A survey conducted by Baltimore school officials showed that vandalism in 1967-68 cost the public schools $2.7 million in New York City; $940,100 in Los Angeles; $716,600 in Baltimore; $683,500 in Tampa; $535,000 in Boston; $410,500 in the District of Columbia; $407,000 in Milwaukee; $346,400 in Newark; $309,000 in Oakland; and $253,800 in Kansas City.

Much of the damage consists of window breakage from rock throwing, a familiar form of schoolboy mischief which the schools have long had to contend with but never to such a degree. Even more ominous are outbreaks of pupil rioting—rampages through school corridors, the smashing of furniture and equipment, overturning of office machines and files, setting of fires, etc. The monetary cost of damage so caused, including the rise in insurance rates that results, is the least of the problems. The sheer nihilism of such acts baffles school authorities, widens the breach between school and student, and injects an atmosphere of guerrilla warfare into the schoolhouse, vastly complicating the educator's task.

Schools, of course, are not the only targets affected by the increased incidence of vandalism. But school-age children are responsible for a large percentage of all willful destruction of property, private as well as public. Perhaps nothing else so dramatically underlines the weakening that has been taking place in the authority of schools to enforce student discipline.

Weakening of Authority Over Pupils

A body of principles on student discipline, developed by American education over the past half-century or longer, appeared until recently to satisfy nearly everyone as reasonable, humane, educationally productive and eminently suited to the goals of a democratic society. Almost overnight, the entire edifice of institutionalized procedures, developed to implement the principles, came under attack and students themselves were prominent among the attackers. Suddenly the rules on discipline in the standard teachers' manuals became, if not obsolete, at least not pertinent to the instant problems presented by unorthodox student behavior. Teachers who were taught how to deal with long-familiar types of difficult kids— the class clown, the back-talker, the unwilling worker, etc.—found themselves facing a new breed of misbehavers: rebels who challenged the entire institutional structure that supported the authority of the teacher and the principal.

The challengers were not mere deviants from the norm, the "bad boy" or "bad girl" who is likely to appear in any class and who can be singled out for special disciplinary action. Often they were junior authority figures themselves, capable of calling on a large sympathetic constituency in the classroom and even beyond it. The young rebel's supporters might include parents, preachers, politicians, even teachers. In Washington, D.C., militant black students found a sympathizer on the school board who encouraged their use of disruptive tactics to gain their ends.

Inapplicability of Old Disciplinary Rules Today

A student rule-breaker of this kind can scarcely be dealt with effectively by a reproof from his teacher or by the issuance of a detention hall slip. In a classroom confrontation the young disrupter of the educational process may have a better grasp of strategy than his teacher. He may counter an effort to discipline him by leading a sit-in, organizing a class boycott, or going to court to establish his legal rights. In the atmosphere that prevails in many schools today, what begins as an ordinary case of misbehavior may blow up into a full-scale disorder. Police have been called and schools shut down for trouble that began when a teacher sought to discipline a pupil for a minor rule infraction.

This is particularly true in schools where there are tensions based on race. Racial unrest in senior and junior high schools results from "long-brewing black resentments against racism," the Urban Research Council in Chicago noted last May. "Almost always the triggering incident is minor and innocuous in itself." The sensitivity of minority race students to real or imagined prejudice in school personnel or in the application of disciplinary procedures adds immeasurably to the inflammatory possibilities. The teacher or principal, in his efforts to carry out normal disciplinary procedures, may be accused either of disciplining the black student too severely out of prejudice or of disciplining him too leniently in order to avoid a charge of prejudice.

But the new breed of student may be white or black, rich or poor. "The most visible trend of secondary education today," said the principal of a high school in the Bronx which was the scene of considerable trouble during the past school year, "is the change in our students":

> Language becomes harsher and profanity is now coeducational. A subtle kind of defiant posture masks the normal tendencies of adolescents to be cheerful and cooperative. Absenteeism and cutting have mushroomed. The new breed of parent glories in the individualism of the child. . . . Narcotics invade the most respectable of our high schools, and marijuana is obviously in high fashion among the most sophisticated and intellectual of the young.
>
> High school students are eager to catch up with college students. The apathy we used to deplore is now replaced by acute social consciousness.

To deal with the new breed requires not only patience but also "an open-minded commitment to explore new directions, freed from the shackles of the conventional wisdom, and from the inertia of the status quo."[9]

Past Reliance on Fear of Corporal Punishment

Teachers in the more difficult schools may long at times for the autocratic methods of keeping order and forcing obedience that were available to schoolmasters in earlier times. But even if today's students would submit to the harsher disciplines of the past, these methods would hardly suit the goals of modern education. The old disciplinary procedures served a society that held submission to authority to be a prime goal of modern education. Today the ideal product of the mass schooling system is expected to possess an independent mind and a cooperative spirit, traits not likely to flourish in an atmosphere of institutional coercion.

For most of the years of American education, fear of the rod was a major instrument of student discipline. Infliction of physical pain was justified on the same grounds as were the harsh penal codes of the day for adults. "Fear was conceived as the only force which would make men amenable to dominion. . . . It was natural [to believe] that children, too, should be controlled by violence or the threat of violence."[10]

An historian of childhood, Philippe Aries, has traced the great change in educational style that took place between the late Middle Ages and the 17th century, from a comradely association of teachers and learners to prisonlike schools where "the birch became the mark of the schoolmaster, . . . the symbol of the subjection in which [he] . . . held his pupils."[11] The authoritarian school was the product of an authoritarian society, the power of the schoolmaster over pupils reflecting the power of the king over his subjects. And where authority became absolute, harsh penalties to uphold it usually followed. Thus "a humiliating disciplinary system—whipping at the master's discretion, . . . became widespread" in the schools of France and England. The American colonists, coming from a land where flogging had become common in schools, took it for granted that corporal punishment would be used to control children in the schools they established in the New World.

The child in pre-Revolutionary America suffered not only pain of the flesh but the tormenting threat of eternal damnation. A catechism told him he would be "sent down to everlasting fire" if he were naughty. Evangelist preachers told him children were born sinful and graphically described what awaited them in the afterworld. "This repressive attitude toward life, this insistence on conformity to a moral and ethical code based on purely religious sanction, was naturally reflected in the colonial schools and in the discipline of children."[12]

The libertarian ideas and the humanitarian movements of the 18th and 19th centuries were slow to overcome the authoritarian spirit that prevailed in schooling of the young. Though whipping posts and other harsh instruments of adult punishment gradually disappeared, "the tradition of the rod remained fixed in the educational practice."[13] The Rev. Francis Wayland, president of Brown University, expressed the prevailing view in a public address in 1830: "The pupil . . . [is] the inferior. . . . [he is] under the obligation of obedience, respect and reverence. . . . It is the duty of the instructor to enforce obedience and of the pupil to render it."

Even Horace Mann, who crusaded during the 1830s against excessive application of corporal punishment, did not approve of abolishing it altogether. Another educator, lecturing in 1843, said, "With the present conditions of society . . . there are cases in which the good of a school and the good of the offender . . . demand a severe application of the rod. Some teachers may use it . . . too frequently. In our attempt to prevent this, let us not rush to an opposite and equally pernicious extreme."[14]

The pros and cons of corporal punishment were extensively debated in the decades following the Civil War, but its use persisted. A record kept in Boston in 1889 showed 11,768 cases of officially reported physical punishments in boys' grammar schools, which then had a pupil population of 16,198. A number of writers who grew up in the 19th century recalled in memoirs the numerous cruelties inflicted on them for offenses that would be considered trivial, if offenses at all, today—squirming, nervous giggling, whispering, slowness to come forth with the right answer. Ears were twisted or boxed, noses pinched, skulls rapped with a thimbled finger; children were closeted, tethered, made to wear neck yokes that hampered their head movements, and ordered to hold uncomfortable positions until their muscles became cramped. The physical conditions in many schools made it all the more difficult to abide by the universal rule of the schoolroom to sit still and be silent until called on.[15]

Corporal punishment never quite dies as an educational issue. The rise in juvenile delinquency in the decade following World War II revived public support for it. A scholarly study of corporal punishment in the early 1960s showed it was "still a factor in the schools," that "it is still practiced even in areas where regulations forbid it." The author found a "strong trend" of public opinion "away from the permissive and toward the authoritarian point of view in discipline of pupils in the public schools." This was due to concern over "ever-mounting unruliness and disorder in the schools."[16] However, corporal punishment hardly presents itself as an answer to the disciplinary problems of the schools today.

Progressive Education's Approach to Discipline

Vast social changes which took place in the early decades of the 20th century modified considerably the authoritarian atmosphere of the public school classroom. The teacher was still "boss" but the prevailing principle on discipline leaned more to cultivation of self-discipline than toward rigid conformity to specific rules of conduct. Advances in the study of child psychology and the measurement of intelligence, growing recognition of emotional factors in learning, the rising influence of the scientific spirit, and the declining influence of Puritan morality over public education all helped to free the student from the stern discipline of earlier days.

Loosening of controls over student life was apparent in the growth of student councils, the provision of playgrounds and other recreational facilities, the institution of elective courses, and the decline in adherence to the punishment principle as an aid to learning. New guidelines on student discipline were embodied in the progressive education movement, which became increasingly influential in the post-World War I era. Progressive education held: "The conduct of the pupil should be governed by himself according to the social needs of his community, rather than by arbitrary laws. Full opportunity for initiative and self-expression should be provided."[17]

John Dewey, high priest of progressive education, described the shift of direction: "To imposition from above is opposed expression and cultivation of individuality; to external discipline is opposed free activity; to learning from texts and teachers, learning through experience." The "external authority" of the teacher was not rejected, Dewey explained; it was rather a question of finding "a more effective source of authority" than imposing facts and rules of conduct on the young.[18] This statement, made in 1938, might well sum up the problem of school discipline today.

New Concept of Students' Rights; Court Tests

Something new has been injected into the turmoil in the schools, something which is likely ultimately to have an important effect on the entire question of student discipline. This is the concept of students' rights. As used by students today, the phrase can mean anything from their right to wear their hair as they please to the exercise of a student veto over the school's instructional program. In the main, however, "students' rights" constitutes the rallying cry of a crusade against what remains of the autocratic spirit in the public schools as it affects the life of the student.

Much of the students' rights crusade is directed at freeing the high school pupil from pettifogging regulations that routinize his day, deprive him of small freedoms, and subject him to nuisance penalties for infractions of what the pupil considers "stupid" rules. The students' rights movement has also challenged the arbitrary right of the school to suspend or expel students—a punishment more fearful for many of today's college-bound students than a birching at the hands of an old-fashioned schoolmaster—for offenses which students do not consider offenses at all. Still another important direction of the crusade is toward the demand for a more "relevant" education, that is, the provision of courses and the reform of instructional programs to bring them more closely into line with student interests.

What students' rights will come to mean in actual fact is currently in process of formulation, in part through action of the courts and in part through responses of school authorities to student demands. In an address to the seminars on student activism sponsored in July 1969 by the Institute for Development of Educational Activities, A. Edgar Benton, Denver attorney, advised school administrators that students' legal rights were not clear cut. So long as students remain "inactive, nonassertive, submissive, . . . conforming, . . . ," he said, "the question of student rights will never come up." Obviously, that happy day is over for many school administrators. To an increasing extent, students and their parents are raising the issue by taking legal action against disciplinary penalties imposed by the schools.

The courts used to uphold school officials unless their action could be proved arbitrary, capricious, or based on faulty information. The *in loco parentis* principle —giving schools the right to exercise their judgment as parents would in disciplining children—prevailed. Recent decisions have moved away from that principle and toward a more positive definition of the student's rights under the Constitution.

The U. S. Supreme Court on Feb. 24, 1969, struck a major blow for students' rights by reversing a lower court decision upholding suspension of two junior high school pupils in Des Moines.[19] The two had been disciplined for wearing black armbands, signifying their opposition to the war in Viet Nam, in defiance of a school rule prohibiting the wearing of badges or emblems without permission. If the school had been able to demonstrate that wearing the armbands caused disorder or disruption of school activities, the decision might have gone differently. But the High Court held that in the absence of evidence, the "undifferentiated fear or apprehension of disturbance" on the part of school administrators was insufficient reason for denying the students what was in effect an exercise of their right to free speech under the First Amendment. Neither students nor teachers "shed their constitutional rights to freedom of speech or expression at the schoolhouse gate," the Court said.[20]

The trend of lower court decisions also is in the direction of protecting students' rights and requiring school officials to justify disciplinary rules as pertinent to the school's educational function. A Superior Court in California found in 1966, for example, that dress regulations must be based on considerations of student health or safety or the orderly conduct of school business, not on the mere desire of school authorities to enforce conformity with particular standards of propriety. An Alabama court ordered reinstatement of a student editor who had been removed from his post for disobeying a rule forbidding publication of editorials critical of the state governor and legislature. Other decisions have forbidden search of students' lockers or cars without a search warrant. Summary dismissal of a student without a hearing can be interpreted as failure to observe due process of law. "In short, the courts are rapidly beginning to define the rights of students and the limits of legitimate disciplinary authority for the school official."[21]

The American Civil Liberties Union spelled out in detail the rights of high school students (and teachers) in a pamphlet, *Academic Freedom in the Secondary Schools,* published in September 1968. Eight amendments to the U. S. Constitution

(First, Fourth, Fifth, Sixth, Seventh, Eighth, Ninth, and 14th) were found applicable. The pamphlet constitutes a guide to the new freedom in public schools.

Response of Schools to New Challenge

American schoolmen appear to be urgently searching for new ways to turn off, or to redirect into more manageable channels, the rising flow of youthful antagonism to the status quo in public education. There have been, and apparently will continue to be, a host of educators' conferences—national, regional, local—dealing with the problem of student unrest and the weakening of standard disciplinary controls. The session with this theme was by far the best attended of 46 group discussions held during the seven-day convention of the National Association of Secondary School Principals in San Francisco, Feb. 28 - March 5, 1969—"a good indicator of how concerned principals are about this problem," the association reported.[22]

The National Educational Association recently published a collection of articles from its journal on classroom discipline. Although many of the articles were written before disruptions reached the 1968-69 level, they were republished because "student unrest [is] spreading downward to many high schools" and "maintaining pupil discipline is one of the most persistent problems teachers face."[23] Several N.E.A. organizations—the Association for Supervision and Curriculum Development and the National Committee on Secondary Education—sponsored meetings or seminars on student unrest last April.

Guidelines for Dealing with Student Disruption

The Institute for Development of Educational Activities plans to publish around Oct. 1 a handbook on student activism prepared from material developed at the four seminars it sponsored earlier in the year for administrators of schools in various parts of the country.[24] N.E.A.'s National Center for Human Relations is scheduled to meet in October with teams—that is, groups representing various segments of a school community—from a number of schools which have had serious trouble. From the experiences of these schools, it is hoped to develop guidelines for meeting the problem of student dissent in constructive ways.

High school principals, so often the chief target of student disruptions, have been particularly active in preparing for the expected onslaught in the 1969-70 school year. The principal is in a particularly difficult position because he must not only take the brunt of the student protests, but also contend with rising militancy among teachers and parents, who often disagree among themselves on what should be done. With student unions pressing for reform on one side and ad hoc "Concerned Parents" organizations pressing conservative positions on the other, the principal is "clearly the man in the middle," as the executive secretary of the National Association of Secondary School Principals put it in his annual report last spring.

"As you well know," the Ohio Association of Secondary School Principals wrote in a message to its members in May, "it is becoming increasingly difficult to operate the public schools." The message accompanied a "position statement . . . on student unrest" and a copy of a sample "Resolution Supporting Teachers and School Administrators," suggested for adoption by boards of education. A number of boards, it was said, had adopted such resolutions. That they were needed was sufficient commentary on the shaken authority of the principals.

The national high school principals' association expects to publish this autumn a report on a study that probably will be of use to its members in coping with problems of student unrest. The study, conducted by Dr. Kenneth Fish, principal of the Montclair (N.J.) High School,[25] included analyses of the situation in 15 selected high schools, including some which had as many as 100 policemen patrolling their corridors, and others where there had been no trouble "even though the ingredients of conflict" were present—"bigness, urban location and a racially mixed population." Dr. Fish has already offered the nation's high school principals a number of "tentative" recommendations:

> Muster in advance of conflict the resources of faculty, administration, student body, and community in cooperative efforts to resolve differences.
> Communicate, continuously and fully, with students.
> Make needed reforms in student council.
> Expand activities program.
> Call for and use outside help when needed.
> Develop an emergency plan.
> Work positively with news media.
> Reform the curriculum.[26]

The N.A.S.S.P. is expected to draw up a position paper on student unrest, based on findings of this study.

Trend Toward Reform of Educational Programs

On the whole, public school administrators who have been through the fire of student unrest evince considerable willingness to meet the more reasonable demands of young militants and to give students the greater responsibility that the new freedom entails. A number of schools have relented on dress and grooming, allowing students to set their own standards within general bounds of modesty and cleanliness. Freedom of the press is also being extended to the innovating journalists of the high schools with only the stipulation that they skip the obscenities and libelous attacks on individuals.

To reach an accommodation in the case of student demands for a share in control of the instructional program presents a more difficult problem, but many of the student complaints about "irrelevant curriculums" are only echoes of what has been said for years by educators and school administrators. Criticism of public school education in its every aspect has been flowing steadily from the education "establishment"; it fills the professional journals and is sounded repeatedly from the numerous platforms of the education fraternity. "Today's schools fail the middle class as much as they fail the deprived and the affluent," Dr. J. Lloyd Trump, associate secretary of the national high school principals' association, said in a typical utterance of this kind before a meeting of school administrators in July 1969. "The present school curriculum emphasizes content and skills that many pupils neither need nor want."

Receptivity of Educators to Disciplinary Changes

Many schoolmen sympathize with the student challenge of what they consider an obsolete disciplinary system. It was not a student activist or the editor of an underground newspaper, but the superintendent of the Rockford, Ill., schools who said in an address to fellow educators last May:

> Our schools are organized on a semi-prison approach. We have lack of trust, sign-in and sign-out slips, detention systems, wardens and jailers, fear of escape, regimentation, limited opportunities for choice, barricaded or locked toilet rooms, cell-like classrooms. Why are we surprised that some youngsters rebel? Is it not surprising that more of them do not?[27]

The road to reform is not expected to be easy. Conflict on many fronts is inevitable. A New York teachers' union local, which has called on union leaders around the country to develop "plans of action to deal with disorders in the high school," has criticized school officials "who out of fear or guilt . . . seek to find answers in accommodation to . . . anti-democratic behavior. . . ."[28] The New York Civil Liberties Union attacked the New York Principals' Association report for having "lumped together" student vandalism and assaults with activities like "peaceful distribution of political literature."

The national secretary of the Students for a Democratic Society told an interviewer that nothing a school administrator could do to appease student radicals would satisfy them because the whole system was oppressive; that "administrators oppress young people"; and that "whether they do that liberally or or conservatively, they are still doing it."[29] And a Concerned Parents Association of a high school in Arlington, Va., called on parents on Aug. 5 to mobilize against efforts of radical militants to "introduce new procedures into the educational system . . . under the guise of personal 'freedoms' of speech, press, assembly, appearance, conduct and behavior."

These are only some of the aspects of the conflicts that lie ahead in the struggle for acceptance of new modes of maintaining student discipline. The consensus is that changes will come about nonetheless, and that when the schools have actually become better adjusted to the needs of the students, in both their instructional and their disciplinary functions, the anger and the alienation that lie behind adolescent violence will recede from the foreground of public education.

FOOTNOTES

[1] C. Edwin Linville, "New Directions in Secondary Education" (address at convention of National Association of Secondary School Principals, San Francisco, Feb 28 - March 5, 1969), *The Bulletin* (of the N.A.S.S.P.), May 1969, p. 205.

[2] The maximum penalty for assault was fixed at $1,000 fine or one year in prison: for bad language, $300 or 30 days.

[3] *American Teacher*, May 1969, p. 4, and June 1969, p. 2.

[4] Quoted in report of Institute for Development of Educational Activities, Inc. (I/D/E/A) on its 1969 Fellows Summer Institute for School Administrators, held July 7-12, 1969, on four college campuses.

[5] J. Lloyd Trump, Associate Secretary, and Jane Hunt, editorial assistant, of National Association of Secondary School Principals, report presented at San Francisco convention, Feb. 28 - March 5, 1969.

[6] "Nothing Administrators Can Do Is Right," and interview with Michael Klonsky, *I/D/E/A Reporter*, Spring Quarter 1969, p. 67. According to *I/D/E/A Reporter*, a publication of the Institute for Development of Educational Activities, the S.D.S. leader demanded a fee for the interview and said he would not have granted it at all except that he was very low on funds.

[7] C. Edwin Linville, *op. cit.*, p. 204.

[8] Dian Divoky, "The Way It's Going to Be," *Saturday Review*, Feb. 15, 1969, p. 89.

[9] C. Edwin Linville, *op. cit.*, p. 203.

[10]Herbert Arnold Falk, *Corporal Punishment: A Social Interpretation of Its Theory and Practice in the Schools of the United States* (1941), p. 3.

[11]Philippe Aries, *Centuries of Childhood* (First Vintage Edition, 1935), pp. 245-253.

[12]Herbert Arnold Falk, *op. cit.,* p. 42.

[13]*Ibid.,* p. 48.

[14]Charles Northend, quoted by Herbert Arnold Falk, *op. cit.,* p. 69.

[15]A School Committee report of 1868 described the schools of Cambridge, Mass., as overcrowded, unventilated "hotbeds of consumption."

[16]Keith Franklin James, *Corporal Punishment in the Public Schools* (1963), pp. 88-89.

[17]From *Progressive Education,* reprinted in *Readings in American Educational History,* Edgar W. Knight and Clifton L. Hall, eds. (1951), p. 538.

[18]*Ibid.,* p. 535.

[19]Tinker v. Des Moines-Independent Community School District.

[20]The Court's opinion was written by former Associate Justice Abe Fortas. Associate Justice Hugo L. Black said in a dissenting opinion that the decision virtually transferred power to control pupils from the schools to the courts. He predicted that "After the Court's holding today . . . some students . . . in all schools will be ready, able, and willing to defy their teachers on practically all orders." This was particularly unfortunate, Black added, because "Groups of students all over the land are already running loose, conducting break-ins, sit-ins, lie-ins, and smash-ins."

[21]"The School and the Courts," *I/D/E/A Reporter,* Spring Quarter 1969, p. 2.

[22]"Ring Around the Convention," *The Bulletin* (of the National Association of Secondary School Principals), May-June 1969, p. xvii.

[23]National Education Association, *Discipline in the Classroom* (1969), p. vii.

[24]The seminars were held July 7-12 at the expense of four colleges: Mills (Calif.), Southern Utah, Milford (S.C.), and Rockford (Ill.). The institute, better known as I/D/E/A, is an affiliate of the Charles F. Kettering Foundation; it has offices in Dayton, Los Angeles, and Melbourne, Fla.

[25]The Ford Foundation and the Montclair, N.J., Board of Education are co-sponsors with N.A.S.S.P. of the study.

[26]"Montclair Principal Studies Unrest," *NASSP News Letter,* May-June 1969, p. 1.

[27]Thomas A. Shaheen, quoted in report on seminar held in Columbus, May 15-16, 1969,

"Principals Tackle Student Activism at SMI (School Management Institute) Seminar," *Ohio Schools* (Journal of the Ohio Association of Secondary School Principals), May 22, 1969, p. 20.

[28] *American Teacher,* June 1969, p. 8.

[29] "Nothing Administrators Can Do Is Right," *I/D/E/A Reporter,* Spring Quarter 1969, p. 8.

9

PROBLEMS TEACHING LOW INCOME GROUPS

STRENGTHS OF THE INNER CITY CHILD

Leon Eisenberg

The view that poverty is the result of stupidity or indolence is like saying that large shoes cause big feet. The key issue in looking at the strengths of the inner city child is the importance of not confusing difference with defect. Any teacher who has taught a grade in the middle-class section and a grade in the lower-class section of the city can certainly testify to the difference. Inner city children's clothes, their accents, their activity level, their classroom behavior, their type of verbalization, their health standards, all do differ. Depending upon the type of test you use, they do test defective—notice that I said "depending on the type of test."

If we look at what we are and what they are as an anthropologist might, and total up the assets and the liabilities in the patterns of each group, then we find that all of the virtues are not on our middle-class side.

Some inner city children show positive attributes that we don't succeed in conveying to ours. Let me make it clear: I don't mean to suggest that the inner city child is a paragon of all virtue.

I'm calling attention to the positives because they're so often overlooked, but I don't suggest these children are without their difficulties. For, surely, they enter our schools poor in vocabulary, limited in ability to abstract, hampered even in capacity to sit still. They are children who are angry—angry perhaps for a good reason, but with an anger that takes it out on them and on us as well.

The behaviors the inner city child displays, however, are not entirely inside him. They emerge in response to the setting and values we supply and there is a way to alter what comes out. There is the possibility of change in the presence of what one might call an educational or a therapeutic environment.

For instance, the Harlem Project in the New York City Schools put extra services in a high school for a three-year period. As a result, it was possible to lift the group IQ ten points, to triple the number of graduates, and to double the number who went on to take some further type of education. If this can be done in

*Eisenberg, Leon, "Strengths of the Inner City Child," *Baltimore Bulletin of Education,* Vol. XLI, No. 2 (1963-64, pp. 10-16), Baltimore City Public Schools.

high school where the children are certainly in worse shape, think of what could be accomplished at an elementary school level. The success of the program stemmed from a saturation of educational services; just a little bit here and there will not get the job done.

Cooperativeness–Mutual Aid

If we are to succeed in changing these children, we have to build on what their strengths are. And what are some of them?

To begin with, the family of the inner city child is marked by a degree of cooperativeness and mutual aid between family members that extends beyond the nuclear family typical of the middle class. It embraces uncles, aunts, grandparents, cousins, and so on. The child has a sense of being part of a large and extended family which becomes as large as the community in which he grows up, and these are people available to him as a resource in times of crisis.

In our work in the Children's Psychiatric Service, it is not uncommon to have a child brought to the clinic by someone who is not a blood relative of the child but has taken him in. This goes back to customs in the rural South, customs which still characterize some of this area, whereas in the neighborhood in which I live, it's almost unknown to take in children who aren't within the immediate family.

In consequence of the cooperativeness and mutual aid in the lower-class family, these children display a feeling for people which may be more extensive and widespread than is found in the group we're used to. Inner-city children frequently enjoy each other's company more freely and fully than do children who are more individualistic and self-oriented. As a rule, they show less sibling rivalry than do middle-class children. There isn't the struggle for mother's or father's love—the family situation is more diffuse.

Family and Group Values

Psychologically, these youngsters are less marked by an individualistic competitive orientation, a characteristic which may be either a deficit or an asset. It does mean that you have to find other ways of challenging them in the classroom, ways that differ from the ones suitable with the middle-class child who's out to start his bank account of grades and money as soon as possible. You need a different approach with the inner city child who doesn't think of himself as setting aside wheat in his granary so that he can eat while others have to struggle.

Inner city children tend to have collective, that is family and group values, rather than individualistic ones. Again, this is a clue to what the teacher has to strive to work for with them. These children come from families where the parents feel that if there's to be any advance, it has to come out of social group forces, not individual activity. They're not oriented toward individual success because, in general, there is a feeling that you can't succeed anyway; the odds are stacked against you. There is a feeling that if we are going to get anywhere, all of us have to do it at one time. We've got to act as a group. A kind of fellow-feeling comes out of that which you don't get from people who feel "I'm going to make it on my own."

I might point out that collective or group values can have an extremely potent motivating force if you can tackle them and put them together. There is good evidence that one nationalistic group has succeeded in rehabilitating a number of people who had criminal records, were drunks, or addicts, thus indicating the potency of belonging to something which is meaningful.

Also, evidence is pretty impressive that during the bus strike in Montgomery, Alabama (the first shot in the current Negro resistance campaign), the rate of crimes committed by Negroes dropped sharply. Once people had a collective, socially positive way of expressing their antagonism, it was channeled to this constructive goal; people didn't commit the individual acts of violence which represented their antagonism, anger, futility, and defeat. Here is a tremendously potent educational force, if we can find a way to catch the child up into it so that his aggressive energy is channeled into positive classroom work, not into throwing stones at the school after classes are out.

Equalitarian Values

Inner city children and their families are less readily taken in than are we by status and prestige. They have more genuinely equalitarian values.

This is part of your problem, too. My child, having been raised to believe that teachers are good and should be respected, is likely to listen and to believe the teacher, to assume that what the teacher did was for the right kind of motive. On the other hand, the inner city child feels that people are what they are on the basis of what they show and not on the basis of their titles. This child, when the teacher walks into the classroom, is likely to think, "Who is this woman? Is she like all the other adults I have known? The ones who slapped me, punched me, didn't give me candy, failed to provide dinner, threw me out of the candy store, etc., etc.?" What I'm saying is that the inner city child isn't so readily taken in by a person who has all the right credentials but isn't a genuinely deserving person. You've got to prove yourself.

Responsibility for Family Chores

Typically, inner city families are somewhat disorganized. The parents have so much to do, they can't watch over their children the way we watch over ours. Consequently, inner city children are free from parental overprotection. They are more ready to accept responsibility and many begin babysitting at the age of five, six, and seven, and keep the baby out of trouble. They'll make mistakes because no seven-year-old ought to have to take care of the baby. But they often show more responsibility for family chores than I see in my child—it's my fault not his.

In effect, these children learn to negotiate the jungle of the slums. If we put 100 children from the inner city and 100 children from the suburbs into the slums of another city, our children wouldn't make it because they haven't learned something that inner city children have. Some of the things inner city children have learned are terrible—how to steal candy from the store and so forth. But on the other hand, there is a certain kind of know-how for survival, and this is an intellectual art, not just an exercise in an Oliver Twist environment.

Some years ago, a prominent psychologist went to Africa to study the chimpanzee. He took along some geometric form tests which are standard for cross-cultural studies. During the rainy season, he tested his native guides on the form tests. He found, as had been demonstrated by others before him, that primitive peoples do poorly on the form boards. If you were to use American standards, they would be mentally defective. When the rains stopped, he went out with his guides to look for the chimpanzees. Day after day, the native guides deduced where the chimps would be found that day and led him to the right spot. They did this by observing details of the environment that the psychologist could not learn to see in all the time he was there.

Obviously these people were not mentally defective as you might have concluded from the test score. They hadn't learned the geometry of Euclid that is in our environment from the beginning—houses with square corners, streets built in straight lines—they hadn't seen triangles and diamonds. What they'd learned is a kind of non-Euclidean geometry with relation to Nature about them.

Concreteness Without Flexibility

Likewise, a Guatemalan eleven-year-old girl, who can't put circles and triangles in place on a form board, can weave geometric designs on a rug—she's learned to do it one way but not the other.

This is another characteristic of the inner city child to which you have to pay attention—the concreteness of his learning and the lack of flexibility in mental sets. Having learned to do something according to way "A," he can't do it according to way "B," at least not until he's been given extensive experience. This is something to which the teacher has to be alert.

Let's not jump to the conclusion that the inner city child is inadequate because, having lacked the early experiences our children have had, he cannot do the things that our children do. The inner city child is responsive, he has learned, but the trouble is that we haven't yet got a curriculum that pegs the things that he has learned so as to start from where he is.

Another point about these youngsters is that they're angry. It's anger expressed directly and not in devious ways. If one can get anger expressed verbally rather than physically, it can be channeled and redirected. These children are less verbal and this is one of our serious problems. But it's also true that they're less word-bound, they don't sit around just talking and not doing.

Physical Skills

Finally, these children show superior physical coordination and skills. They have had to learn to survive by doing rather than talking; they possess a kind of body language and grace, a style that is physical rather than verbal. This was demonstrated as long ago as the 1920's at Teachers College, Columbia, when groups comparable to inner city children, although they fell way down on verbal items, had higher test results on performance items than did middle-class children.

Other traits could be listed. Perhaps such a list misses the point. The issue isn't who is better, but what are the differences. Teacher understanding of the differences provides the basis for more effective teaching.

What we need, and someday we'll get, is teacher training that prepares teachers to use Methods A, B and C for Children of Category 1; Methods D, E and F for Children of Category 2; and so on, instead of feeling it's got to be one way. No system works for all children. You have to know a variety of methods so that you can reach the child with his particular needs.

Physically and Visually Oriented

As I've indicated, the inner city style of orientation to the environment is physical and visual rather than auditory. You can sit here and listen to me talk. I've caused sound waves and they are more or less effective. For other groups of people, this would be a total waste of time.

The style of inner city children is physical and visual. To engage these children in watching a movie where they see it, or a class play where they act it out, or a role-playing exercise where they pretend to be the storekeeper and customers if you want to teach them behavior in a store—these techniques have been demonstrated to be effective. There is much greater likelihood of getting the children to be able to give you verbal descriptions of what happened than if you simply challenged the children with a verbal stimulus.

If you say, "Johnny, what do you think about George Washington?" you'll get an "O.K." if you're lucky, or nothing. If you get Johnny to play George Washington in a little drama in the classroom or watch somebody else play it, he may not give you a very accurate picture of George Washington, but you'll get him involved, it'll matter to him, he'll care. George Washington will have seemed to have been a real person. Johnny will begin to talk and talk around something constructive, and then you have your avenue.

Experiences Concrete

Just reading stories is not enough. If you read stories, you have to have pictures, the children have to have something to do. What they can see is better than what they can hear, at least as a beginning to build on. People have examined this by asking children to tell stories under different circumstances and counting the number of words. The response to "tell me a story" is absolutely minimal in these youngsters, whereas with a middle-class child you can get a fair amount.

The more clues you give them, the more you show them, the more you make it a personal kind of experience, the better the inner city child's response. Some of the apparent verbal poverty disappears when the conditions are changed. Then the teacher can work with the child's inner world, which he could not have done while the child was sitting there mute, sullen, and unresponsive. But the primers and the readers will have to deal with the issues of slum life and not a lily-white fairybook family the like of which he's never seen.

Externally Oriented

These children are externally oriented rather than introspective. Questions about how people feel and think are less meaningful to them than questions about what people do. The lower-class society, in general, is a doing society. These children have had relatively little training toward thinking about the self, meditating about one's feelings. These children are all on the outside; they're doing. If they feel angry, they run; they don't talk about why they're angry. This is unfortunate because talking to some extent would help them.

This action rather than word and feeling orientation suggests that play and games with children like this are a more effective spur to thinking and finally to talking than are verbal exercises. It's a challenge to design games that really do lead the child in a kind of direction.

The thinking of inner city children tends to be concrete rather than abstract. The logic they display is inductive rather than deductive. These youngsters have to be taught something very specifically, then after a number of specific teachings led on toward the generalization.

Thinking Concrete Not Abstract

In a study being carried out at New York Medical College, a simple test is applied to lower-class and middle-class children. The child is given picture cards which have a number of objects on them. Commonplace objects are chosen so that both the lower-class and the middle-class children can describe them with about equal adequacy. The first card in the series has a doll, a ball, a toy gun, a drum, and so on. Then you say, "Tell me what's on the picture." Then you take away the card and you give it to the child again. This time you say, "Give me a *title* for this picture." The word "title" means "what class" the objects in this picture belong to, only that would be too complicated an idea for a first-grader, so you say "give me a title."

The middle-class child will call it "toy," "things I like," "things for children," or something like that showing the subsumption of objects under a generic term as a generalization. The lower-class child will say "drums," because there was a drum on the picture, or "balls," because there was a ball on the picture. Usually, he cannot see that all of these objects have in common some abstract characteristic. This inability to abstract from the particular the characteristics of the general class constitutes a major barrier to learning in school. And we have to give the inner city child this ability which the other children come into the classroom with. Of course, it would be great if we did it at three and four, but until we get that, we've got to do it in kindergarten and first grade.

Slow Not Facile Cognitive Style

The cognitive style of inner city children tends to be slow, careful, and patient as opposed to clever and facile. A conclusion that the child is stupid is easily drawn by an examiner who will not wait to let the child arrive at the goal toward which he may be slowly progressing. What's your rush? You know he's got sixty-five years ahead. It's true you've got a certain amount of work to get done in the classroom. But when you cut him off from a path at which he would have arrived, you tell him he can't get this and he becomes convinced of what you were convinced of in the first place, that he's stupid. Then he acts stupid, and you're on your way to defeat, and he will be, too.

So these children need time. Holding up a flash card to see who's the first one to shout out the right answer isn't an appropriate exercise for them. They do poorly, particularly if there are some facile and clever children in the classroom. They have to be protected from the kind of competitiveness where speed is the major requirement. Certainly, we all agree we'd prefer to have the child arrive at the right answer even if it takes him longer than give the wrong answer quickly.

These and other characteristics that could be listed suggest a need for modification of the classical educational methods which have been developed on the pattern of the middle-class child.

These are children with insufficient verbal and experiential stimulation who have not yet formed the learning sets necessary before formal learning in school can begin.

The principle of learning sets is illustrated in the work of Harry Harlow at the University of Wisconsin.

Lack of Learning Sets

Harlow presented to a hungry monkey in a cage a little tray on which there were three geometric objects, two triangles and a circle. If the monkey lifted off the circle, the one that was different, there was food underneath the circle. Harlow brought in a tray with two squares and a triangle. Again, the food was under the one that was different, the triangle.

Isn't this what you do with the first-grader in reading readiness? Which is the one that's different?

Since you can't ask the monkey and the monkey can't tell you, you put food under the one that's different and he has to learn how to pick out the one that's different. He will learn although it takes an inordinate amount of time. It's really easier working with people than with monkeys when you're trying to teach them something. But psychologists are very patient people and finally the monkey learns the problem.

If you then give him another problem of the same general class but with different constituents, it will take him a long time, but not as long a time. By the time you get to the two hundredth problem with the monkey, he will be able in one or two trials to solve that problem where it might have taken him 500 trials to solve the first problem. He has acquired, in Harlow's term, a "learning set"—he has learned how to learn.

That is what inner city children don't know how to do, because of lacks in their experiences. They learn other things outside the classroom, some things we wished they didn't learn. But in a classroom setting they have to learn how to concentrate, how to look, how to narrow attention, how to abstract from the situation its general properties, and so on. Each thing you try to teach isn't as important in itself as it is preparation for learning more.

The teacher of the inner city child needs more than techniques, though I've talked at some length about techniques. Above all else, the teacher needs a respect for and serious interest in the child and his family, demonstrated not by word but by dedication to service of the child and patient interest in his family. If the principal or the teacher says, "Oh, how nice to have you here, Mrs. Jones," but really hoped Mrs. Jones never showed up because her dress isn't the finest and her language isn't the best, Mrs. Jones will get the unspoken message and she will disappear. They're better judges of motives than we are. I don't mean to put all the responsibility on the teacher, but I do mean to suggest that the teacher's attitude is a very important variable in this.

Impact of Teachers

A significant change was reported to me in the case of some children who are bussed into one of the schools in the northwest section of the city. Several weeks ago, the children were behaving well but were silent, there were not many smiles, and not much output. A group of PTA parents organized a carpool to bring in the mothers of these children because they didn't have cars. And so some thirty or forty mothers whose children were bussed in came to the gathering. The next day the change in the atmosphere of the school was remarkable in terms of the behavior of the children who finally felt that someone cared about them. This story illustrates a point that has been demonstrated elsewhere.

You will have respect for inner city children if you understand the relationship of their behavior to their environment. Teaching these children is the most effective form of psychiatric therapy that I can imagine in terms of making constructive people out of them. The rates of mental illness and antisocial problems are very high among this population, but they don't need a psychiatrist, they need good education. Of course, you'll need not only yourself but the help of more teachers, and more specialists, than the school system at the moment is providing. It is only this, a knowledge of competence, that can restore the child's self-respect and give him a sense of potency. The most dreadful thing about these youngsters and young adults is the feeling, "There's just no use in this world, no matter what I do it's not going to make any difference. If I have the chance to make a quick buck, I might as well take it. Why be a fool?"

The only way to change that is to create the reality that will give the child the feeling that he can do something. Obviously, part of this task is beyond the public schools. If you have good vocational education and he learns to do a job but when he comes out he can't get in a labor union or he can't be hired in a factory, then it's going to feed back negatively. But we have a job, too. It requires that we involve the child in direct activities that make sense to him as producing benefits to his family, to his neighborhood, and hence to himself.

The effective teacher is one whose concern for these children extends beyond classroom activities to citizen participation in efforts to upgrade the neighborhood, to abolish discriminatory practices, to provide more recreational facilities, to support social action for human betterment. Such a teacher will have an impact on her pupils and engage them to the end that they realize the talents they have in the same measure as children elsewhere, but that they cannot develop without her help.

It is no trick to teach the middle-class child—the odds are all with the teacher; and I suspect that even if we took the teachers out, the middle-class children would learn, but a little more slowly and a little more clumsily. The real challenge is to lead forth the disadvantaged child to a place in the sun, because he isn't learning by himself and he isn't learning in the way we have been teaching him. Here is the challenge. If you accept it, if you use your ingenuity, if you have faith in the child's capacity for growth, you will succeed. And society will owe you a debt that money and prestige can never repay.

THE SELF-CONCEPT: BASIS FOR
REEDUCATION OF NEGRO YOUTH

Jean D. Grambs

The human personality is a bundle of dynamic forces about which we have many conjectures and few certainties. Like the inner particles of the atom, which are seen only by the shadows they cast, so we have only the shadows of the workings of the human psyche. We are not always sure, and certainly not always in agreement, as to what these shadows represent. But whatever components there may be to personality, in the words of Park and Burgess, "it is an organization of traits and attitudes of which the individual's conception of himself is central."

There are unresolved differences of opinion among psychologists as to the sources of behavior. Whatever it is that impels an individual to act or not to act, a significant role is played in this determination by what the person thinks about himself. He may be able to tell us something about his view of himself, or he may be able to tell us very little. What he tells us may be what he really thinks, or it may be a selective version for a particular public; on what appears to be safer ground, he may reveal a different version of what he thinks he is. Or he may be completely unaware of what his true feelings about himself are. We are assuming, however, that the person acts and can only act in terms of what he thinks about himself in a given situation, and he cannot assess that situation and its action requirements except in terms of his own view of himself.

Contemporary research in child growth and development has highlighted the central significance of the individual's concept of himself. The way a person views himself is the way he will behave. If he sees himself as successful, as someone whom others like, as good-looking, then his behavior will reflect these views. If the person considers himself to be inadequate, as someone whom others probably won't like, as unattractive, then again his behavior will reflect these valuations. The factual truth of any of these statements is irrelevant. A very beautiful girl may consider herself unattractive; children with adequate intellectual endowment may do poorly in school because they perceive themselves as not able.

The source of one's self-image is, of course, not internal; it is learned. The way a mother responds to her newborn baby—with delight or with weary acceptance—will be apparent in the behavior of the baby before very long. A child whose parents trust and love him will be a loving and trustful individual who will tend to go out to greet the world and its many new experiences.

We have some research insights into the differential treatment that parents accord their children from the very beginning. It is true, too, that different cultures produce different personality types. The ways in which children are reared, the things that they are told to do or not to do, the rewards for various kinds of competencies or their lacks, differ from one culture to another. This produces, as Kardiner has pointed out, what might be termed a basic personality type consistent for a given culture.

Venturing outside the family provides the child with additional clues to his self-worth. As he meets teachers, policemen, and storekeepers, he is told what these powerful persons think of people like him. He learns about himself from other children on the block who report to him how they feel on seeing him and playing with him. Out of countless messages, the individual contrives a picture of who he is.

It is obvious that individuals develop different concepts of themselves and that the concept of self is always in terms of degrees of *adequacy*. Everyone must have some sense of adequacy, no matter how minimal, or he cannot cope with his own existence and then must escape into psychosis or suicide. *"We can define man's basic need, then, as a need for adequacy."* Jersild refines this further: "The needs associated with a person's idea and appraisal of himself include both desires for enhancing his self-esteem and also striving to preserve the integrity or consistency of the self."

There is agreement that the contemporary situation of the American Negro is deplorable. A nationwide, continuing debate is concerned with ways of ameliorating this condition. As educators, we need to develop strategies for change which will aid the individual in achieving more adequate adjustment to and control of his environment. The role of the concept of self in achieving this sense of adequacy thus appears to be central. The questions that must be considered are these:

1. How do Negro children and youth now achieve a sense of who and what they are?

2. What is the role of education in the school in developing this sense of self?

3. What is the potential within the educational setting of achieving a desirable shift in self-image?

These questions can only be answered by further research. Our purpose here is a brief review of the relevant research and speculation.

The Question of Differences Between Negroes and Whites

One of the clearest differences between Negro and white is that society in the contemporary United States continually tells the groups that they are different. Not only are the groups different, but the Negro group is considered inferior to the white group. This message has been communicated in different ways via different social media ever since the Negro was first brought to America. It is obvious that this kind of differential social communication is going to have a differential impact on the personality. As Allport asks:

> ... what would happen to your own personality if you heard it said over and over again that you were lazy, a simple child of nature, expected to steal, and had inferior blood. Suppose this opinion were forced on you by the majority of your fellow-citizens. And suppose nothing you could do would change this opinion—because you happen to have black skin.

Or, stated in the words of the late President Kennedy:

> If an American, because his skin is dark, cannot eat lunch in a restaurant open to the public; if he cannot send his children to the best public school available; if, in short, he cannot enjoy the full and free life which all of us want, then who among us would be content to have the color of his skin changed and stand in his place?

The self-concept of the Negro is contaminated by the central fact that it is based on a color-caste complex. The American color-caste system was evolving at the same time that the brave concepts of the American and French revolutions about human equality were also born. It was thus almost inevitable that the racial situation would cause trouble. The first drafts of the Declaration of Independence contained a clause objecting to the imposition of slavery upon the American colonies by the English power. The clause was stricken from the final version for fear of alienating Southern support. Shades of contemporary political maneuverings over civil rights legislation in Congress!

In order to cope with the obvious discrepancy between Christian beliefs about the oneness of the human family, slaveholders had to resort to the idea of the supposed inferiority of the Negro, preaching in some instances that he really was a subhuman breed of animal. Even today there continue to be strenuous efforts to convince those who require scholarly evidence that the Negro is, in fact, inferior.

The social system that emerged out of the need to rationalize the owning of slaves and, following the Civil War, refusal to accord the Negro full citizen status was a clear development of a caste system. Unlike the caste system of India based on religious beliefs, the caste system in the United States was based on color and on the assumption of inferiority due to color. The Brazilian melting pot, unlike that in the United States, classifies anyone with any amount of white ancestry as white; in the United States, the smallest amount of Negro ancestry classifies an individual as Negro.

In the evolution of institutions, those provided for the Negro in the United States, therefore, had to be *separate,* but also *unequal.* It is possible that there are caste systems in which parallel caste-class groups exist without any presumption of superiority or inferiority for one caste over another; this certainly has not been true in America. Of course, the South had to refuse to provide equal educational opportunity for the Negro; the Negro was *not an equal.*

The Impact of Inequality in Valuation

It does not take much imagination to understand what generations of being told one is unworthy do to a group's own valuation of its worth. From the first slave revolts, Negro leaders have continually fought against this self-view; but there have been relatively few leaders, a condition also produced by the effect of inferior caste status. Only in recent decades have there been enough Negroes who have overcome these multiple barriers to challenge the general valuation of the Negro.

To quote Dollard, whose original study of caste first focused general attention on this problem:

> Nothing has happened since 1936 [the date of the original study] which has served to unconvince me about what I saw. It seems as real now as then. We are still in the hot water of conflict between our democratic ideals and our personal acceptance of caste status for the Negro. We are still deliberately or unwittingly profiting by defending, concealing or ignoring the caste system.

Interestingly enough, a recent comprehensive review and evaluation of the research in the area of self-concept does not include any discussion of research that considers race as an aspect of self-concept, though research relating to other factors, such as sex, religious affiliation, social-class status, is discussed. Blindness to, or avoidance of, the implications of the caste system on the self-concept of the Negro, and of the white, which is thus seen to occur at the most- and least-sophisticated levels of society, is symptomatic of the difficulty of dealing with color discrimination in American life and thought.

The Negro personality *cannot* be unmarked by the experience of caste discrimination based upon color. One of the first family learnings of the Negro child has to do with his color. The more white a Negro child is, the more he will be accepted by his family, the greater his opportunity will be to use his talents, the more likely it is that he will be able to make the most of the limited opportunities of his environment. The love that his family will accord him can be calibrated on the same scale as one calibrates color differences. To be most loved as a Negro child, one has to appear least Negro.

In one of their cases, Kardiner and Ovesey describe the reactions of a middle-class Negro woman, herself light, on giving birth to a dark baby. She was sure she had been given the wrong baby; later she tried to bathe it in bleaches of various kinds; she refused to appear in public with it. She reacted almost the same way with a second baby.

In the early drawings and stories and dreams of Negro children appear many wishes to be white. Negro children have a harder time than white children in identifying themselves correctly in terms of race. This identification is also related to color: the darker Negro is able to see himself as a Negro earlier than a light-colored one. In the latter instance, is the nearness to being white such as to make the acceptance of being Negro that much harder?

The self-esteem of the Negro is damaged by the overwhelming fact that the world he lives in says, "White is right; black is bad." The impact on the Negro community is to overvalue all those traits of appearance that are most Caucasian. Evidence is clear that in almost every Negro family, the lighter children are favored by the parents. It is interesting to note that most of the Negro leadership group today are not Negroid in appearance, many being almost completely Caucasian in terms of major physical appearance.

What effect does this have on the child? Of course, his own color becomes extremely important to him. As Dai points out, ". . . the color of one's skin, which does not occupy the consciousness of children of other cultures, is here made an issue of primary importance, and the personality problems thus created are almost as difficult to get rid of as the dark skin itself." The Negro press is replete with advertisements for skin lighteners and hair straighteners. It strikes some Negroes as ironic that, while they strive to become lighter and to make their hair less curly, whites go to great pains to stay out in the sun in order to become darker and spend endless amounts of money on getting their hair to curl! Unfortunately, the efforts of the whites do not assume an acceptance on their part of the features of the Negro which appear to be desirable: darker color and curly hair. But the efforts of the Negro do spring from a deeply ingrained view regarding appearance: it is better to be more white.

One interesting feature of the current Negro revolution has been a small but persistent insistence that the Negro cease trying to make himself white. The Black Muslim group is an almost pure expression of the need to reject all that is white and replace Negro self-hatred with justified hatred of whites, including the dominant white Christian religion. With some Negroes, it is now considered a matter of racial pride to refuse to straighten the hair or to use cosmetics to lighten the skin. It is possible that this movement will reach other Negroes, and with it will come a lessening of the rejection of color and the personal devaluation that this has carried. But unfortunately it hardly seems possible that a reversal of the value system will occur for many, and certainly not for a long time to come.

Thus we see the central ambivalence that makes the world of the Negro so baffling, frustrating, confusing, and demeaning. On the one hand, he is told that white is better, and he relates this to his own social system in which the Negro who is most white, but still a Negro, has highest status. But to *be* white is not good. Whites are not to be trusted; they are, in fact, hated as much as they are feared.

Hatred breeds aggression. Aggression seeks an outlet. A major focus of the hatred of Negroes is the white group, but this group is almost completely protected because of the potency and immediacy of white retaliation. One must remember that the antilynch laws are quite recent. Pictures of burning buses, fire hoses; mounted police with electric cattle prods, and attacking police dogs show only too well that the Negro still is not protected from the quick and vicious reactions of the white group when this power is challenged in any way. Incapable of attacking the white group, the Negro has several psychological alternatives: to hate himself, to act out his aggressive needs within his own group, and to escape into apathy and fantasy. All these paths are utilized, and often by the same individual, depending on the situation. As Combs and Snygg point out, responses to feelings of inadequacy range from the neurotic through perceptual distortions and may result in actual psychosis. The production of "multiple personalities" is, as they see it, one response to feelings of loss of self-esteem. This splitting of the personality in response to the social disvalue placed on being a Negro is graphically stated by Redding:

> From adolescence to death there is something very personal about being a Negro in America. It is like having a second ego which is as much the conscious subject of all experience as the natural self. It is not what the psychologists call dual personality. It is more complex and, I think, more morbid than that. In the state of which I speak, one receives two distinct reactions—the one normal and intrinsic to the natural self; the other, entirely different but of equal force, a prodigy created by the accumulated consciousness of Negroness.

As the gifted Negro writer James Baldwin puts it, in commenting on his own childhood:

> In order for me to live, I decided very early that some mistake
> had been made somewhere. I was not a "nigger" even though you
> [whites] called me one. . . . I had to realize when I was very
> young that I was none of those things I was told I was. I was not,
> for example, happy. I never touched a watermelon for all kinds of
> reasons. I had been invented by white people, and I knew enough
> about life by this time to understand that whatever you invent,
> whatever you project, that is you! So where we are now is that a
> whole country of people believe I'm a "nigger" and I *don't*.

It does not escape the Negro observer that Negro crimes against Negroes are considered far less serious by the law in many areas than similar crimes of whites against whites, and certainly not nearly so serious as Negro crimes against whites. And white crimes against Negroes are the least serious of all. Again, these social symptoms report to the Negro that he is not valued as a person; he cannot, against such massive evidence, counter by his own feelings of self-esteem, since in truth he can typically show little factual support for a contrary view.

Crucial Social Forces Creating the Negro Self-Image: The Family and Poverty

The potency of the family in producing the culturally approved person has tempted social manipulators since the dawn of history. Sparta intervened at a very early age in the child-rearing functions of the family. Recent attempts to supplant the family have been unsuccessful. The most enduring such contemporary situation, the Kibbutz of Israel, appears to have produced a rather special kind of person whose social potential can be questioned. So far, no adequate substitute for the family has been found, despite Huxley's predictions.

That there are unique stresses and strains in the modern family is agreed; but the stresses in a Negro family are qualitatively different from those in a white family, even when we hold socioeconomic status constant. The poor have never lived in comfort, and the struggle for material survival has certainly made psychologically adequate survival extremely problematical anywhere in the world. The situation of the Negro family today in the United States is qualitatively different on a number of important counts.

The Negro family is much more likely than the white family to be on the lowest economic rung. Furthermore, we could say that no more than a very small percentage of Negroes is more than one generation removed from abject poverty, so that "Negroes have [a] deeply ingrained sense of impoverishment." It is a rather special kind of impoverishment, too; it is almost inescapable. Although we have seen in recent generations the rise of a Negro middle class, and even a few very wealthy Negroes, most Negroes remain in the "last hired, first fired" category of employment—and if not this generation, their parental generation. Most Negro children, then, inherit a family which is economically insecure from the very start. Most of them live at the edge of survival; and those who have moved a little bit away have a constant fear of a future which may reduce them, too, to desperation.

It is almost impossible for one not reared in a slum to understand its awfulness. Middle-class America flees from a true picture of slum degradation. But as Riessman points out, children reared in these environments will soon constitute 50 percent of all children enrolled in schools in large cities. Most of these children will be Negroes, unless something drastically changes the housing situation which exists in urban centers.

The Negro slum child is far more liable than a white slum child to experience also an unstable home. The self that the Negro child learns early in life is one exposed to the most difficult of all situations for the human being to cope with: an inadequate family living on the edge of economic insufficiency. The impact of family disruption is accentuated by the incapacity of those involved in the rearing of the children to do an adequate job of it because they have had few experiences with family stability and adequacy to guide them.

The circle is indeed a vicious one. The case studies reported by Riese provide appalling accounts of generation after generation of defeat in Negro families. Often neither mother nor father is able to provide the minimum of affection and attention that an infant needs in order to grow into a person able to like himself and others, because, of course, his parents do not like themselves. Too many of these marriages are the result of impulsive escape wishes and lack a secure base in personal regard for the marital partner. Poignant testimony to the difficulties facing the Negro wife and husband is given by talented Negro singer Lena Horne.

As she describes it, her marriage was an effort to get away from the miseries of being a Negro singer in a white man's world. Yet she was not able to accept her role as a Negro wife. The needs her husband brought home from his work, mainly with white colleagues, she felt quite unable and unwilling to deal with. Not only had she to cope with the ordinary problems of running a home and rearing children, she had to absorb the anger and hurt her husband bore on his job, the countless humiliations and degradations that he, a Negro, experienced daily in his contact with white people.

What Lena Horne tells us provides a needed window into the inner reality of Negro family life. The normal hazards of the working world are multiplied many times over by the pervasive insecurity attendant on almost all of the Negro's economic activities. Not only is the Negro the last to be hired and the first to be fired, but he pays more for insurance premiums, he has a much harder time obtaining home mortgage money and any kind of bank or credit loans. Even the slum store preys upon the poor with higher prices for shoddier stuff. In such an environment, it is hard indeed for the Negro male to achieve a sense of self-worth as breadwinner and provider for his family.

The woman typically is aggressive and hostile; the man is hostile and dependent. Because his economic situation is so insecure, the husband-father cannot be sure that he will provide the economic base for a family; and in a majority of cases, he is right. He cannot assure his wife of support or his children of food and shelter. Who can feel pride of self in such circumstances, and who can pass on feelings of adequacy to anyone else?

The economic security of the Negro family rests primarily with the mother. This is one outgrowth of slavery, when at least the mother could keep the children with her until they could be physically independent and able to work, while the father was often not even accorded the recognition of paternity. Certainly the family as the white population knew it was prohibited for slaves. The patterns of employment in today's urban centers have continued to make economic stability more available to the women than to the men. The significance of this family situation appears in study after study.

The home life reported in many case studies of Negro youth is one of constant bickering and fighting. One father leaves; a stepfather or father substitute appears. The family conflict continues. Because of death or illness or desertion, children often are left with grandparents or other relatives. If an attachment occurs, it may not last until adulthood. Thus many Negro children have few experiences with stability, warmth, attention—all the things that are taken for granted as part of the necessary environment for healthy personality development.

The important point, of course, is that while many of the conditions reported are a result of acute and continued poverty, a major ingredient is also the color-caste of the Negro. One of the child's early racial learnings is that he cannot turn to his parents for help and retaliation if he is hurt.

> A white man yanked me off a streetcar because I got on ahead of a white woman. He shook me good and tore my clothes. I walked home crying, knowing that my father would do something about it. (But his father could do no more than remark, "You should have known better.")

The denial to a parent of his role in protecting his own child is deeply destructive, not only to the parental feeling but to the possibility that the child will look to his parents as adult models. Nor will the growing child be able to internalize the parental feeling without which having children of one's own is a dangerous enterprise.

What the Negro child is likely to learn is that no one is to be trusted. He is given such small ingredients of affection and attention that he has too meager a hoard to share with anyone else. He learns, too, that his family is only partly responsible for the horrors of his existence; it is the whites who have created this situation, and it is they who keep him in abasement. The burden of hatred for the whites is increased because he is also told that he cannot do anything about that hatred; in fact, he must be particularly careful and watchful in all his relations with whites. These persons hold the key to all that is desirable and good. If only one were white, too!

The earliest learnings, then, of the Negro child, particularly one in the rural or urban slums, is that the family is not a source of basic nurture and support. He seeks his gratifications, therefore, on the street and among peers. But as Kardiner and Ovesey point out, at no time are these relationships such as to produce a feeling of comfort and safety. No one can find in the street a substitute for parental and adult guidance and parental affection. If the child does not necessarily become antisocial, he is asocial.

The damage to the child's self-esteem appears greater for Negro boys than for girls. Though it is debatable whether, in general, it is more or less difficult to grow up as a boy or as a girl in our culture, it seems clear from the evidence that during early childhood and school years, the Negro girl accommodates better to the circumstances of existence. Certainly in school performance the Negro girl exceeds the Negro boy. In most measures of social disorganization, the Negro boy appears to be far more vulnerable. This can be accounted for in part by the fact that the male models available for the growing boy are themselves demoralized. A father who feels defeated by the world is not in a good position to give his son a sense of optimism and a feeling that he can achieve something himself. The fact that the father is most likely to be the absent member of the family and often is replaced by a succession of fathers or father substitutes also tends to militate against the establishment of a view of the male as a reliable, responsible individual. If the boy sees around him men who are unable to sustain a consistent and positive social and economic role, it is hard for the youngster to build a different pattern out of his limited experiences.

Recent efforts to equalize educational opportunities for Negroes in the South should not obscure the fact that these efforts are indeed very recent, and still fall short of providing, even on a segregated basis, an adequate education for all Negro young people. The fact that even today many Negro children and youth have far from adequate schooling, whether they live in the rural South or the urban North, Midwest, West, or Southwest, should not make us forget that, with few exceptions, the story of Negro education to this day has been one of gross lacks. As Horace Mann said over a hundred years ago, "No educated body of men can be permanently poor;" and the obverse is that no uneducated group can expect to rise out of poverty.

Although the Ausubels state that "Negro girls in racially incapsulated areas are less traumatized than boys by the impact of racial discrimination," further evidence is needed to support such a statement. On the surface, Negro girls seem more able to cope with some of the demands of middle-class society: going to school, behaving in school, keeping out of serious trouble with the law, showing responsibility for child rearing, and keeping a job. It is nevertheless possible that the impact of their situation is just passed on to the men in the household. Certainly a mother is a prime source, as we have stated, of the child's self-concept. It is communicated to Negro boys, somehow, that they are less wanted, less able to deal with their world, bound to fail in their efforts to be men. We cannot lay the major blame for the way Negro boys develop on the lack of adequate male models. It is highly probable that the trauma suffered by Negro females is passed on and displaced upon the males in the situation. Certainly the case material of Kardiner and Ovesey shows much personal trouble experienced by female as well as male Negroes. The fact that so many Negroes become contributing and stable members of society is an extraordinary tribute to the resilience of the human psyche.

Educational Processes and Self-Concept

It is clear that the life experiences of the Negro child are not such as to aid him in developing a positive sense of himself or of his place in his world. What does this suggest to us? It would seem that a very compelling hypothesis is that *the Negro child, from earliest school entry through graduation from high school, needs continued opportunities to see himself and his racial group in a realistically positive light. He needs to understand what color and race mean, he needs to learn about those of his race (and other disadvantaged groups) who have succeeded, and he needs to clarify his understanding of his own group history and current group situation.*

At the moment, these are missing ingredients in the American public school classroom. Numerous studies of textbooks have shown them to be lily-white. Pictures do not show Negro and white children together; when Negroes appear they are usually either Booker T. Washington, George Washington Carver, or foreign. Neither whites nor Negroes have an accurate picture of the American Negro and his history. One observer noted that a commonly used contemporary civics book had no index entry for *urban renewal, transportation, transit, or Negro.* The lily-white nature of text materials is true also of other visual aids used in the schools. If Negroes appear in school films, they are in stereotyped roles. One film, for instance, showing "community helpers" illustrated the work of repairing the street with a Negro crew and a white foreman. The educational consultant, incidentally, who worked with the film company to produce the film was surprised at his own blindness. This kind of presentation merely reinforces the many communications to children that Negro work is inferior work.

That these materials can and do have a strong impact on the child's perception of himself and others was well documented in the study by Trager and Yarrow. When a story describing a Negro child as a funny savage (*Little Black Sambo*) was read aloud to young children, white and Negro children's feelings were affected, particularly when the white children pointed this out in the schoolyard. The only thing that is surprising about these findings is that educators and others have consistently ignored them. It is interesting that the Trager-Yarrow research report is probably the only study made of the differences in education (textbook) content that is reported in the literature. As a matter of fact, it is claimed by one of the very knowledgeable experts in the field, that *no* experimental study has been done of differences in textbook content, despite the fact that the textbook is the most consistently and constantly used educational aid in the classroom, other than the teacher.

If teaching materials present a slanted view of him and his place in the world to the Negro child, what does the teacher tell him? It is not a very startling piece of news that teachers, too, bear the majority version of the Negro. Studies of their attitudes toward children show that the Negro child is rated lowest in all rankings of groups on a Bogardus-type social-distance scale. The original study was completed thirteen years ago; teachers in training in 1963 give the same responses. Attempts to change teachers' attitudes through human relations workshops and special courses have reached very few. In formulating some guidelines for the education of the culturally disadvantaged, Niemeyer stated:

> Our hypothesis is that the chief cause of the low achievement of the children of alienated groups is the fact that too many teachers and principals honestly believe that these children are educable only to an extremely limited extent. And when teachers have a low expectation level for their children's learning, the children seldom exceed that expectation, which is a self-fulfilling prophecy.

Nor is the situation made easier where Negro teachers are employed. The Negro teacher represents a middle-class position, and there is evidence that virulent anti-Negro feelings are expressed by middle-class Negroes for lower-class Negroes. Unfortunately, most Negro children come from lower-class homes. Dai makes the point that, denied access to other rewards in life, the Negro tends to put an overemphasis upon status. The Negro professional, who may have many contacts with white professionals, must even in these professional relationships maintain an etiquette which prevents showing resentment or rage; but this is not necessarily controlled to the same extent when dealing with fellow Negroes. Children, particularly, are available targets of all the displaced self-hatred of the professional middle-class Negro teacher. If they are lower-class children, they typically will demonstrate everything the middle-class Negro most despises about the race from which he cannot dissociate himself. The warmth, welcome, and support which children should find, particularly in the early elementary school grades, and which the Negro child needs in abundance because of so much deprivation at home, is exactly what teachers, Negro or white, as presently oriented, can least provide.

In this necessarily brief discussion of the factors that enter into the development of the self-concept of the Negro, we have utilized only a small sampling of the wealth of research literature and other documentation which bears on this subject. We have merely tried to suggest some of the crucial situations which help to mold the Negro child. It is these of which educational practitioners must be aware.

Educational Intervention

The child with a negative view of self is a child who will not be able to profit much from school. Once a child is convinced that school is irrelevant to his immediate needs and future goals, the task of education becomes almost impossible. As one junior high student said, after having failed all his subjects for two years:

> I just don't like it. It seems to bore me. It seems silly just going there and sitting. And most of the time it is so hot and they don't do anything about it and the teachers just talk, talk, and you never learn anything.

Deutsch's research points out that the lower-class Negro child probably received about one half to one third less instructional time in the primary grades than did white children from the same slum environment: "our time samples indicated that as much as 80% of the school day was channeled into disciplining, and secondarily, into ordinary organizational details. . . ."

Conclusion

If today we note a change of tone, a militancy and impatience on the part of Negro youth, it is not because schools are any different. For the first time, the Negro, via TV, is beginning to see that the world of comfort, luxury, and fun is all around him. He wants some of it, too. As Hayakawa pointed out in a speech at a recent American Psychological Association convention in Philadelphia, the ads that beckon one to join the fun on the picnic do *not* add "for whites only."

But the militancy, welcome as it may be, cannot erase the burden of self-hatred that has accumulated through so many generations. And many who most need to hear the call to challenge the racial status quo may already be too deeply sunk in despair and apathy. These feelings are so quickly communicated to the infant and child that intervention by the school even as early as kindergarten or the first grade may be too late. But if many older adolescents can respond to a new concept of their role in the world, then certainly the younger child can be reached, too, by deliberate efforts to change the way in which he views himself. These, then, are the challenges we must meet.

CULTURE CONFLICT

William Madsen

The Plight of the Hyphenated Citizen

A casual visitor traveling through Hidalgo County today could see little overt demonstration of tension between Anglos and Latins. Stores and restaurants welcome Latin trade. On the streets, Anglos and Latins exchange friendly greetings. One cannot fail to notice that some of the leading business and professional men bear Spanish surnames that are mentioned with respect in the newspapers.

The outward feeling of friendliness pervading the area may be illustrated by the experience of a Mexican-American friend of mine who came to the valley from California. He commented on the smiles and greetings he received from Anglo strangers. Experimenting with this Texas informality, he took the initiative one day and greeted a lanky Anglo wearing a Stetson hat and cowboy boots. The sour-looking Anglo broke into a smile and replied, "Why howdy son! It sure is nice of you to say hi to me." It took my Latin friend half an hour to disengage himself from the resultant conversation.

In many ways Texas is a friendly place but sometimes this friendliness masks areas of suspicion, distrust, and even fear between the two major ethnic groups. To a large extent, the mistrust accompanied by subtle discrimination is a matter of class rather than race. The majority of Anglos in Hidalgo County are middle class while the majority of Latins are lower-class manual laborers. Class differences reflect cultural differences that distinguish the Hidalgo situation from the class hostilities found in regions of a common ethnic background. The recognizable physical differences between Anglos and Latins accentuate their separateness. As one anglicized Latin said to me, "I think like an Anglo and I act like an Anglo but I'll never look like an Anglo. Just looking at me, no one could tell if I am an American or one of those blasted Mexicans from across the river. It's hell to look like a foreigner in your own country."

The Mexican-American who has had little education is even less identifiable as a United States citizen. In a border area, resembling a foreigner can be inconvenient. Pablo is a United States citizen born in Texas of Mexican parents. His dark complexion and Indian features indicate his foreign ancestry. He is a field hand who has never been to school and knows only a few hundred words of English. Pablo has a birth certificate to prove his citizenship but seldom carries it with him for fear of losing it. On several occasions he has been picked up by immigration officials on suspicion of illegal entrance into this country. Each time he has persuaded the officers to take him by his home so he could show them his proof of citizenship. Each time he was released immediately and once an officer apologized for the inconvenience. Another time, the officers drove him back to his job in the field. Pablo is not too bitter about these incidents but he does admit that they are embarrassing.

In the past, the Mexican-American resemblance to Mexican nationals has been dangerous as well as inconvenient, especially during crises between the United States and Mexico. Such a crisis period existed in 1914 when United States marines seized the Mexican port of Vera Cruz in retaliation for the Mexican military refusal to salute the United States flag in Tampico. Diplomatic relations between the two nations were severed. The Mexican-Americans of south Texas were frequently identified with the enemy just as loyal Japanese-Americans were suspected of traitorous potentialities during World War II. The Texas Latins were not interned but they learned to avoid the Anglo part of town if they disliked being involved in violence. The Anglos also found it advisable to stay out of the Latin community. A wall of fear grew between the Anglo and Latin communities. Recalling this period, a Mexican-American said, "All our people were afraid. And we were in our own country but the Anglos thought that we were not from here."

The plight of the Mexican-Americans grew worse when the Texas Rangers and United States Army troops entered the area to pursue revolutionary bandits from Mexico who were making raids across the United States border. Throughout the valley, gory sagas are told and retold about the "Hora de Sangre"—the Bloody Hour—when Texas Rangers reportedly shot innocent Mexican-Americans instead of the Mexican bandits they were supposed to be chasing. Some Anglos remember this period with shame. The Anglo widow of a prominent businessman commented, "All the Rangers had to do was get a suspicion on somebody, any little thing, and they would take 'em out and shoot 'em down."

Spatial and Social Separateness

The historical past is not forgotten despite the growing tolerance and friendliness in the valley. Incidents such as the Bloody Hour reinforce the barrier between Anglos and Latins created by differences in appearance, language, custom, and class. This division is both social and spatial.

The larger towns in Hidalgo County still maintain the planned geographical separation of Latin and Anglo populations initiated by the land development companies in the early part of the twentieth century. Today, each town and city is neatly divided into an Anglo and a Latin community. Today, the dividing line is usually a railroad or a highway. Until the end of World War II, this boundary commonly served as effectively as an electrified fence to socially separate the two ethnic groups. Mexican-American entry to the Anglo side was restricted to employment situations or shopping expeditions. A Latin crossing the line at night was subject to police questioning or taunts and violence at the hands of Anglo teenagers. Similarly, the Latin side of town was regarded as unsafe at night for Anglos, especially women. However, groups of Anglo males made occasional slumming trips to the Latin cantinas in search of beer and excitement.

The geographical division of the community is marked by speech differences. English is the predominant language on the Anglo side of town while Spanish prevails on the Latin side. The Spanish dialect of this region is commonly called Tex-Mex because it includes many hispanicized English words. Each side of town has distinctive labels. The Spanish-speaking population refers to the Latin community as *el pueblo mexicano* (the Mexican town), *Mexiquito* (Little Mexico) or *nuestro lado* (our side). They designate the Anglo section as *el pueblo americano*. The Anglos also refer to "our side" and "their side" and speak of the Latin community as being "over there." They generally designate the Latin side as "Meskin town."

The two sides of the tracks reflect the class differences between most Anglos and most Latins. Most Anglo homes are well-constructed and well-equipped with luxuries such as TV sets, washing machines, and air conditioning. They are situated in shady, well-kept yards. On the Latin side of town, homes are smaller and obviously of cheaper frame construction. Some are drab shacks with peeling paint, bare yards, and rundown outhouses. Others display fresh coats of paint in the lively pastel colors so loved in Mexico. Even the poorer homes maintain an appearance of brightness by decorating the yards with arrays of gaily-colored flowers neatly arranged in earthen pots or painted tin cans.

There is a noticeable difference in the pace, atmosphere, and noises characteristic of each side of town. The Anglo commercial area buzzes with the traffic din and the hustle of busy shoppers. The determined look of an Anglo housewife may be seen on the faces of women out to buy particular items of clothing in the near panic of a department store sale. People hurry along the streets with an appearance of definite purpose. Even coffee breaks are marked by the concentrated effort of purposeful conversation.

The Latin shopping areas lack the plush department stores of the Anglo side of town. Small stores sell produce, Mexican magazines, cotton clothing, or sundries. There may be a tiny hole in the wall specializing in medicinal herbs. The shoppers are more relaxed and there is more casual visiting. Pleasantries are exchanged between buyer and seller. From the cantinas come the strains of the gay-sad music of Mexico played on juke boxes. Traffic noises are less pronounced on the streets, many of which are dusty and unpaved. The Latin side is poorer but it seems gayer than the Anglo side. There are more children and dogs and more laughter on the Latin side.

Since 1946, the apartness of the two sides of town has been decreasing. Today, almost any Anglo neighborhood may have some Latin residents. In the evenings, Spanish-speaking families may be seen strolling to the movies in the Anglos downtown section. During the day, increasing numbers of Anglos go to Mexican town to eat enchiladas and tacos and drink beer. In one town, a Mexican-American judge settles complaints brought by Anglos and Latins.

Cultural Images

Despite the growing tolerance and intermingling between the two ethnic groups, each is still keenly aware of the differences that divide them. Feelings of resentment stem from a mutual lack of understanding and stances of superiority. Each group finds the other lacking in propriety of behavior and each feels superior in some respects. These attitudes are manifest in the labels by which each group distinguishes the other. Each group has polite terms for the other to be used in face-to-face contact and in press releases. These respectful terms include: Anglo, Anglo-American, Latin, and Latin-American. Anglos refer to themselves as Americans and use the term Mexican or Meskin for both the Mexican national and the Mexican-American. Depending on the particular usage, the term Mexican may be merely descriptive or derogatory. A decreasing minority of Anglos still use the face-slapping term "greaser" for the Latin citizen. Derogatory terms used by Latins to designate Anglos include: gringo, *bolillo*, and *gabacho*. Among themselves, Latins may refer to a respected Anglo as an *Americano*. Mexican-Americans[1] call themselves *tejanos* and sometimes speak of the Anglos as *extranjeros* (foreigners). Latins use the words *mexicanos* and *chicanos* for both Mexican-Americans and Mexican nationals.

Anglos reserve the racial term "white" for their exclusive use in the valley. This tendency is deeply resented by the Latins who see themselves lumped together with the Negroes as colored. The only similarity the average Latin sees between himself and the Negro is that they both belong to minority groups. Neither Latins nor Anglos have much direct contact with Negroes—who constitute less than one percent of the population of Hidalgo County. Until quite recently, the Negroes attended their own segregated schools. The Negro district in one urban center is often called "Niggertown" by both Anglos and Latins. Most Mexican-Americans say that they feel no hostility toward the Negroes but one Latin added, "Of course, I wouldn't want my daughter to marry a Negro." Negroes are almost never entertained in Latin homes.

There can be no doubt that the Anglo has a higher regard for the Latin than for the Negro. As an uneducated Anglo put it, "The Meskin's not a white man but he's a hell of a lot whiter than a nigger." Anglos regard the Latin field hand as superior to the Negro although they sometimes complain about the unreliability of the Latin. Many Anglos claim that the Latin is basically lax and unreliable but does a good day's work once he starts. An Anglo farmer pointed toward a group of Mexican-American crop pickers in a carrot field and commented, "They're all right if they have their own boss supervising them. Basically, they're lazy." This particular crew had been working at stoop labor for hours without a break. Another Anglo regarded Latins as the best of all farm laborers, "Man for man, a Mexican can out-plant, out-weed, and out-pick anyone on the face of the earth." Most Latins would agree with him. They think the Negro is too clumsy and the Anglo too weak to do a good day's work in the fields.

Anglos express different opinions on the Latin contribution to the development of Hidalgo County. Some say the area would still be a desert if it had remained Mexican. Another point of view was expressed by an Anglo rancher, "We've got to give them a lot of credit. They conquered the Indians and had ranches going here while much of our West was still wild." Perhaps the most common Anglo sentiment was voiced by a rancher, "If it were not for those hard working Meskins, this place wouldn't be on the map. It is very true about the Anglo know-how, but without those Meskin hands no one could have built up the prosperity we have in this part of the nation."

Although the Anglos fully recognize the economic importance of unskilled Latin labor, they tend to regard the Mexican-American as childlike, emotional, ignorant, and in need of paternalistic guidance. The American zeal for bettering people leads to the popular conclusion that the Latin should be educated and remade in an Anglo mold. At the same time, employers do not want to educate the Latin to the point of losing their labor force. The Anglo white-collar worker sees the educational upgrading of the Mexican-American as a threat to his job with the increasing employment of Latins in office and mercantile work at lower salaries.

The Mexican-American resents the economic dominance of the Anglo and his associated air of superiority. The Latin also objects to Anglo intolerance of Mexican-American ways and the pressures put on minority groups to conform to the American way. A Latin high school teacher summed up this attitude:

The Anglo-American sees himself as the most important being that ever lived in our universe. To him the rest of humanity is somewhat backward. He believes his ways are better, his standard of living is better, and his ethical code is better although it is of minor importance. In fact, he believes that his whole way of life is the best in the world. He is appalled to find people on the face of the earth who are unable or unwilling to admit that the American way of life is the only way.

Many Latins believe that Anglos lack true religion and ethics and are concerned only with self-advancement. When one Mexican-American expressed the opinion that Anglos were not religious, another protested by saying, "Look at the number of people in their churches every Sunday." The first man replied, "But have you looked at the altar? No crucifix. Only a bank book." As the conversation continued, a third man said, "The Anglo will do anything to get ahead, no matter who gets hurt. Of course, it's usually one of us who is hurt." A similar view came from the teacher quoted above, "Personal gain and achievement are the main Anglo goals in life and the ethics used to attain these goals will be worked out along the way." A Latin crop picker phrased the same sentiment in more transcendental terms, "The Anglo does what his greed tells him. The Chicano does what God tells him." He added somewhat hopefully, "I think that Anglos will be discriminated against in heaven."

The Latin feels that blind dependence on science and the ceaseless push for advancement have fettered the Anglo's integrity and intellectual ability. The Latin male sees himself meeting life's problems with intelligence and logic, which he finds lacking in the Anglo. An educated Latin pointed up the contrast in these words, "The Mexican-American has no disdain for thinking, no mistrust of it. He wants to arrive at his own convictions, do his own thinking. The Anglo-American will fit into almost any organization in most any way if he can only get ahead. He is often so overworked that even if he had faith in thinking, he would have little time for it. He accepts many facts although he does not understand them."

Decreasing Discrimination

Despite such unflattering images, the overt relationship between Latin and Anglo shows signs of improvement. Latins are well aware of the fact that discrimination is becoming increasingly rare. All can remember the days of segregated schools, direct insult, and unequal rights before the law. The Mexican-American sees the current change as a result of his efforts rather than a product of increasing Anglo democracy. "When we stand together for our rights, we will get what we should," is a common sentiment. The Anglo knows that when Latins do stand together they will control 75 percent of the votes. This realization makes Anglos more considerate of Latins.

Latins are listened to when they stand up to the Anglo now. Francisco advised a younger Latin to stand up and hold still in order to get the respect of the Anglo:

> We never used to do this. Instead we would take our hats in our hands and look at the gringo's feet. It was bad in those days before the war. The Mexicans suffered very much. They discriminated against us more than now. So, when the law came to make me go to war, I told them that before I was not good because I was Mexican. I was not treated as a citizen. Why was I good enough now to go to war? I told them I would go on not being good, just a Mexican. I said I wouldn't go to war. They went away and left me. Later I was a soldier and a good one. But I went to war because I wanted to. No Tejano runs from a fight. I went because I wanted to, not because anyone told me to. It pays to be a man.

As opportunities open for economic advancement and social acceptance of the Mexican-American, he still resists complete conformity to Anglo patterns. This resistance puzzles, and at times, angers the Anglo-Americans. Nevertheless, many Mexican-Americans are unwilling to abandon their cultural heritage from south of the border. The Latin pride in heritage was espoused by a college student:

> We're not like the Negroes. They want to be white men because they have no history to be proud of. My ancestors came from one of the most civilized nations in the world. I'm not going to forget what they taught me. I'm proud of being an American but I won't become a gringo. Now they're offering us equality. That's fine. I want to be equal before the law and have a chance to make money if I choose. But the Anglos are denying me the right to be myself. They want me to be like them. I want the chance to be a Mexican-American and to be proud of that Mexican bit. The Anglos offer us equality but whatever happened to freedom?

I asked the same Latin gentleman why the Magic Valley seemed so friendly when so much emotional hostility boiled beneath the surface. "I think," he replied, "that the Anglos smile at us because they need to be liked. We smile back because we're polite."

FOOTNOTE

[1]Mexican-American and Latin are interchangeable terms.

10

HUMANIZING EDUCATION

THE PERSONAL DISCOVERY
OF WAYS TO TEACH

Arthur W. Combs

The search for methods of teaching which are "good" or "right" in themselves is fruitless. Modern psychology tells us that methods are but ways of accomplishing purposes. They are not good or bad, right or wrong, by nature. They are vehicles for achieving results. Whether their effects on others are good or bad depends on who is running the vehicle, what he is trying to do, and how this is perceived by those he is doing it to. This personal approach to the problem of methods helps us to understand why so much of our former "logical" approaches to teaching did not produce the results we so earnestly hoped for. And looking at methods in this way, one may see new directions for attention and experimentation which hold promise for more efficient production of the kinds of teachers we so desperately need.

Part of our former difficulty in respect to teaching techniques came about because we tried to find "general" methods, ways of operating that would get results "across the board." Many educators still do. They keep hoping for methods that will work in all times and places and for every variety of teacher. They gather round some methods like political party banners and will fight to the death for heterogeneous grouping, the self-contained classroom, team teaching, phonics, or the particular fad which happens to be in vogue at the time. But skill in teaching, as we now know, is not a mechanical matter of using the right methods at the right time. It is a creative act involving the effective use of one's self as instrument. Preparing teachers is not a question of teaching them "how." It is a matter of helping each to discover his own best ways. The problem is not, What is the right method? but, What is the most *appropriate* method to fit the individual's personal perceptions of the following?

*From Arthur W. Combs, "The Personal Discovery of Ways to Teach," from *The Professional Education of Teachers: A Perceptual View of Teacher Preparation,* Boston: Allyn & Bacon, Inc., 1965, pp. 98-111. Reprinted by permission.

1.   The nature and content of his subject;
2.   What he believes his students are like;
3.   How he sees himself;
4.   His own and society's purposes;
5.   His understanding of the nature of the learning process.

If there were but a single factor to be taken into consideration under each of the five headings above, the task of finding the "right" methods appropriate to these categories would be within the realm of possibility. But within each of these categories there may be hundreds of variations, and the chances of finding the right methods become astronomical. Even the behaviors we call "habits," which most of us are used to thinking of as repetitions of an action, are now described by psychologists as never being done the same twice. Each human behavior is a creative act, a reaction of a person to the situation he sees himself to be in. So it is with methods. Each teacher must find his own best ways of teaching. To make this discovery most effectively, student teachers need

1.   Rich opportunities for involvement with students and with teaching;
2.   Concurrent opportunities to plan for such experiences and to discover the meanings of them after they have occurred;
3.   An atmosphere that actively encourages and facilitates self-involvement and personal discovery.[1]

A Facilitating, Encouraging Atmosphere

The Importance of Feeling Safe

For most people there is a natural reluctance to giving self over to untried and unknown circumstances. When one is involved, one is also vulnerable. When one is committed, one can be hurt. Many young people have been sufficiently humiliated in their previous experiences both in and out of school to make them approach with caution new situations which hold a potential for further self-damage. They have a real need to play things safe but the discovery of methods requires of the student that he risk himself. As we have already seen in our discussion of the atmosphere for learning, such exploration is most likely to take place when the individual feels safe and secure. Only the foolhardy take risks which are not likely to pay off. It is important, then, that a warm, friendly, understanding, and encouraging atmosphere characterize all aspects of the student's exploration of methods. Every effort must be expended to make his experiences as challenging and unthreatening as possible. Students should be given major responsibility for their own learning, and encouraged to "stick their necks out" in all kinds of experimentation and to dare to get involved to the very limits of their capabilities. If this is to happen, however, it will require a high-grade staff of sympathetic people, able to provide support and assistance when needed and skilled in protecting students from humiliation, embarrassment, and failure.

Since it is the student's self which must be fashioned into an effective instrument, the atmosphere for personal exploration must begin with an acceptance of the self the student brings with him. It is the function of professional education to produce changes in the self, to be sure. There is a world of difference, however, in a program which begins by giving the student a feeling that his self as it stands is enough for now and can be helped to become adequate, or a program which diminishes and degrades the self by continual harping upon its insufficiencies. Acceptance of self, as any psychotherapist is aware, is essential to personality change. One can only progress from where he is. He cannot start from where he is not. So it is necessary that professional students begin with the feeling, "It is all right to be me," and "This self with which I begin can become a good teacher."

The atmosphere we seek involves accepting each student's self as it is, including his preconceived notions about teaching. Instead of rejecting these out of hand, they are taken as the place where this student begins and are accepted, considered, discussed, tried, tested, and modified by his own experience. Each person's beliefs about teaching serve as his point of departure.

The principle of readiness which governs so much of what teachers do in their daily jobs must also be applied to the teacher's on experience in learning to teach. Teachers-in-training need to explore and try out what they are ready to do. The methods with which they experiment need to be those they can feel comfortable with and with which they have a chance of success. No matter how clever or sophisticated a method may be, its value to the student is dependent upon whether it works *for him.* The things which will *not* work for a given personality are so many that it does not really pay to explore them. The precious time available to help a student become a teacher is much better spent on things that fit than things that do not.

It is important, also, that the consideration of methods be approached in relaxed fashion. It is not necessary that all possible ways be considered or tried or even thought much about. Too much pressure to make a choice, especially if it must be the "right" one, may have the effect of impeding any choice whatever. Who has not had the experience of walking into a bookstore or record store and being so swamped with the thousands of choices available that he walked out again without buying anything, or worse still, with a purchase he didn't really want? The opportunity to try a few is much more likely to be helpful than standing immobilized before a thousand, unable to make a choice. Record and bookshop clerks have learned from experience that the browsing customer is more likely to buy than the hurried one. The same principle seems true when applied to shopping for methods.

The Importance of Eliminating Barriers

To bring about an atmosphere conducive to the personal exploration and discovery of techniques, instructors need to root out barriers which lie in the path of such exploration. It goes without saying that a program oriented about helping the individual find himself has no room for invidious comparisons or competition among students. Learning to be a teacher is a developmental task of increasing uniqueness. As with an artist, we cannot compare his pictures with others'. We look at the changes occurring from picture to picture of one artist and value each artist for his difference from others.

The failure of students to understand the personal character of methods may create an additional barrier. Most beginning students share the commonly held conception that there are "right" methods of teaching. This belief may seriously interfere with the very learning we hope to produce. When methods are stressed, the student's attention is directed to the wrong place for solving his problems. When methods are practiced, it is methods which are the center of attention, rather than the goals of teaching. Psychologists point out that only one thing can be in the center of attention at one time. With attention centered on method or procedure, the teacher cannot properly respond to the individual needs of students with whom he is working or to changing conditions in the classroom which call for changing techniques. It is even possible that preoccupation with methods may seriously interfere with the student's success as a teacher. The use of kinescopes by which student teachers could see themselves in action, for example, did not produce noticeable differences in skill.[2]

There is a little rhyme I remember from my youth:

The centipede was happy quite
Until a toad in fun
Said, "Pray, which leg goes after which?"
That worked her mind to such a pitch
She lay distracted in a ditch,
Considering how to run![3]

So it is with teaching: over-concern with method may get in the way of the smooth operation characteristic of good teaching.

Actually good teachers are rarely concerned about methods. It is a fascinating thing to watch an expert teacher, doctor or counselor as he goes about his work. He thinks about problems, ideas, goals, purposes, beliefs, understandings, and proceeds about his business by doing what comes naturally! His methods are like language. They are the expression of his thoughts, hopes, and goals, not chosen from his bag of tricks and applied. He operates by a kind of ad-libbing, adapting to events as they occur. The methods he employs flow naturally out of his knowledge and understanding of the problems and the goals he has in mind, so that what he does has a quality of "of course." It is appropriate. It fits. This genuineness opens lines of communication with students, creates a stable "expectancy" in the minds of students, and makes the teacher "visible" and human. Preoccupation with methods seriously interferes with these important aspects of the teaching relationship. An understanding of these principles about methods can save beginning students many headaches and lead to more efficient use of time and energies.

Common misconceptions about children may often create additional barriers to exploring techniques. One of these is the belief that children are basically evil, the natural enemies of adults. With such a feeling about his pupils, the beginning teacher can hardly afford to do much experimenting with methods. Seeing children on the other side of every question, he is likely to be so busy hanging onto his power and authority that he does not risk trying anything new. It often comes as a great surprise to student teachers that children can be trusted, that most of them are not scheming to embarrass or destroy their teachers. Even some experienced teachers never get over this fear, even after fifty years of service. The fact is, however, that children, like everyone else, want to be adequate. They even *want* to learn if they can be freed to do so. They really want the same things their teachers do for them—to grow up to be worthwhile, important people.

Another misconception has to do with children's fragility. They are often assumed to be delicate and likely to be irreparably harmed by any single thing a teacher may do. This notion has been fostered by some psychologists' stress upon the traumatic events in a child's life. The consequence of such emphasis on trauma has been to make many parents and teachers afraid of children. It is interesting to see how many teachers who fear doing something that will destroy a child at the same time will hold an equally firm, but inconsistent, belief that the child is entirely the product of his parents and what teachers do does not matter! Actually, what teachers do does matter, but not so much that any one event is likely to destroy a youngster. Children are tough, and can take a great deal. If they could not, they would never grow to adulthood.

Finally, it is essential that the atmosphere for exploring methods be one which values and encourages experimentation. It must give students the feeling that mistakes are of minor consequence and the really important thing is trying. Whatever gets in the way of the freest possible opportunities to experiment, even with the wildest, most far-out notions, should be eliminated. Students who are afraid to experiment fall back on the methods used on them. This is not so bad when those methods fit, but the attempt to adopt someone else's methods when they do not fit can be disastrous.

When students are afraid to *try*, they rely on crutches of one sort or another, like the age-old advice to beginning teachers, "Start out tough! Don't let them get away with a thing!" Unhappily, once having come to rely on such crutches, some students are never able to give them up. The future of the profession is dependent upon the production of teachers deeply ingrained with the experimental attitude. It should begin with the very first teaching experiences.

Personal Involvement with Students and Teaching

For a very long time our teacher-training programs have operated on a philosophy of "preparing to teach." Students were taught the "good." methods or "right" methods with the expectation that after they had learned them well, they would then apply them, first in practice teaching and then on the job. For most students this meant little or no contact with live students until the day they entered the classroom for their practice teaching experience. Practice teaching was regarded as a kind of examination at the *end* of learning rather than a learning experience in itself. This is a dreadful waste of a wonderful opportunity.

Participation in teaching should be the occasion of learning, not of testing methods after learning is finished. Young teachers ought to be involved with students and teaching at every step of their training. The laboratory for the student teacher is interaction with people in all kinds of settings and particularly in educational ones. Long ago we learned that the gradual approach in teaching children to swim or breaking horses to the saddle was superior to throwing them in the water, or riding the bronco down. In similar fashion the learning of methods needs to be a slow process of discovering solutions to problems and one's own best ways of working. This calls for continuous opportunities to be involved in teaching activities rather than a single traumatic plunge at the end of professional training. Ideally, this kind of program would begin with students "helping" teachers at the very outset of their professional training, with the time and responsibilities involved smoothly increasing throughout the period of professional training.

Each teacher-education curriculum can give different kinds of opportunities for involvement, depending upon local conditions. Some programs make full use of these opportunities, but others are not even aware of what resources exist in the local area, beyond those officially established for practice teaching or internship experiences. A great deal more imagination needs to be devoted to searching out and contriving involvement experiences for all students in every phase of their training and at every level of participation, whether it be observation, working with single individuals, with small groups or with large classes.

In recent years we have come to appreciate the importance of early involvement for quite another reason. Increasing technology and industrial automation has created a world which demands more and more knowledge and skill of all our citizens in order that they will be able to pull their proper weight. We have also launched a national effort to eliminate poverty, and we are looking to our public schools for ways of helping persons from every class of our social system to achieve the maximum of which they are capable. These are bold and exciting goals. Whether we achieve them will depend very largely on our success in training teachers to work effectively with the most needy of our citizens.

This calls for teachers who are ready and able to get out of their familiar ruts and confront aspects of the world they did not know existed. In the past we have characteristically drawn our teachers from the upper middle class. Many of them do not know what it is to be poor, or hungry, or rejected, or subjected to minority group pressures like discrimination. Yet many of these teachers will find their first positions working with just such people. We cannot afford to prepare them to teach in a world that does not exist. To help them discover their own best ways of teaching, they need to be immersed in educational and human problems just as deeply as they can take it, with the security and help of friendly persons around them to help when the going gets rough and to provide encouragement and assistance as it is needed.

The Personal Approach to Supervision

The "self as instrument" concept of good teaching calls for a new conception of the role of supervisors in the education of student teachers. The task of supervisors is usually conceived of as one of helping students learn how to teach. Often such instructors are chosen because they are master teachers able to teach extremely well. This very expertness can, however, get in the way of helping teacher-education students to discover their own best ways of teaching. The supervisor's task must be to help another person find *his* best ways of teaching. Lindsey comments on this point:

> Being a master teacher does not, by itself, quality one for leadership in the field of teacher education. To work with the prospective teacher as a colleague in guiding learners calls for special competence, no small element of which is the ability to teach "through" another person. Many a master teacher finds it very difficult, if not impossible, to share his skills with a novice, to recognize and appreciate ways of guiding learning other than his own, to safeguard the interests of learners, while at the same time

giving the teacher-to-be, freedom to "try his wings."[4]

The master teacher who conceives of his job as a matter of helping the student learn to teach as he does will defeat the very purposes of teacher education as we have outlined them.

Conant suggests the use of "clinical professors" as supervisors of teachers-in-training. These are persons "prepared by training to understand what other specialists have to say, and inclined to listen to them, and prepared by continuing experience in the elementary or secondary school to demonstrate in concrete teaching situations the implications of expert judgment."[5] There seems much merit in this suggestion. Supervisors who do not themselves engage in front-line activities can all too easily slip into the trap of teaching students *about* teaching rather than helping them find their own appropriate ways of teaching. Indeed, this error is so easy to make that even active involvement in teaching will not of itself insure escape from it.

It is a rather frustrating experience to ask a good teacher about his methods because he often cannot tell you about them. Since he rarely thinks about methods, questioning him about them is very likely to be embarrassing because he probably believes he *should* know good reasons for his behavior. Consequently, he will make up some for you which will almost certainly be *only parts* of the real reasons. Let us take an example of a good teacher whom we have observed doing "just the right thing" with a child. She behaved the way she did because, among other things, of the ways she saw him, how she saw herself, how she saw the problem the child faced, how it looked from his point of view (empathy), how she saw the rest of the class, how she was feeling, how she felt the child was feeling, where they were in the lesson, where they were in the hour, how far along this child had come in his studies, what he is ready for and what is too much for him, and so on. Impressed with what she did, we ask her, "Miss Brown, why did you do that?" The answer we get is not at all why she did that. She tells us why she thinks she *must* have done that! What we get is a psychologist's explanation of the historic reasons bearing on the problem, the child's performance, past history, what he needs, *some* of which had a bearing on what she did, to be sure, but which are only a pale excuse for the warmth, color, vitality, and sparkle of the real thing. A preoccupation with what teachers do may only serve to point the student's attention to the wrong places for change and destroy the effectiveness of the supervisor as well.

Focusing on Causes Rather Than Results

Formerly, we have conceived the task of the supervisor as a "critic teacher," someone who would assist the student to evaluate his performance and find new and better things to do. Emphasis was on the teaching act, what the teacher did. The effect of this concern with the student's behavior, however, is to focus attention on results rather than causes. As modern psychology tells us, behavior is only a symptom of internal states of feeling, seeing, believing, and understanding. To help people change behavior, it is on these factors we must concentrate. This calls for a shift in the basic orientation of supervisors. Instead of focusing attention on what students *do,* they must learn to concentrate on how student teachers feel, think, believe—about themselves, their students, their purposes, and the subject matter they are charged with teaching.

Supervisors in many other fields have learned they are more likely to get results by bypassing the question of methods to deal with the more important questions of the student's beliefs, feelings, and understandings. The counselor-trainer, for example, explores with the student such questions as "How do you feel about your client?" "How do you suppose he feels about that?" "What is it you are trying to do in the time you have with your client?" The supervisor sees his role not as one of teaching methods and techniques, but of helping the student-in-training to explore his own perceptions and beliefs about the critical questions which govern his behavior. Supervisors in teacher education must learn to be concerned with similar problems.

To help students in this way calls for supervisors who are more than master teachers. They must also be skillful in establishing warm, nonthreatening relationships with student teachers and must possess clear understanding of what is needed to be truly helpful in assisting students to explore and discover their own best ways of operation. This calls for supervisors whose own thinking about what is important and what constitutes good teaching is clear and enlightened. They will also need to be people capable of much self-discipline so that they do not make the mistake of imposing their own values on those whom they are supervising. In addition to being knowledgeable in their own right, persons chosen for these kinds of responsibilities will need to be people with respect for the dignity and integrity of others, who will value difference, and who are able to respect the right of student teachers to find their own best ways.

Rich Opportunities to Explore and Discover Appropriate Teaching Techniques

The "self as instrument" concept of professional work which I have advocated requires helping the student find and use the very best methods of teaching which will suit him. Teaching methods is a question of helping students explore and discover purposes, technique, self, and subject matter. These must be encountered as a whole, not in unrelated bits and pieces, as the discovery of methods is not a matter of putting things together in the most logical form. Rather, it is a question it is a question of finding those techniques which best fit a unique individual operating in a complex and changing set of circumstances. To my mind, this calls for a laboratory approach to the question—a workshop type of operation.

What is needed is not courses in methods, but curriculum laboratories, places where curriculum materials are available in abundance and where students can explore and try out all kinds of equipment, supplies, and materials. Such laboratories may operate in close conjunction with libraries, but should also provide space for experimenting with materials needed by teachers in carrying out their jobs. They should also be available when students need them, open at all times so that students can browse as they wish or work by themselves or with others. There should even be opportunity, if the student wishes, to set up materials and leave them for a period of time while he continues to experiment with them. Some medical colleges now provide small offices within the college assigned to medical students. Working in their own offices, students can get the feel of professional work in a professional setting. Perhaps the day may come when we will regard similar facilities as important aspects in the training of teachers as well.

Teachers-in-training need to be surrounded with rich opportunities to see the kinds of methods and materials other people have found useful. This can be provided by observing teachers in action, by opportunities to examine curriculum materials through reading, demonstrations, and the whole gamut of audio-visual devices now available to us. It is important, however, that the student be given opportunities to explore these materials at his own speed and in terms of his own needs and without prejudice. The moment labels of "good" or "bad," "right" or "wrong," become attached to methods and materials, students are no longer free to explore at will. The pressure to be on the "right" side restricts choices. Worse still, if he has the misfortune to be seduced into trying a method which does not fit him, he may reject the method forever because "it doesn't work" when the real difficulty was that he wasn't ready. The student subjected to many such experiences may even end with the conclusion that his instructors "don't know what they are talking about," that "educational theory won't work," or that "this progressive education jazz is 'for the birds.' "

An attitude of critical appraisal should reign in the laboratory in order to avoid either blanket acceptance or rejection of methods. There *are* things that can be taught very well by lectures, television, teaching machines, and the like. There are also things that cannot. To deal with all methods as dichotomies—as though they were good or bad—only compounds the problem and makes it less likely that we will find adequate solutions. Good teachers cannot afford either to go overboard for a method on the one hand or to resist what it honestly can do on the other.

The kind of laboratories we have pleaded for in the paragraphs above, where students can be free to experiment in whatever ways they choose, will provide important opportunities for students to interact with teach other, to see what others are doing, to involve themselves in argument and discussion, and to test ideas in the open market place. Additional opportunities for this kind of exploration can be provided in the various kinds of demonstration and group discussion activities provided by the college as a part of its regular curriculum.

The supervisor or teacher of the kind of laboratory we have been describing will himself have to be a first-class teacher with a wide variety of skills, sensitivity to the needs of students, and an enthusiastic willingness to share himself and his skills with student teachers. The kinds of teaching he does should be demonstrations in action of the best he knows about teaching so that students not only talk about teaching techniques but experience them as well. What is more, the supervisor should be sufficiently secure so that he can permit, and even encourage, students to critically examine his methods and procedures without fear of reprisal. At our university it is interesting to note that when students come in from their field experiences or internship, they do not ask to see the expert teachers in our Laboratory School. They want to talk to each other about very practical matters of the most elementary sort. It takes real understanding on the part of supervisors to let students be and to set aside their own pet methods and ideas while helping a beginner find his. All things need to be open to discussion in the curriculum laboratory, including the supervisor himself.

In the search for personal techniques for teaching, there should be no unreal distinctions between what is good for public schools and colleges. Teacher-preparation programs are often criticized because some of the things taught, particularly in classes preparing elementary teachers, seem a far cry from traditional college procedures. Education students learning children's games, learning how to make papier-maché figures or number boards for teaching arithmetic, or gathering files of useful materials are sometimes disdainfully regarded by nonprofessional students as engaging in "Mickey Mouse" activities. But every profession has its simple techniques as well as its profound and scholarly aspects, and one is no good without the other. Such criticism should not dissuade the teacher-preparation programs from engaging in whatever is necessary for the production of teachers. Whatever is useful and helpful, no matter how simple or bizarre, should find its proper place in the curriculum laboratory, as long as it contributes to the exploration and discovery of useful techniques for the students involved.

FOOTNOTES

[1] Irvine reporting on the Project I studies of Buffalo, Syracuse, Cornell, and Rochester universities states, "Project I is concentrating on the differences in prospective teachers with a view to helping each student discover ways to use his unique self in the competent performance of a variety of roles as teacher-scholar." W. L. Irvine, "Project I: An Experimental Program for the

Preparation of Secondary School Teachers," in *Changes in Teacher Education* (Washington, D.C.: National Commission on Teacher Education and Professional Standards, N.E.A., 1963).

[2]H. Schuler, M. J. Gold, and H. E. Mitzel. *The Use of Television in Teacher Training and for Improving Measures of Student Performance. Phase I, Improvement of Student Teaching.* Mimeographed (New York: Hunter College, 1962).

[3]Mrs. Edward Craster in *Pinafore Poems* (1871).

[4]Margaret Lindsey, *New Horizons for the Teaching Profession* (Washington, D.C.: National Commission on Teacher Education and Professional Standards, N.E.A., 1961).

[5]J. B. Conant, *The Education of American Teachers* (New York: McGraw-Hill, 1963).

IS THIS WHAT SCHOOLS ARE FOR?

Kathryn Johnston Noyes and Gordon L. McAndrew

"We go to school because it's the law," a latter-day Holden Caulfield told us. He was sixteen, intelligent, and had hair too long and eyes too wise for the comfort of either parent or teacher. "They make you stay until you are sixteen, and by then you may as well go on since you probably only have another year or two, anyway. The point of it, I guess, is to get a diploma so you can go to college."

In the course of dozens of interviews with students from coast to coast, and many other conversations with teachers, school administrators, and parents, we have asked the simple question: "What are schools for?" Oddly enough, there are many and conflicting answers. Although most people can agree on the general purpose of a bank, a hospital, a court of law, or most other institutions in our society, Americans seem to have very disparate views on the purpose of their schools.

Adults are likely to say that the schools are designed to prepare young people for full and meaningful lives, to train skilled manpower for society, to prepare youth for constructive adulthood or for self-realization or economic self-sufficiency. But the large majority of students—the consumers of education—are convinced that the purpose of the school is simply to prepare them for college. And most of them also believe that the student who does not enter college is, *ipso facto,* a failure at the age of eighteen. Since less than half of all American young people enter college, and only a fraction of these graduate, it is small wonder that so many students have a jaundiced view of the schools.

"It's pretty stupid really," our "Holden" went on, "Most of what you have to learn isn't worth the time or trouble. It's mostly memorizing, which in this day and age is so much wasted effort. Information is available everywhere, except maybe in the jungle or someplace like that. And if you were in the jungle, you wouldn't be worried about the kind of information we have to memorize. Even my little brother knows it's stupid. The other night—and he's only ten years old—he asked my mother why he had to memorize all those dates about the Civil War when we have an encyclopedia and he could look them up in five minutes any time he needed to know. She couldn't answer him." He shrugged his shoulders and laughed. "Oh, well, I won't put you on. I could give you some pretty spooky answers to what school is for, but the fact is that aside from the college thing, I really don't know. It's a system, that's all."

The interview seemed to be ended and then, quite suddenly, he began to talk again: "It's a system, you have to understand that. I guess it's because there are so many kids and they all have to be in school so many days a year, for so many hours. Or maybe it's because the people who run schools finally get to the point where they don't like kids and don't want to have too much to do with them. Anyway, it's a system. It's like a machine. One person, a person like me, say, can't beat it.

"Let me tell you about it. I'm failing math and science, see? My second-year algebra teacher told me she took the exact same course I'm failing now when she was a sophomore in college. But that was a hundred years ago, and now they won't even let you in college unless you've already had it. I'm in the eleventh grade, and if I fail these two subjects, I probably won't get into college. So I look around and I see that other kids are passing them who aren't any smarter than I am. So I figure the trouble has to be with me. So I need guidance, right? I decide I should go talk with the guidance counselor.

"But you see, that's where the system comes in. The guidance counselor has the whole eleventh grade to worry about in my school—642 students. So he keeps this sign on his door: DO NOT ENTER WITHOUT AN APPOINTMENT. I guess he's in there, talking with some kid who's in trouble or something, and doesn't want to be interrupted. I go down there before school, after school, and during my lunch break. The sign is always there.

"Finally, I go to the main office and ask how I can get an appointment with the guidance counselor. The girl behind the desk, a student, looks at me like I'm not all there and says that I have to make an appointment with him, personally. I explain that I can't get into his office to make an appointment, and she says that the sign's only up before and after school and at lunch period, and that I can get into his office during study hall, if I get a pass from the main office to leave the study hall. Are you following me?

"OK, fine. The only trouble with this is, I don't have a study hall. I'm carrying a full load and I'm in some class or other all day. Well, the girl didn't know what to do about this, so she went and asked the old lady who works in the office. The old lady comes over to me and starts in again at the beginning and tells me that appointments with the guidance counselor must be made during the student's study hall. I ask her what happens if the student doesn't have a study hall, and she says that it always works out all right because students who don't have study halls don't have them because they are carrying a full load, and the only kids who are allowed to carry a full load are the smart ones who don't need the guidance counselor anyway.

"You see what I mean? You just can't beat it. It's kind of funny when I tell it like this, like a comedy of errors or an old Laurel and Hardy comedy on TV. But it's not funny to me because it's my *life*. If I don't get into college, I'll probably get drafted and get my head blown off for reasons I don't understand. I don't know what's going to happen to me. How can I keep my sense of humor when I'm going to get ruined by a damned *system?*"

We couldn't answer his question and didn't try. He let us off the hook by shrugging again and saying, "Oh well. My mother finally went and talked with my teachers. They don't think I'm trying. She was all right about it—I guess she's as worried as I am. But I *am* trying and I'm still failing and God knows where it will all end."

Two thousand miles away, another boy picked up the "system" theory. This one was slicker than "Holden" and far slyer in terms of "getting through" (a significantly universal term, by the way). "School is like roulette or something. You can't just ask: Well, what's the point of it?" he explained. "The point of it is to do it, to get through and get into college. But you have to figure the system or you can't win, because the odds are all on the house's side. I guess it's a little like the real world in that way. The main thing is not to take it personal, to understand that it's just a system and it treats you the same way it treats everybody else, like an engine or a machine or something mechanical. Our names get fed into it—we get fed into it—when we're five years old, and if we catch on and watch our step, it spits us out when we're seventeen or eighteen, ready for college.

"But some kids never understand this, and they get caught, chewed up, or pushed out. I'll give you an example: The other day this other guy and I had to make up an English test we'd missed because we were absent. The English teacher said she'd give it to us at 8 o'clock in the morning before school begins. Well, I knew that if the test made me late for my homeroom period at 8:30, that teacher would send down an absent slip on me to the office. So I went to my homeroom at five of 8 and wrote a note on the blackboard to the teacher, telling her where I was and that I might be late.

"This other guy, though, he didn't know enough to do that. He hasn't studied the system. So we go and make up our test and sure enough before we are through the late bell rings for homeroom period. I can see he's nervous and he doesn't know what to do, so he tries to hurry up and finish the test so he can get to his homeroom before the absent slips get sent down. He tears through the test and probably marks half the multiple-choices wrong. Then he takes off just as the first bell for first period is ringing.

"I saw him later in the day and he was all shook up. He couldn't catch the absent slips so he had to go down to the dean of boys' office to explain that he wasn't really tardy or absent. But the dean's office had a long line, and while the guy's waiting in line, the late bell for first period rings. So now he's half-way out of his mind, you know? By the time he gets up to the dean of boys, he really *is* late for first period and another absent slip about him is already on its way down from *that* teacher. The dean of boys tells him to come in for detention after school, one hour."

Our narrator stopped and laughed uproariously and then went on. "Well, the guy gets all uptight and tries to explain why he now has two absent slips going when he wasn't even tardy. He loses his cool and says some things and the dean says some things and the next thing you know, the guy's got *two* hours detention, for being rude and smart-alecky. But wait, it gets worse. I swear he hasn't got a brain, that kid. Anyway, as it happens, the day he was absent and missed the English test, he also missed a math test. And he's scheduled to make that one up after school, when he's supposed to be in the detention hall. If he misses the math test, it won't be given again, and he doesn't know if his grade can stand a zero for this marking period. But if he misses detention, he might be suspended and have three days' worth of stuff to make up when he gets back.

"I don't know what he did, finally. Probably just had a nervous breakdown. It was really pathetic. But the point is that he should have foreseen all that and made arrangements for it. I'll be surprised if he makes it through school. He just doesn't understand the system."

The speaker obviously did; he had learned well. The only question is, is that what he went to school to learn?

Our last example is shorter and more succinct, but it is one we heard many times, from both boys and girls. It goes like this: School was invented to bug kids.

These were high schoolers, and their stories were depressingly the same from one coast to the other. The system syndrome turns up in junior and senior high schools of all shapes and sizes and, contrary to what might be expected, seems as prevalent in relatively small schools as it is in schools with 2,000 or more students. The same two words were spoken in all the regional accents of America: *system* and *machine*.

The elementary schools are no more human in their dealings with students. Although the self-contained classroom allows more opportunity for the teacher to know her students, this is balanced by her determination to "mold" them into what she and the school authorities think they should be. And what they should be, at the end of any given year, is ready for the next year. In the final analysis, the first-grade teacher's aim is to prepare her students for the second grade, and so forth from elementary school to junior high, from junior high to college.

Generally speaking, the typical first-grader is inclined to be outgoing, uninhibited, and candid. He arrives at the schoolhouse door eager and primed for what lies ahead. If he has the verbal tools and inclination to communicate with you at all, he is likely to tell you early in your acquaintance that he goes to school now. It's a big thing in his life and, psychologically speaking, he is probably far more interested in school at this point than he ever will be again.

What happens to him next will be a series of little things, none of them especially traumatic, but all of them together sufficient to turn his enthusiasm down, if not off. By the end of first grade the child is no longer excited and proud to be a schoolboy. By now, he probably doesn't like school half as well as he likes home or the streets, and his favorite subject is recess. And the chances are that he doesn't like school very much because, somehow, he has gotten the idea that school doesn't particularly like him. He is too often corrected and reprimanded, too infrequently challenged, and too consistently bored. The exceptions to these schools that turn off their students so effectively number in the hundreds. But the American public is supporting more than 100,000 schools.

No child can think well of himself if the individuals with whom he comes in contact do not seem to think well of him; no one who thinks of himself as fodder for a machine—or a "system"—is likely to have a comfortably good opinion of himself. Simply because nobody else seems to think he matters at all, he must spend a good deal of time and energy proclaiming that he does. If he is not able to do this, if he cannot make himself believe in his own worth, he will soon be broken.

As presently organized, the inescapable truth is that our schools seldom promote and frequently deny the objectives we, as a nation, espouse. Rather than being assisted and encouraged to develop their own individuality, our children are locked into a regimented system that attempts to stamp them all in the same mold. The student is filled with facts and figures which only accidentally and infrequently have anything whatsoever to do with the problems and conflicts of modern life or his own inner concerns. What he needs and wants are matters of no apparent interest to anyone associated with the schools.

In sum, we run our schools almost totally without reference to the needs of the children who attend them. What we teach, how we teach it, and even when and where we teach it are far too often based upon the needs and convenience of the school, upon the comfort of the administrators, and the logistics of the system. And the students are all too aware of this; in all of our dozens of conversations with students in all parts of the country, not one boy or girl ever answered our initial question with: "The schools are for kids."

THE HUMAN DIMENSION IN TEACHING

Ernest R. Hilgard

It is surprising that, after all these years of doing it, we know so very little about effective teaching. The payoff of careful studies, such as those reviewed by [W. J.] McKeachie in the Nevitt Sanford volume on *The American College,* is very slight indeed. It is surprising that studies of class size, discussion vs. lecture, and teaching aids such as motion pictures and TV point to so few differences in the effectiveness of teaching. These studies, therefore, give us little guidance.

It is not that these studies are poorly done, and even studies which show little differences in effectiveness leave us with freedom of choice. My guess is that they fail, however, to understand the subtle differences made by kind of student, kind of teaching setting, and kind of long-range goals that are operative. If one looks back on his own experiences, or inquires a little of others, a number of paradoxes within effective teaching come into view. I shall give a few examples. When I was in high school, they decided to introduce a senior course in economics and assigned it to the history teacher as the only social scientist on the faculty. It so happens that she had great difficulty in understanding economics, but one of my best learning experiences in high school was getting together with other members of the class in order to explain economics clearly to our teacher, who was, in fact, quite ready to learn. I am not joking about this: we went to the bank for statements to *prove* to her that capital was listed as a liability and not as an asset. (She knew capital was an asset because her wealthy aunt occasionally had to dip into capital to pay her bills.) In overcoming her objections, economics became clearer to everybody.

My second illustration is the graduate teaching of psychology at Yale during my student days there. We took only a couple of courses and a seminar, and some of us, like myself, had come without any undergraduate work in psychology. So beyond a course on the history of psychology—which took two years to work up to the time of modern psychology beyond Descartes—and one course on dissecting a

*Ernest R. Hilgard, "The Human Dimension in Teaching," American Association for Higher Education, *College and University Bulletin,* Volume 17, No. 11, March 15, 1965.

dogfish and a human brain—we were largely on our own. So we arranged a little study group without including faculty to work up contemporary psychology. That little group has produced a number of department heads, deans, a university chancellor, journal editors, and four presidents of the American Psychological Association.

One additional illustration. Truman Kelley, an early teacher of statistics at Stanford (later at Harvard), one of the original authors of the Stanford Achievement Tests, and one of the originators of factor analysis, was a very poor but very effective teacher. He was poor in the sense that he always got mixed up in the midst of a derivation he was working out on the blackboard. But, as in the case of my economics teacher, the students learned a great deal in helping him find his errors and putting him back on the track. As a consequence, his students, such as Hotelling, McNemar, Dunlap, Kurtz, Tryon, and Franzen, have gone on to take leadership in statistics in the next generation.

These illustrations are used to point out how occasionally *bad* teaching can have *good* results. This is not to be construed as a recommendation for bad teaching, but only as a warning that we have to be careful about pat answers concerning teaching effectiveness.

I think I could go on almost as well to show how *poor* students often become our best products. I know a dean in one of our liberal arts colleges who would almost certainly have been rejected for graduate study if the standards of selection in his day were those of today. One of my ex-students failed in college his sophomore year, came back and was graduated, took a master's degree under my supervision, went on to be the leading Ph.D. student at Harvard in his group, and is now a distinguished professor in a first-rate university.

If then *bad* teachers may in some sense become *great* teachers, and *unsuccessful* students may turn into *successful* professors, we are dealing with a pretty complicated set of relationships.

It is facts such as these that have led me to choose to discuss personal and motivational matters. We are in an age of intellecutal and cognitive emphases—but I prefer to stay off that bandwagon, for the present at least.

The Ethics of Selfhood

Teaching is an ethical profession; that is, it is concerned with the preservation of historical values, and with their inculcation. No matter how "objective" we become, our ethical responsibilities are inescapable. I wish to discourse a little about ethics, but in order to remain within my role as a psychologist I shall address my remarks to the ethical implications of promoting the growth of *selfhood* in our students.

A popular developmental psychology, one proposed by a leading psycho-analyst Erik H. Erikson, distinguishes between the *identifications* that help shape a growing personality, and the *identity* that is later achieved. That is, the child incorporates attitudes, ideals, and personality styles from important people around him, chiefly his parents. He develops a conscience based on these internalized values and feels guilty when he does violence to this conscience. But he must eventually become himself, because these influences upon him are not altogether harmonious, nor are they necessarily appropriate to the realities of life as he must live it. This proposal is important for us, because our students come to us still dependent economically, and to some extent emotionally, on their parents and they are here trying to find themselves and to establish their identities.

If we are really helpful in this growth process, we find ourselves in the ethical dilemma of either enforcing parental values, and thus playing safe, or taking the risks of permitting experimentation with life experiences, through which the new identity will emerge. If our teaching is effective, it cannot avoid the awkwardness of being caught in a cross fire at this point, for we can be neither fully on the side of the parents, nor fully on the side of a defiant youth.

Our skill comes in permitting exploration—and error—with a minimum of risk. Erikson speaks of the "moratorium" which many cultures allow during the transition between adolescence and adulthood—a period of wandering about, per-haps sowing a few wild oats, with, for a time, little social responsibility. In America the early years of college often provide something of this moratorium, although we have not learned quite how to manage it without undue risk. One way is, of course, to make as much as we can of vicarious experience. Much great literature has a kind of sordid quality about it; without recommending the degrading experiences it pictures it gives an opportunity for a kind of emotional experimentation that keeps established our own orientation to values. The censorship of literature would often deprive us of this protection against the need for personal experimentation which is provided when our fantasies are worked out and evaluated by others. That great literature and drama is mostly tragic has something of this psychological meaning: The people who die in tragedy, unlike those who die in the who-done-its, are commonly people we wish would not have to die, but often their confused values, as in Hamlet, let us examine our own confusions to avoid related pitfalls.

So if we are to do our job for keeps, we must know what we are doing to the self-development of our students. One of the great teachings of psychoanalysis is that self-deception is far more prevalent than was earlier supposed. The mechanisms of defense will preserve self-esteem at all costs; we need, therefore, to bolster self-esteem in realistic ways, so that the mechanisms can dissolve because they are no longer needed, and self-knowledge can replace self-deception.

I know that what I am saying is a mixture of psychology and ethics—we "ought" to do this or that in order to achieve this or that end, recommended, somehow, by psychological considerations. I am not denying the ethical component; I am asserting that it is inevitable, and we had better know that this is a part of teaching.

To carry this assertion a step further: Focus upon self-development and the achievement of dignity need not be, indeed must not be, egocentric. How is this dilemma to be avoided, so that enhanced self-esteem remains distinguished from selfishness and self-interest? The answer here is that respect for oneself is a condition for having respect for others—unless one has personal integrity, he doubts, by projection, the integrity of others. Gregory Vlastos some years ago analyzed this problem and solved it for himself in the concept of mutuality. A mutual relationship between two people, he asserted, was on a high ethical plane if each person preserved his identity and derived some growth through the relationship, without one person exploiting the other. This is a good way to characterize the relation between husband and wife, parent and child, or teacher and pupil. That is, the teacher gains satisfaction and becomes enriched through the interplay with students, just as the students, in varying ways, grow under the teacher's influence and become increasingly themselves, in a form acceptable both to themselves and others.

The enhancement of selfhood is, in this sense, a primary aim of education. If this proposition is accepted, some implications follow and to these I now turn.

A Proper Vocationalism

It is fashionable these days to favor general or liberal education and to deplore vocationalism in education. I wish to talk on the other side and expand a little on the theme of a proper *vocationalism* in education.

Before deploring vocationalism, let us pause to think a little of the original meaning of vocation as a "calling." A vocation as a calling is not a trivial bread-and-butter matter, but an important avenue through which one fulfills one's destiny as an individual.

This is a special problem for women and hence for a college devoted to the instruction of women. I do not propose to plow over the ground covered by the *Feminine Mystique* ([Betty] Friedan, 1963), it is quite a good book, even though its message would have come through better had it departed more from the defense of the thesis in favor of the analysis of the problem.

As I see it the contrast between the homemaker role and the outside-of-home employment of a woman rests largely on the lack of differentiation *within* the homemaker role. That is, all women are assumed to be essentially alike in their abilities to perform the duties associated with, and in their capacities to derive satisfaction from, rearing children, doing housekeeping, acting as a hostess for the

husband, and raising the cultural level of the community through voluntary services. No man's role is so undifferentiated and uniform—not even his lesser responsibilities as a husband and father. Special considerations are made for his share in
these responsibilities dependent upon his outside obligations—his office hours, his
time in travel, and so on.

By contrast, work outside the home for both men and women is highly
differentiated according to the capacities and training of the worker. Some work is
itself little differentiated, as in being a typist in a pool, or a routine machine
operator, but even those have their own occupational hierarchies, one different
from another. If one thinks of marks of individuality as signs of identity and
self-esteem, it is no wonder that the homemaker role is not satisfying to many
women.

These are not newfangled ideas. The homemaker's role is probably less differential today than in any period of history, when, with home industry, the woman
was commonly skilled at making pottery, or baskets, or weaving rugs. In modern
life we often have to go to extremes to recover something that was commonplace
when technology was at a lower level. I recall an account of a community in the
Virgin Islands where a small colony of middle-class people have their homes a few
months of the year. There is one caterer who takes turns bringing his hors d'oeuvres
and casseroles from one house to the other as each in his turn has his opportunity
to be host by paying the bill. What kind of differentiated role for a housekeeper
does this provide? With frozen meals adding to the uniformity of life, there is every
reason why some form of self-expression should be sought by the bored housewife.

My own preference is for an early exploration of the vocational problem.
There is a danger that should be noted. This I may call *premature vocationalism.* By
premature vocationalism I mean the entering early upon a course of narrow training
that almost precludes a change of direction. Going to a secretarial school beyond
high school, instead of college, for a bright girl would often constitute such a
premature vocationalism; perhaps going to an IBM school to train to be a key
punch operator would represent the same kind of thing. Premature vocationalism
aside, I favor an early effort at reaching a decision, including the exploration of a
possible commitment, if only to reject it.

There is an interesting psychology of choice that has recently been explored
by one of my colleagues, Alex Bavelas. He finds that a choice actually made is
examined much more carefully than one merely contemplated. Let me explain by
an illustration, and then return to vocational choice.

One of Mr. Bavelas' demonstrations is as follows. He holds a fairly large book
and then riffles through the pages to call the size of the book to the attention of his
class or other audience. Now concealing the book behind the lectern he asks each
member of the audience to write down his estimate of the number of pages in the
book. This having been done, the papers are traded, and he now asks the class

members to correct the estimates before them, although they do not see the book again and have no new information. It invariably turns out that the corrected estimates are more accurate than the original ones, even though made by the same people with the same background information. There is no magic in this. The concrete choice having been made and written down, it is examined more carefully than the mere "guess" that was earlier written down. Estimates obviously too great or obviously too small are appropriately changed; plausible ones are preserved, and the total result is a better average estimate than before.

Another problem is given to class members. This is to describe what Professor X will do *tomorrow* if his car breaks down on the way to the airport; these answers are compared with those given by a corresponding class in answer to the question, "What did Professor X do *yesterday* when his car broke down on the way to the airport?" The answers, based on the same information (or lack of it) are very different in the two cases. The answers are very "iffy" and general regarding what he will do tomorrow, but full of vivid detail on what he probably did yesterday.

The suggestion, then, is this. If you act as if you have already chosen, the situation becomes more concrete to you than if you think about it as lying uncertainly in the future. Committed to medicine, the boy or girl who works in the hospital as an orderly during the summer knows "what it feels like" to be a physician in the way an orderly merely earning his living does not. The advantage of early choice is that a negated choice is not costly, and a substantiated choice becomes a focus of integration.

Studies at Yale a number of years ago showed that students, equated for ability, did better in courses perceived as relevant to their major than in other courses. We have postponed some general education courses at Stanford to the junior and senior years on the assumption, for example, that an engineering student will see the relevances of economics as a senior more than he would have seen it while impatient to get on with his engineering.

[Jacques] Hadamard, the distinguished French mathematician, used an expression that I have often quoted. He said that specialization is a good thing, through giving direction and keeping you on the track, provided you learn also to "look aside" as you go down the road. That is the way I feel about having a vocational goal.

A vocational goal need not be a money-earning goal. I suppose a life-plan is what I am talking about, but life-plan has a kind of sentimental sound about it, whereas vocation is getting down to brass tacks. Were we able to get down to brass tacks on life-planning, I would prefer that. Perhaps we can.

Teaching as Contagion

My theme is a developmental one. I have thus far stressed the growth of the individual and the importance of vocational roles in providing some of the necessary differentiation. Now I wish to get a little closer to the teaching and learning process, for I am sure that you are wondering when I am going to get back into the classroom.

First I am going to wander even further afield, into child training and psychotherapy.

We have been finding out some interesting things about individual development through our research in the personality backgrounds of those susceptible to hypnosis. This phase of our program is largely under the direction of my wife, Josephine R. Hilgard, a medically trained psychiatrist and psychoanalyst. We find that the capacity for deep involvement in novel experiences, so important in hypnotic susceptibility, often has its roots in the close relationship with parents who can themselves become deeply absorbed in music, religion, or communion with nature, and this learning by the child is more a matter of contagion than of instruction.

Basing some of her conjectures on these hypnotic results, Josephine Hilgard and her colleagues have been experimenting with a kind of psychotherapy which she has called *affiliative therapy*. Very disturbed adolescents, who have not been helped by ordinary therapeutic practices and are on the verge of being committed to custodial institutions, have turned the corner toward good adjustment through this procedure. What is done is to find some source of strength, some interest on which to build, such as a skill and interest in swimming, for example. It is important that the college student, as affiliative therapist, must enjoy swimming and think he is getting paid for something that he would like to do without pay. He thus takes the patient along with his enthusiasm but demands consistent effort. The consequence is a spread of self-respect and effort in other areas, such as school work, without the affiliative therapist taking on any interpretive role.

The lessons to be learned from this illustration of contagion are that one way of understanding teacher-pupil relations is through contagion. The strange illustrations of bad teaching that I gave at first can be reinterpreted in this way. Even my high school economics teacher was intrigued with the new subject she didn't understand; there was no boredom in her interchange with the class. My Yale professors were all strongly identified with psychology, and we got apprentice training in research under them, even though the formal instruction was somewhat casual. What courses we took were never superficial—including the long-drawn-out historical one. And Truman Kelley was teaching on the forefront of statistics as he derived (with errors) formulas that were not yet published.

Reports of great teachers commonly stress their personalities, rather than their scholarship or technical teaching skills. William James used to sit on his desk, dangling his feet, telling the class to read the book while he would share some of his recent thoughts with them. John Dewey put his students to sleep by his delivery, but they took notes avidly to try to keep awake, and these notes on review brought out the freshness of his thought.

Some years ago [E. G.] Boring published in the *American Journal of Psychology* an article on masters and pupils among American psychologists. This has been republished in a book of his collected papers that has recently appeared. I have taken a look at the table to see if any generalizations were possible.

This table consists of eminent psychologists and their eminent pupils— eminence defined by being starred in *American Men of Science*—a practice since cancelled.

While the quantities are not enough to make very firm assertions, it seems possible to classify masters as those who sought *narrow allegiance* and those who produced *divergent* excellence.

Thus [E. B.] Tichener's pupils, while often struggling to throw off his yoke, continue to show his influence on the topics they preferred to study—the Pillsburys, Borings, Dallenbachs, and Bentleys.

James' students diverged as widely as [J. R.] Angell, [Edward L.] Thorndike, and E. B. Holt, while Angell produced not only such "animal" men as [J. B.] Watson, [Walter S.] Hunter, and [H. A.] Carr, but human learning experts like [E. S.] Robinson, and individual difference people such as [W. V.] Bingham and [June E.] Downey.

[R. B.] Cattell, too, produced diversity in the first clinical psychologist [H. L.] Witmer, the great experimenter [Robert S.] Woodworth, the brain investigator S. I. Franz, and the applied psychologists [E. K.] Strong [Jr.] and [A. T.] Poffenberger.

Thus the enthusiasm of a teacher can encourage breadth or narrowness—the *model* is not defined by its specific content.

I am sometimes puzzled as to what my own students get from me. Most of them who have had an opportunity to reach some eminence in the profession took their degrees with me when I (and they) were working in the experimental study of learning. Yet only one of them, now the editor of a leading psychological journal, has stayed with the experimental study of learning, though another is within learning experiments in education. Several have achieved eminence in social psychology; one department head of a major university is essentially a factor-analyst; one is president of a major private foundation; and another is deputy director of one of the larger governmental foundations. Whether or not my avocational interests in public problems and social responsibility were more influential than the substantive teaching I did would have to be investigated by someone else. I am proud of these ex-students, and in some roundabout way their careers reflect something for which

I stand. There is some suggestion that what happens is *caught* rather than *taught*.

Some Practical Counsel

Now let me see what practical counsel to teachers derives by logic or free association from the things I have been saying.

If we are to be concerned with the student's development of *identity,* in the direction of seeing himself as a competent, effective, creative, and socially responsible person, capable of achieving mutuality in relation to others and *if* we believe that this will come about, in part at least, through a contagious enthusiasm generated by his teacher, then we do, indeed, have some general suggestions for teaching.

1. *Don't try to teach what you aren't interested in: it's no use.* What can this mean? Surely we have "service courses" that we teach because they are assigned to us; surely we have to cover some material that we have been over so often before that the excitement in it has gone out for us. But I say "no" to these "surely's."

If teaching is routine, and material familiar, so that you can't have any enthusiasm for it, assign it for reading, or get it programed; in other words, don't stand in its way. It may be fresh to the student; let the student see for himself. Find something new in it yourself, discover a new angle in which *you* can be interested. A common fallacy in teaching is that the teacher must *cover the ground* in class. This is never essential; there are many ways of "covering the ground," and usually a block-and-gap method, in which *some* ground is well covered and others ignored, is quite satisfactory. The teacher can choose the "blocks" that interest him and leave the dull parts as "gaps" as necessary. If we believe the contagious enthusiasm theory, the best way to *destroy* a topic is to teach it out of duty, without any interest in it.

2. *Don't be afraid of showing feeling.* One advantage of talking together is that the spoken language, accompanied as it is by inflections, gestures, and facial expression, *permits* the communication of feeling. Show that you like something; show that you dislike something. Dislike is not the same as boredom; you may dislike something because you think it limits your freedom for enjoyment or enthusiasm. Objectivity can be served by showing that there are those who believe otherwise, but you need not do obeisance to other viewpoints by sterilizing your own enthusiasm into a vapid eclecticism. Even a little dogmatism will not hurt students; they have to learn to make their own corrections in any case, for they cannot be protected from dogmatism.

What I have said thus far expresses the teacher's attitude toward himself and his subject matter. Now the appropriate attitudes toward the students.

3. *If we accept the contagious enthusiasm theory, celebrate and reward student enthusiasm.* Remember that an idea may be original for a student, even if it is

not truly original in the sense that nobody ever had it before. I have known professors so eager to impress students with their knowledge of the history of the subject that as soon as a student says something original he tops it by saying, "You can find the same idea in William James." This may be said in such a way as to put the student in the company of a great mind or to slap him down as an ignoramus. How much better to say, "What a good idea—why don't you see if you can develop it a little further?" Then, later on, you might direct a search for anticipations, after the student's claim to the idea as his own has been anchored.

4. *Finally, encourage growth toward identity by establishing self-criticism based on adequate self-respect.* Modern psychotherapists find their greatest success comes not by first attacking the patient's conflicts and inadequacies, but by first building up his hope through an assessment of whatever objective grounds there are for his own favorable self-image, whatever interest he enjoys. Maybe he was the one his parents always counted on to get the chickens fed, or maybe he taught himself how to swim, or he was brave when big bullies picked on him. Search around, and you always find something, however small, that shows some fiber, some strength, on which to build. Surely our students have a great many accomplishments to their credit, or they would not be here. If an individual, boy or girl, knows he is a valuable person, to himself or others, he is better able to see and correct defects within himself. "Nothing succeeds like success" is an important dictum.

One of my students once performed an experiment with equated classes of night school students in which one group had weekly quizzes graded, as they commonly are, with the same distribution throughout so that students could come to understand the meaning of an A, B, C, or D grade. But note what this does. Even though all are learning, for every student who moves up a grade, another must move down, in order to keep the distribution the same. In the other section he had an artificial grading scheme in which the proportion of higher grades, beginning low, increased throughout the term, so that the average effect was an *increase,* rather than balancing increases and decreases. The result was that, on the final examination taken by all, those who had been encouraged throughout the term scored significantly higher than those graded by the usual method.

In another experiment, not by a student of mine, it was shown that a sentence written on the paper (in addition to a mark) increased student performance— even if all got the same sentence, such as "It is clear you are trying." Thus there was a motivational significance in increased self-esteem that went beyond any diagnostic significance of the sentence.

Anything that can be said in a paper of this kind is, of course, incomplete. I hope that I have not given the impression of being uninterested in content or instructional devices. My own textbook gives, I believe, evidence of my interest in the details of experiences and theories, and a programed workbook that accompanies it shows that I believe also in teaching aids.

In the statements sometimes made, as by Gilbert Highet in *The Art of Teaching* that teaching is an art and not a science, I believe the position tends to be overstated. For instance he says:

> Scientific teaching, even of a scientific subject, will be inadequate as long as both teachers and pupils are human beings. Teaching is not like inducing a chemical reaction: It is more like painting a picture or making a piece of music or on a lower level like planting a garden or writing a friendly letter.[1]

While I am in sympathy with the flavor of his remarks, I do not like to think of teaching as something so precious and special that we cannot do anything about it.

I believe we ought to find out whether or not our enthusiasms are getting accross to our students. If not, the students should not be punished, but our approaches should be changed. I believe that creating a classroom atmosphere by respecting the teachers' interests and enthusiasms, by encouraging students, by building their self-esteem, is something we can go about deliberately, that we can study the effectiveness with which we do it, and we can continue to improve.

FOOTNOTE

[1] G. Highet, *The Art of Teaching* (New York: Knopf, 1950).

11

PROFESSIONALISM IN EDUCATION

PREPARATION IN THE GOVERNANCE
OF THE PROFESSION

David D. Darland

Just as he needs adequate preparation in the knowledge, attitudes, and techniques of teaching, so does the teacher need to understand the principles, policies, and procedures of his organized profession. In some professions, it may not be necessary for a trainee to study the procedures and policies of his professional organization because they are so simple anyone can gain a command of them through daily experience. However, this is not true of the profession of teaching. The teacher and his profession touch the public at so many vital points that the prospective teacher needs to study with care the issues that confront his profession. But before he can work confidently on these problems, he must answer the question of how the profession is to be organized and governed.

The question of what the prospective teacher should be taught about his profession and its government can be answered by reference to issues such as the autonomy of the teacher, or by presenting an outline of professional policies and procedures. Or it can be answered by reference to publications that set forth the status of teaching as a profession. Perhaps elements of all these approaches can be found in the following pages. But the emphasis here is upon how the profession should be perceived and how it should be organized and governed. For unless the profession can put its own house in order, clarify its own sense of direction, and establish its own policies and procedures, it will be ineffective in working with the public and its own members. Furthermore, feelings of self-esteem and commitment to the profession will be enhanced as teachers come to feel that the profession controls itself and is imbued with a sense of mission.

Much is written about the self-esteem and commitment of teachers. But until the teaching profession establishes its own self-government and sets its own patterns of performance and evaluation, there will be too little commitment. The process is

*From B. Othanel Smith, "Preparation in the Governance," from *Teachers for the Real World*, Washington: The American Association of Colleges for Teacher Education, pp. 135-49. Reprinted by permission of the publisher.

under way, but there is much confusion. At the moment there exists a condition which is best described as professional anarchy. The individual teacher often receives little support from his professional associations in his attempt to uphold the precepts of a professional.

This chapter sets forth the status of teaching as a profession, and presents a position on how the profession should be organized and governed, a position doubtless in conflict with the views of some teachers and some elements of the public. But to set forth a few *substantive* propositions on the question seems more desirable than giving a number of issues prospective teachers should consider. This approach offers something to examine; it opens up the issues in ways that questions alone cannot do.

A Concept of the Profession

If teachers are to have control of their own affairs, it is essential that a distinction be drawn between the control of education and the governance of the teaching profession. This assumes that this governance be delegated to a variety of professional organizations, agencies, boards, and commissions with clearly defined responsibilities. Such an entity will establish necessary checks and balances to protect the public interest as well as generate and disseminate the power of the teaching profession. Those who are the best qualified in any given aspect of a profession should be involved in the policy- and decision-making processes in the public interests. Contrary to popular opinion, public and professional interests are usually not in conflict.

The people of the United States are involved in a great social revolution. Teachers have habitually reflected, not led, the forces of society. The setting in which teachers find themselves today demands more dynamic and intelligent leadership, especially in the professionalization of teachers. Their professional integrity is at stake.

If the teaching profession is to acquire and maintain the intellectual strength and the political power necessary in these times, a new concept of the professional must be created. This concept must include new structures and functions—in short, a professional entity.

The importance of the control and proper support of education is inextricably involved with teaching. But the subject here is the teaching profession and its governance, rather than the control of education.

The social revolution in America directly affects the teaching profession. There are two concurrent, related power struggles. One is over who is to control education and the other is how and by whom the teaching profession is to be maintained and governed.

The teaching profession today is highly vulnerable. Because of its lack of maturity as a professional entity, there is neither the backlog of precedent nor adequate professional protection for those who wish to be heard on issues vital to education and the teacher. Of course, teachers should not control education, but they should be in a position to be heard, and they should govern their own profession.

Education at the elementary and secondary levels was organized before there was any semblance of an education profession. It became customary for lay boards not only to control education but to govern the profession of teaching. There was almost no distinction drawn between them. It is only recently that teachers have moved decisively toward professionalization. Yet in many areas laymen are still, today, having to make decisions of a professional nature. Control of the profession by laymen is so entrenched that it is very difficult to understand the importance of differentiating between control of education and governing of the profession. Acceptance of this difference is essential if the teaching profession is to function in the best interests of society.

It is this process of differentiation that is now causing so much concern. Precisely because teachers are moving rapidly toward maturing as a professional force, toward creating their own instruments of governance, is concern being voiced by the traditionalists.

The attention of teachers is easily diverted to the support of a professional organization as an end in itself. Jurisdictional conflicts are thus created. The organization becomes the end, and the internecine conflict among organizations consumes the energy and displaces constructive programs needed for development of an effective profession.

A concrete example is the AFT-NEA feud. This is not to say that the conflict is not real. It is. But it is peripheral to the issue of teaching becoming a professional entity, capable of responsible self-government. Organizations which use their energies to produce such an entity must ultimately receive the backing of the majority of teachers and of the American people. If this is true, there is strong reason for classroom teachers to recognize that jurisdictional battles are a waste of energy and that great professional issues go begging as long as this goal displacement prevails. When enough classroom teachers discover that it is they who are being weakened and divided, not school boards, college professors, or administrators, there will be a more vigorous thrust toward making teaching a professional entity.

Meanwhile, it is urgent that attention be given to evolving a conceptual design for a professional entity. This idea requires careful delineation and must be viewed in the context of its assumptions. Some of these assumptions are:

1.   Teaching is a highly complex endeavor involving ever greater techniques and never-ending knowledge of the highest order.
2.   Teaching requires continuous education relevant to the needs of the

practitioner.

3.   Teaching assumes the necessity of the involvement of practitioners in establishing their own patterns of self-improvement and patterns of professional governance. (Intrinsic motivation is essential.)

4.   Teaching assumes that the vital point is what takes place between teacher and child or youth. (It involves both the affective and cognitive domains.)

5.   Teaching assumes the need to have a supportive staff of specialists for the teacher to draw upon at all times for assistance.

6.   Teaching assumes the inextricable relationship between the conditions in which children attempt to learn and a teacher to teach, and success in these endeavors.

The above list could be expanded but these assumptions are enough to illustrate the imperative need for the practitioners of all areas, levels, and specialties in the teaching profession to recognize that none of these can be accomplished unless there are ways to support them with continuing action programs. For example, perennial education for teachers will hardly be relevant to their needs unless teachers are involved in determining the nature of such education. And that requires professional government.

Currently, the teaching profession is composed of a loose federation of groups and individuals which operate quite independently. It is not uncommon for two groups to have a common, stated goal but, because of the professional anarchy which prevails, one group often neutralizes the other.

Ideally, the teaching profession should build an entity which ensures for all practitioners certain well defined rights and opportunities for effective service. Such an entity is not a single organization. It is rather a profession: a planned integration of interrelated individuals and groups with no fixed physical dimensions, each group with specialized functions, all directed toward common purposes.

In the teaching profession there are dozens of interests and forces to be reconciled. The anatomy or structure of the profession has been defined to include the segments and the practitioners within each segment listed below.

1.   Those who teach or carry out other professional activities in preschool programs and in elementary and secondary schools.

2.   Those who teach or carry out other professional activities in colleges and universities.

3.   Professional personnel in state departments of education and other governmental agencies such as the United States Office of Education.

4.   Professional personnel in organizations directly related to teaching at any level.

5.   Professional personnel in voluntary accrediting agencies involved with accreditation of educational institutions.

Each of the groups mentioned functions in the setting of noncommercial institutions, professional agencies, or governmental agencies. The term "teacher" is used to include all members of the teaching profession and is differentiated from the term "classroom teacher."

The setting in which teachers are employed appears to have had rather profound influence on them. For example, a recent survey reveals that persons employed in elementary and secondary settings tend first to be *loyal to their individual school (or system);* second, to their level or area of teaching; and only third to the precepts and commitment of the profession. One might be a little uneasy if one felt that such a condition prevailed in medicine.

There is considerable evidence that provincialism is a strong force among teachers: for example—

1.   the mutual distrust between people from lower education and higher education,
2.   the state and regional loyalties that emerge at any national educational forum,
3.   the fact that the teaching profession tends to pattern its organization upon the way in which *education is organized* rather than create a new pattern which is independent and autonomous.

The last point is especially troublesome. Great reliance is placed upon the role of local teacher organizations and their relationships with local boards of education in matters which far transcend the capability of much of the currently established professional machinery. Of course, local professional groups could handle many of their own professional problems if they had clear, well defined, and fixed responsibilities. For example, they could develop and carry on an agreed-upon perennial education program, designed by and for teachers.

There is a multiplicity of professional matters that cannot be satisfactorily handled at a local level: for example, serious cases involving competence and ethics. Here the profession must depend upon peer judgment, but such judgment should be made by those outside the setting of the problem and not personally acquainted with or professionally related to the institution involved. Teachers must have professional protection and responsibilities and commitments which transcend their local systems, but there is still a great need for strong local professional groups. These require machinery for professional governance managed by professionals and sanctioned by law. Such a plan does not deny the important role of local groups but illustrates the importance of a design of operation different from and independent of the way education is organized and controlled.

Today there are few considerations more important to a profession than a standard of living which allows a practitioner to have job security and to build an adequate retirement. Security once vested in property is now vested in job security and retirement, but so far the teaching profession has not adjusted to this change.

In a country where teachers must be mobile, little attention is paid to the need for a universal retirement system which makes crossing state boundaries irrelevant. Few teachers even dream of independence in such matters. The best retirement plan for teachers to date sets up reciprocal relationships among states permitting teachers to transfer or buy into state retirement systems.

The teaching profession should design a true retirement system whereby employer and employee contributions are placed in individual accounts and held there till retirement or death. Some large business corporations do this without letting state boundaries inhibit them. But the teaching profession is so tied to the way education is organized that it behaves as though its own pattern must be consonant with that of the state system. After all, the thinking goes, education is a state function.

Teachers are equally inhibited by the fact that teaching is a "public" profession. Therefore, it follows that the "public" may decide upon professionally technical matters such as certification of teachers and evaluation of teachers. But these decisions should be made by the ones best qualified to make them in the interest of the public welfare. If teaching were already a professional entity, such decisions would be made without question by the professionals.

It is important to keep in mind that what is being advocated here is the idea that a profession should govern itself and assume the responsibility for decisions best made by professionals. Of course, the control of all professions is ultimately vested in the people. But the delegation of rights and responsibilities to a profession has substantial precedent in our society. To delegate such rights either by agreement, law, or precedent does not mean that the people give up these rights. It is, of course, implicit that when the right of professional governance is afforded any given profession, it be upon the premise of built-in guarantees, so that self-serving zeal does not supersede the public welfare. This is why the teaching profession must be a functioning entity rather than a monolithic organization. The very nature of successful teaching derives from the involvement which the process of self-government provides. This is the essence of intrinsic motivation which provides the dynamics of self-fulfillment, improvement, productive change, and intellectual liberation.

Since structure and machinery should accommodate function, we will begin with the essential functions of any profession in our society and attempt to evolve a workable concept of professional entity.

Function 1. Educating for the profession. A profession depends to a large degree on a wide range of intellectual abilities to carry on its services. Furthermore, professional education and training must be continuous if competency is to be maintained. Educating teachers should be viewed as a never-ending function of the profession, and designs for accomplishing such a function should be created.

The details involved are not relevant here but the great number of vested interests are. These include the interests of educational personnel from each of the settings in which teachers serve, as discussed above.

Local school personnel, especially classroom teachers, are particularly concerned, since they are often expected to supervise teachers-in-training in addition to carrying a full teaching load. Very little effort has been directed toward organizing programs for the initial preparation of teachers so that mature practitioners working with teachers-in-training, or interns, are assigned such responsibility as a part of their regular teaching load. This function is typically assigned to a teacher *in addition* to his regular teaching responsibilities. This would not be the case if the teaching profession had charge of its own affairs. Currently, there is some interest in providing school systems which assist in teacher preparation with a differential state grant of money for classroom teachers to work with prospective teachers as a part of their regular teaching load. This will be done only if the profession presses the issue; it serves here to illustrate the type of issue in which the organized teaching profession must become more involved.

In the future, some initial preparation of teachers should be done in training cadres of people for a variety of educational positions. The Education Professions Development Act emphasizes the important of preparing education personnel in teams. This implies the acceptance of the concept of differentiation of staff and of experimentation with the deployment of educational talent, both designed to provide greater opportunity for individual programs of study and learning for children and youth.

Such a concept requires a new emphasis on the interrelationships between professional personnel in teacher education institutions and in the schools. Not only are such relationships necessary for the initial preparation of teachers, but they are necessary to build relevant perennial education programs for teachers. A profession should surely be responsible for policies governing the adequate initial preparation of personnel and those governing further education for its members.

Function 2. Maintaining machinery for policy formulation and decision making for the educating of teachers. The people have delegated the primary control of state education to state legislatures and state departments of education. Local boards have been delegated certain parallel and specific powers. But the right to educate, certify teachers, and accredit teacher training institutions rests with the state government. It is important to remember here that local school boards are also the creations of the state government.

In the interests of the public welfare and the teaching profession, the following teacher education functions in each state should be delegated to the teaching profession:

1.   the licensure of teachers
2.   the revocation or suspension of license procedures
3.   the review of waiver of any certification requirements

4. the accreditation of teacher education institutions
5. the power to develop suggested programs, studies, and research designed to improve teacher education, including advanced education of teachers.

These functions, with few exceptions, are now vested in the respective state departments of education[1] which are most often controlled by lay boards. The legal right and power to establish policies, develop procedures, and make decisions regarding the functions mentioned above should be vested in a professional standards board in every state. A few states have moved in this direction, but there is great reluctance to ask that such responsibilities be placed in the hands of professionals.

For purposes of interrelation and coordination, the administrative officer of such boards should be an ex-officio member of the staff of the state department of education, and the staff should be housed in state department offices. There should be clear recognition, however, of the importance of the staff's responsibility to the teaching profession. Rather detailed guidelines for establishing such boards are already in existence.

It should be clear that the major responsibility of any such board would be policy formulation and decision-making power over the administrative machinery that carries out the above functions. Since these boards would be creatures of state legislatures, they would be under constant legislative review. This is a very substantial check on any profession. But the technical dimensions of the functions under consideration require the attention of the professionals who are wholly responsible.

Obviously, teacher education, certification, and accreditation are three separate functions and should be administered as such. Each should continue to have its separate machinery. Teacher education should be vested with higher education institutions in cooperation with the common schools. Institutions should be offered greater autonomy and should be encouraged to experiment with new programs of teacher education. Teacher certification and the accreditation of preparatory institutions should reflect this flexibility.

An important function of a professional standards board would be to encourage the creation of study and research teams preparing teachers for the various educational levels and academic areas of teaching. This would provide opportunity for meaningful involvement of liberal arts personnel.

As teaching becomes a more mature profession, quite probably there will be only an initial licensure. Advanced standings in level of teaching or specialties will be administered and controlled by the appropriate specialty group. Professional standards boards should have the power to experiment with such procedures. It would be interesting, for example, if every state in the union had a broadly representative study and research team working on the improvement of programs for training mathematics teachers. The same could be said for all parallel academic and specialty groups.

Everyone in teaching knows that accreditation of teacher education continues to be a complex problem. Recently the Mayor study reaffirmed the need for the National Council for the Accreditation of Teacher Education (NCATE). Nevertheless, there is much foot-dragging in this matter. If the profession were really in charge of its own affairs in the various states, accreditation could probably become national, as in other professions.

Function 3. Establishing and maintaining machinery for protection of competent and ethical teachers, establishing tenure, and protecting the public welfare. Few things are more in the public interest than the protection of the continuity of service of competent and ethical teachers. This requires tenure laws as well as administrative machinery where the profession assumes responsibility for the protection and discipline of its own ranks.

There should be in each state an effective tenure law, administered by a legally established professional practices commission composed of personnel broadly representative of the profession. It is widely held that tenure laws overprotect the incompetent teacher. Many people charge, in tenure cases involving competence, that another person, often an administrator, is placed on trial rather than the accused. This may well be the case because there are few well established procedures for due process involving tenure cases. But the minimums for such due process are well known and well established in other areas of national life, although too often representative professional personnel are only indirectly involved.

Most tenure laws for teachers are obsolete; they need constant revision. But a backlog of useful precedent is developing, and there are some recent innovations which are proving helpful. One is a change in an Oregon law permitting a tenure teacher, who is charged, the right to a professional hearing before a body of his peers before any recommendation is made to the hiring agency. This procedure may be worth following elsewhere.

It is important that every teacher have the right of hearing before his peers. This can be accomplished by a legally established professional practices commission, in each state, with the power to subpoena witnesses and hold hearings as prescribed by law. This procedure can protect as well as discipline or eliminate the incompetent. An effective commission probably requires a frame of reference, such as a code of ethics, as a point of departure in ethics cases. A code which has been ratified by most educational groups whose members are likely to be involved already exists.

A frame of reference is also needed as an orientation in answering questions of competency. Such a framework would necessarily be broadly gauged because competency will vary with individual cases. There is not substantial precedent in this area, but a backlog of rulings will grow as commissions are established and begin to function effectively. Several states have made beginnings in this direction, but most of these do not connect tenure law with the responsibilities of such commissions.

Function 4. Establishing and maintaining the machinery for the profession to negotiate collectively with hiring agencies regarding matters of welfare, conditions of work, and all matters affecting the effectiveness of teachers. The right to collective bargaining or to professional negotiation is being universally demanded by teachers. The right of organizational jurisdiction for such collective action has become a most bitter battleground.

The great controversy in this matter has prompted some to consider adopting a plan now operating in eight provinces of Canada. In each province, all certified teachers must automatically belong to their respective provincial teachers' federation as well as to the Canadian Federation of Teachers. Provincial federations are authorized and directed to develop collective bargaining procedures and assist local units in bargaining. Provisions are made for impasses, but they seldom occur. It is interesting to note that in several provinces the same law requires the teachers' federation to lobby in the provincial legislature for better education.

With regard to the right to negotiate, few actions taken by teachers anywhere have incurred greater wrath. Teachers are being accused of turning their backs on the children. They are said to be militants without altruistic causes, interested only in their own welfare. But teachers have for years, through low salaries and the loss of adequate retirement, been subsidizing the education of their pupils. The economic plight of teachers is overt and obvious. Because of the close tie-in with the finance of education, property taxes, and local politics, teachers must necessarily be concerned with their own welfare.

However, there are many other aspects of teaching where collective action is needed and is proceeding. These include conditions of work, teacher assignment, perennial education, leave policies, clerical assistance, and the assistance of teacher aides.

Function 5. Maintaining effective professional organizations. Teachers' organizations in the United States are in a revolutionary transition. In both major national teacher groups—the NEA and the AFT and their affiliates—there is obvious turmoil. The one-man, one-vote Supreme Court decision will very likely change the nature of state legislative bodies. Urbanization will be more and more in evidence in these bodies. This will affect state educational organizations, their policies, and programs. Moreover, the breakthrough at the federal level, in more open-ended financial support, the civil rights laws, the 18-year-old vote movement, city renewal, the move for decentralization of city schools, and similar forces, will greatly condition the nature and programs of national education associations, learned societies, and other such organizations.

Moreover, as the evidence mounts that many public schools are not only inadequate but in many cases failing, especially in the inner city, teachers' organizations will realize that they must become more and more concerned with changing the system.

Teachers must become much more concerned with education in general, not merely formal and institutional education. The lack of adequate access to instruments of mass communication for educators is a major deterrent to more effective educational effort. Teachers have not felt enough professional security to battle effectively in the political arena. When issues are outside the halls of formal education, educational groups tend to follow a hands-off policy. Teachers' organizations have only recently been willing to be counted among vested interest groups, even though democracy depends and thrives on open and constant struggle among such groups.

Education associations are almost notorious in their defense of the *status quo* in education. Historically, they have spent much more time in this endeavor than in helping teaching to become a major profession. Moreover, teachers seldom distinguish between education per se and the distinctly different matter of governing their profession. Even constructive criticism of schools is likely to be viewed by teachers as an attack upon themselves. The overwhelming percentage of education association budgets is spent on matters directly related to education and very little on putting the profession's house in order. Both are important, but teachers have neglected their own professionalization.

Accordingly, associations should place a higher priority on creating a well defined and functioning entity for the teaching profession. These associations cannot carry out all the functions necessary for a self-governing profession, but they can create the design and cause such governance to be established.

There are certain minimum functions for which a profession must assume responsibility. These functions must be viewed ecologically and must be defined and fixed accordingly.

Teachers might work for the development and passage of, in each state legislature, a single professional regulations act for teachers which will do the following:

1. Establish a single organization for certified[2] educational personnel in each state in which membership is mandatory. This organization will be responsible for developing appropriate subunits, and will have the specified legal responsibility to:
   a. work to improve local, state, and national education,
   b. work for the welfare of teachers at the local, state, and national levels,
   c. negotiate with local boards for salaries and all welfare matters,
   d. negotiate with local boards regarding policies and conditions which influence teaching effectiveness,
   e. establish a system of grievance procedures,
   f. establish an equitable local, state, national dues system,

g.   maintain an appropriate and adequate professional staff, and

h.   carry on research in the improvement of the professional entity of the teaching profession.

2.   Establish a professional standards board, broadly representative of the profession, appointed by the governor. This board should be autonomous and independent of any association, organization, or institution. Its function would be to establish and administer procedures for each of those responsibilities mentioned above related to licensure and accrediting of teacher education.

3.   Establish tenure regulations and an autonomous and independent professional practices commission, broadly representative of the profession and appointed by the chief state school officer. This commission should administer tenure law and protect and discipline members of the profession when necessary.

4.   Establish and authorize a universal retirement system for teachers.

5.   Establish Save-Harmless Laws (affording protection to teachers in negligence cases).

There are undoubtedly other practice regulations which would be added as time goes on. Items 1 through 5 above are an attempt to suggest a legal basis for the teaching profession as an entity.

It is suggested that state organizations be assigned responsibility for negotiating with local boards. This assumes the use of local negotiating teams. It is obvious that an appeal system of several levels is a necessity. There is a growing body of literature on this subject since several states have moved toward establishing local negotiating teams. The idea of negotiation assumes mutual trust, and decision making should be kept at the level of those directly involved. However, if an impasse occurs, there should be machinery provided to cope with it. But such machinery should encourage diligent negotiation at the initial level.

To date, no state has established the legal requirements of one single organization as indicated in item 1, but the idea is being discussed and, though very controversial, it is not without precedent.

It has been stated here that a professional entity is more than an organization. There should be no monolithic control over a profession. Accordingly, items 2 and 3 recommend *two separate, autonomous, independent bodies,* one appointed by the governor to deal with licensure and accreditation of teacher education, and the other appointed by the chief state school officer to deal with tenure, competence, and ethics. These would provide the necessary system of checks and balances.

Obviously, any professional regulations act will have to be carefully written so that various boards and commissions do not have conflicting legal jurisdictions. The number of such state bodies should be held to a minimum. This also argues for a single act covering all the practice regulations for teachers, including the financing and administration of such activities.

But if teaching has a legal undergirding this does not mean that there exists a professional entity. There is a multiplicity of functions which are voluntary, extra-legal, and assigned by tradition: for example, the initial preparation of teachers, research activities, lobbying for better education, and curriculum improvement. In short, there are roles and responsibilities being accepted by several types of institutions, agencies, and organizations in the interests of the teaching profession. There is a need for all of these, but their roles and responsibilities must be rethought. The roles and responsibilities of teacher organizations are in great transition. No one doubts that all levels of organization are essential, but clarification of roles, inter-relationships, and responsibilities is direly needed. If states were to systematize the legal undergirding of the teaching profession this would give new emphasis to organizational élan.

If something like the above were established in each state,[3] then the work at the national association level would assume new dimensions and would be more assertive in other areas. A profession has universal dimensions. Accordingly, some national accreditation of teacher education must become universal, but states must be involved. If each state did have a professional standards board, such a board might endorse accreditation of teacher preparation institutions by NCATE. NCATE is already approved by the majority of state departments of education in the United States. It should be remembered that NCATE is governed by an independent and broadly representative professional group. Accordingly, under such adjusted auspices for accreditation of teacher education in states, the national association's work would take on renewed importance in encouraging more productive procedures, studies, and experimentation.

A national association should meet the exigencies of unexpected problems related to the profession. This requires much greater agility than has been the case. Such an association would continuously run seminars directed to anticipate problems. In addition, financial reserves should be held to facilitate the convening of *ad hoc* professional specialists to meet exigencies. No professional staff can accommodate all such needs. But, when problems arise which are outside its competence, the staff should know the best and wisest persons to consult. Such organizational agility should require some serious rethinking on the part of most members of the teaching profession.

At the moment there is considerable emphasis upon a variety of forms of decentralization of inner-city schools. The implication of this for teachers is considerable. To cope with related professional problems will require strong local, state, and national approaches. Each level will have a role to play. But teachers need not fear such educational reforms if they are organized to protect the precepts of the profession.

It is the individual practitioner who needs desperately to be heard on the variety of professional matters which affect him. He cannot hope to be heard without established channels and procedures. A major function of organization should be to bring into being a professional entity. This process has begun, but it is being done piecemeal and often without a view of the whole. Teaching will never be as effective as it should be until it governs itself.

FOOTNOTES

[1] The state department of education, as used here, is a collective term including the chief state school officer, his professional staff, and the respective state boards of education (in states having such boards).

[2] Membership should be open to noncertified personnel who are directly involved in any aspect of teacher education, governmental education work, or on accreditation staffs, or professional associations' staffs. (Includes all who teach at higher education levels.)

[3] Several states have some of the above already established, but no state requires a single organization and mandatory membership. Some confusion exists as to interrelationships of existing bodies.

12

STRUCTURE OF EDUCATIONAL SYSTEMS

STATE PUBLIC SCHOOL SYSTEMS

James Monroe Hughes

Basic Administrative Units[1]

As pointed out, ultimate responsibility for public education is vested in the legislatures of the individual states. The controls over public education, therefore, vary from state to state. There are, however, common policies of control among the states, and one of these, familiar throughout the history of American education, is the policy of establishing basic administrative units for purposes of state control. The state exerts its legal authority through these units. Since the framework of administrative units, or the structure for exercising state authority, is about the same in all the states, it is essential to understand the nature of these basic administrative units as a step toward understanding public education in America. standing public education in America.

When the earliest schools were established, a political boundary line was set around each school, designating the area from which its children were to come; the citizens who would support and control the school would be those who lived within the area. This geographical area, or territorial political division, was called a school district. Essentially, this is what a school district still is. Over the years, of course, the states have seen fit to modify the character of school districts—to enlarge the area, include more schools, redefine the prerogatives, add to or take away some of the powers of control. This redefining of a district, as explained later, has been continuous throughout our history, and is even now proceeding at an accelerated rate.

The National School Commission on School District Reorganization defines a school district thus:

A basic unit of local school administration is an area in which a

*From pp. 306-333 (excluding all photos and figures on pp. 311, 317, 327, 329, 331) in *Education in America,* 3rd Edition by James Monroe Hughes. Copyright ©1960, 1965, 1970 by James Monroe Hughes. Reprinted by permission of Harper & Row, Publishers.

single board or officer has the immediate responsibility for the direct administration of all the schools located therein. Its distinguishing feature is that it is a quasi-corporation with a board or chief school officer that has the responsibility for, and either complete or partial autonomy in, the administration of all public schools within its boundaries.

A clear understanding of this definition of the basic administrative unit requires some analysis. What is meant by referring to a state school district as a quasi-corporation? It operates like a corporation, but it does not have articles of incorporation because it is an instrumentality of the state. It is operated under the laws of the state and is created to facilitate the administration of public education by the state government, to execute the state's policy. As the definition points out, the state's authority is executed through a board, or chief school officer, who, like any other important state school officer, is responsible to the state government.

Full agreement among the states as to the relationship between a public school elementary and/or secondary school district and other political divisions is lacking. It should be emphasized, however, that what the relationship is makes a great deal of difference in the way public school systems are organized and administered. The basic administrative units in 29 states are established by the respective state legislatures as *independent* of all other governmental units; in four states the school district has a dependent relationship to the political division in which it is located; in 17 states the relationship is a mixture of both, some being dependent while others are independent. Educational specialists in public school administration almost unanimously advocate the separation of public school districts from municipal corporations. They believe that the boundaries of school districts, the basic state administrative units, can be more logically defined if they can disregard political boundary lines, that the financing of education in the independent district is more favorably considered by a community when costs are not compared with those of other government departments, and that it is much easier to reorganize school districts that are independent of other political ties. Some political scientists, however, for very commendable reasons, believe otherwise. The fact that only four of our 50 states have established dependent districts seems to indicate that independent districts, at least in public opinion, seem best.

Before the present district system of elementary and/or secondary education began to prevail, the pattern set by the Massachusetts law of 1647 was followed. As the frontier moved westward, the northernmost states as far west as Kansas and the Dakotas established similar public school districts, typically one-teacher, one-room, eight-grade elementary schools, called "country schools." These contrasted with the school districts in small towns and in cities, which were allowed to establish complete systems, including secondary schools. Often the eighth-grade graduates of the rural schools were permitted to transfer to a nearby town or city school, their tuition being paid by the rural school district.

As the nation's population increased, the states were kept busy changing district boundaries to meet changing needs—about which more later. in the school year 1968-1969, however, there still remained 19,369 operating basic administrative units in this country. Six states—Nebraska, Illinois, Texas, South Dakota, California, and Minnesota, in that descending order—had almost 40 percent of these units (Nebraska alone had 1,589; Kansas, her "sister" state, only 330).

By and large, school districts in the states on the mainland vary greatly in size, school population, and financial support—that is, in quality of educational opportunities. One large city, for example, operates on a $400,000,000 budget, enrolls over 600,000 pupils, has 25,000 teachers, and 10,000 nonprofessional employees. In contrast, in 1969 there were still 1,037 nonoperating districts, districts that did not operate any school facility but functioned only to transfer their pupils to schools in operating districts. All the states, in varying degrees, place responsibility for conducting the affairs of a school district on the citizens who live in the district.

Reorganization of State Basic Administrative Units

Originally, except for the cities and towns, a district was just large enough to support a single one-room, one-teacher neighborhood school. Eventually larger districts were organized and a number of eight-grade elementary schools were supported in one district. In Indiana, a whole township under a political trustee became the basic unit of school administration. Other states followed other patterns, but very early in American history the movement to enlarge public school districts got underway and has continued at an accelerating pace ever since. Thirty years ago there were more than 100,000 basic administrative units operating elementary and/or secondary schools. By 1969, as stated above, this had been reduced to fewer than 20,000 operating districts; and, as we have also noted, almost 40 percent of these were in six states, where reorganization started later and has proceeded more slowly than in some other sections of the country.

What criteria should be applied to determine whether an area is qualified to be or to continue as a basic state administrative unit to do the job of education? Most educational specialists would agree on the following:

1.   a minimum enrollment of 1,500 pupils
2.   a somewhat homogeneous population
3.   sufficient taxing wealth to support:
     a.   elementary schools and a high school
     b.   such special services as health, guidance, and programs for the handicap-
          ped
     c.   capable administrators and supervisors.

Organizing a school district so that it meets desirable standards of size and support-potential often means removing control over the schools farther and farther from the local citizens, placing it in the hands of fewer citizens, sacrificing some of the considerable advantages that accrue from fostering strong local interest in the schools. This has often led to conflict when efforts are being made to reorganize. The answer by the states seems to be to strike a reasonable balance between the size and efficiency of the district and the preservation of local interest and participation. As pointed out when we examined the contemporary scene, the trend toward consolidation of assets and resources of corporations is a typical current social development. The move by the states to centralize control over public education by enlarging the basic administrative units is consistent with this trend. Although this similarity does not prove that every effort to enlarge a school district is wise, it does indicate that the trend is not likely to be reversed.

1931-32	127,422
1958-59	43,507
1961-62	35,676
1964-65	28,777
1967-68	21,890
1968-69	20,406

NUMBER OF SCHOOL DISTRICTS, 1931–1969. THE DECLINE IN THE TOTAL NUMBER HAS BEEN CAUSED PRIMARILY BY REORGANIZATION LAWS.

The Contemporary Picture

The public school districts that have the greatest influence on education in America, that enroll by far the largest proportion of the pupils, can be classified into three groups: large-city school districts; suburban school districts; and reorganized districts in agricultural centers. Public education is peculiarly different in each of these.

The following discussion deals with these three kinds of districts, omitting the much smaller districts which, although rapidly declining in number and importance, still operate small schools in a number of states.

Large-City School Districts

In present-day America, the school districts of large cities are to the educational world what the cities themselves are to the world in general. Usually, large-city school districts are laid out within the boundaries of the city, although, theoretically at least, they are independent quasi-corporations of the state. The responsibilities placed upon citizens who are appointed or elected to serve on a school board for the public school system in a large city are tremendous. The New York City School District enrolls well over a million pupils and administers a budget of over half a billion dollars. It takes a citizen of considerable ability and unusual civic dedication to share in the direction of such a system.

Currently, journalists are directing many harsh criticisms at America's large cities for their failure to provide adequate education for all pupils. Many criticisms are directed at the leadership of the schools, some at the teaching profession. It is often overlooked that, although educational leadership has at times been deficient, some of the problems faced in the schools today are the outgrowth of broad *social* problems. The city schools did not create the ghetto or disadvantaged pupils. They are not responsible for the extreme heterogeneity of the population. The schools can, with adequate financial and civic support, provide many new and increased services and improve their adaptation to the needs of all pupils. The schools cannot, however, revolutionize the current social climate. Among the biggest problems of the large cities are those related to the socioeconomic structure of their inner cities. Improvement in education in the inner cities is a challenge that the schools must meet.

It is not our purpose here to discuss or even list all the critical problems of education in large American cities today. The reader will find these problems pictured, discussed, analyzed in many current professional and popular journals and books.

Suburban School Districts

We have pointed out that more affluent and better-educated people move in great numbers from the large cities and settle in the suburbs, thus not only creating new, and presumably better, communities, but at the same time contributing to the social, economic, and educational impoverishment of the large cities.

The states have followed a variety of patterns in setting up new school districts in the new locations of rapidly growing populations. In some instances the new districts followed the pattern of the large cities, creating a single unified district with schools from kindergarten through high school and defining the school district boundaries as identical with the city-suburb. In other cases, the boundaries crossed over political boundary lines, thus allowing the school district to be more independent of the influence of a single municipal corporation. Others created small districts for the elementary schools but created enlarged districts for the sole operation of high school education. Generally speaking, the salary scale for teachers in the dual districts was lower in the elementary school district than in the high school district, reflecting, perhaps, the earlier practice of requiring a longer period of training for a high school teacher than for an elementary school teacher.

It is generally held that the best education in America is in the suburban schools. There is much truth in this—suburban districts have many advantages: greater wealth, state taxing systems that favor these wealthier districts, newer and more modern school plants, more favorable teacher salaries and working conditions, more extensive citizenship involvement in the work of the schools, and local pride at a high level. It does not mean, however, that all suburban school districts fare alike in the educational benefits derived from being apart from, but contiguous to, large cities. Some suburbs have so grown in size that they have taken on the characteristics of the large city, the difference being that the offspring has not yet developed an inner city, with its ghettos and substandard living conditions. The extreme range in quality of education provided in the large cities has not yet extended to these suburbs.

Districts in Agricultural Centers

While the problems of education in large-city school districts have grown in number and become more weighty, state programs for establishing school districts in agricultural centers have been achieved more smoothly and successfully. In part because of improvements in roads and other pupil-transportation facilities, it has been possible to enlarge the agricultural school district to a point where it can support schools that match the best programs offered in the cities in facilities and educational services. One can sense the change in education offered in agricultural centers merely by driving through the countryside. The elaborate school plants, beautifully landscaped, surrounded with ample space for parking and playing and, in many instances, located in a setting completely different from the crowded conditions of densely populated communities, are very impressive. From the standpoint of homogeneity of school population, modern facilities, and citizenship involvement, these schools are the greatest improvement in modern education in America. As reorganization in districting continues, the old "country school" or "small-town school" is rapidly fading from the contemporary scene.

Types of Schools

1 Room O   4 Rooms or more ⬗

2 Rooms ▲   High and elementary ●

3 Rooms ▆   High school ⊕

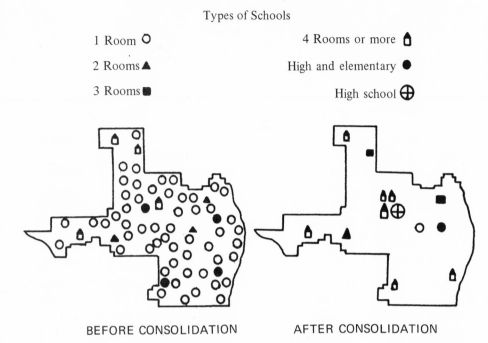

BEFORE CONSOLIDATION   AFTER CONSOLIDATION

If one may judge from these present trends throughout the nation, reorganization of the state's basic administrative units in agricultural areas will have three results:

1. A minimum enrollment figure or standard will be met in all except the more sparsely settled regions such as are found in the Plains and mountain states of the West;

2. Districts that maintain only elementary schools will be consolidated or augmented so that they will be large enough to maintain a complete system up through the twelfth grade, including nursery schools, kindergartens, junior high schools, and all the special services required by such a system;

3. Where districts operated only a four-year high school or a system of four-year high schools, these districts will gradually—and not without opposition—be combined with districts that operate elementary schools, thus creating conditions required for a unified system of schools with no salary differentials among elementary, junior high, and senior high school teachers.

The State Educational Authority

The state, with its units for educational controls, its school districts, has mandatory and permissive laws that *regulate* education. The state also has laws that *insure* the execution of the state's responsibilities for both public and private education. Such laws set up a structure of authority for the express purpose of administering the educational affairs of the state, ordinarily a state office or, in some cases, several offices, with specific and definite functions, with authority and responsibility carefully spelled out. Characteristically, the states differ in the way the state educational office is organized and in the specific responsibilities assigned to it. There are, however, common elements in the national picture. Generally, the state's supreme authority over education begins with a state board of education, an office that greatly influences the character and tone of education within a given state.

State Boards of Education

In 48 of our 50 states, a state board of education has authority over elementary and secondary school districts. (Illinois and Wisconsin are the two exceptions, although there are strong influences in both states that foreshadow change.) The state boards of education—sometimes called by other names such as the Board of Regents in New York State—uniformly constitute the highest educational authority in each of the states, although there is considerable variation in details related to powers, membership, methods of selection, and the like. Since some state policies are considered significantly better than others, a brief survey of current state practices may help in assessing proposed reforms.

1. Functions

Among the functions of the state boards of education, perhaps the most important are to appoint or have elected the chief state school officer, to designate the term of his appointment, to define his duties, and to state his salary. (Where there is no state board, as in Illinois and Wisconsin, this function is, of course, taken care of through state laws.) In broad outline, the responsibilities of a state board of education are somewhat analogous to those of local boards of education. In general, the state board assumes responsibility for carrying out those aspects of education that must be administered at the state level and also for formulating educational

formulating educational policies related to the implementation, control, and supervision of state-wide education.

In most states these functions are divided among several boards, each with
control over some segment of the state's educational program. In only 13 states, for
example, are the state boards vested with general control over all elementary and
secondary education. In many cases a separate board (or several boards) is responsible for universities, for junior colleges, for vocational education, for the education
of the deaf and blind, and so on. Boards originally set up to meet definite and
timely needs have become deeply rooted, resistant to change. A more or less confused, diffused, and inefficient pattern of state boards of education, with overlap-
ping functions and some of the evils that derive therefrom, persists.

2. Membership

The state board of education is an important factor in the welfare of education within a state. Who serves on the board is vital in determining how effectively
the board fulfills its functions.

Currently the states follow different policies in selecting the members. At
present the board is elected by popular vote in only 9 states; board members are
appointed by the governor in 30 states; various methods of election and appointment are used in the remainder of the states.

The number of members on the state board varies, ranging from 21 in Texas
to 3 in Mississippi. Nineteen states have from 8 to 11 members. Ten states have 7
members, while seven states have fewer than 7.

Numerous appointed commissions have made recommendations regarding the
most acceptable membership of state boards. The commissions, almost without
exception, have recommended popularly elected boards of five to seven lay citizens
who serve without pay. No qualifications have been agreed upon other than that
each member should be a prominent citizen who has an unselfish interest in the
administration of education in his state. It is assumed that some kind of preliminary
screening process will protect the office from citizens who are incompetent or have
selfish designs. Obviously, expert opinion about what constitutes the ideal state
board of education has so far had little influence.

Chief State School Officers

It is generally agreed by specialists in school administration that the state
board should select the state's chief school officer, whose title is usually superintendent of public instruction or commissioner of education. In actuality, however, the
chief state school officer is appointed by the state board of education in only 24

states. In 21 states he is elected by the people as a candidate on a political ticket. In the other five states he is appointed by the governor of the state, who, of course, is also elected on a political ticket. The trend, however, is toward a chief school officer appointed by the state board of education—since 1947 the number so appointed has risen from 11 to 24.

In those states where a nonpartisan state board is authorized to select the chief state school officer and to determine his functions, salary, tenure, and the like, it is then possible for the state to attract leaders of outstanding competence.

More than half the states still cling to partisan politics in connection with education. Politicians offer "good" arguments; they invent attractive slogans that influence people to oppose change: "Keep education close to the people"; "Make the chief state school officer independent of the board of education"; "Election by popular vote frees the chief state school officer from obligations to other officials, including the governor"; "If he proves incompetent, he can be recalled." Gradually, however, such political appeals are losing effectiveness—citizens are increasingly aware of the need for expert, not political, state-wide school leadership.

State Departments of Education

In all the states the chief educational officer uses the services of a professional staff. He, with his staff, constitutes the state department of education. It discharges manifold responsibilities in connection with such matters as certificating all teachers of the state, distributing state aid to local school districts, assuming leadership in reorganizing school districts, enforcing various school codes, reporting the status of educational affairs to the public, and distributing large sums of money allocated to the state by the federal government for vocational education or other educational purposes. Responsibilities of a state department of education are indeed extensive. No school or school district in a state escapes its influences.

As is true of other aspects of education in America, there is wide variation among state departments of education in their relative importance in the over-all educational organization. Assuming that importance in, and power over, education are relative to the size of the department, the influence and the extent of responsibilities are much greater in some state departments than in others. All departments, however, are rapidly expanding in power, in size, and in influence. The state department of education in New York State, for example, now has a staff of more than 1,300 professional employees, California more than 435, Indiana more than 165, Wisconsin more than 130, and Connecticut, though a small state, also more than 130.

Judged in terms of time spent administering certain activities in the state, the most important areas are: vocational rehabilitation, vocational education, instructional services, handicapped children, veterans' education, adult education, finance, teacher certification, research, statistical services, and school lunch programs. Obviously, the state department in any state is important and influential.

Planning to improve the organization and services of the state department is in progress in all the states. All 50 states, and also Washington, D.C., the Virgin Islands, and Puerto Rico, have submitted to the United States Office of Education plans and requests for federal funds to help make such improvements. Federal funds are available for this purpose under Title V of the Elementary and Secondary Education Act of 1965.

State Involvement in Public Education

All the states face certain basic questions concerned with the degree of involvement that the state should assume in education and the areas of education where the state should expand its control. Old and new issues that confront state governments include: What is a reasonable balance between the district's control of its education and the state's control? What minimum standards should the state require each district to meet? What financial policy will insure adequate and equitable financial support to each of the school districts? From what sources should the state derive its financial support? What policies regarding distribution of funds to each of the districts are educationally most sound? What minimum, foundation program should be required of all public elementary and secondary schools? These are all urgent issues that challenge the most expert educational statesmanship. Each issue really merits extended analysis, but for our overview purposes, we necessarily choose only a few of the issues for brief discussion. These are, nevertheless, illustrative of the issues in general.

Centralization

One of the most difficult problems as well as one of the longest duration concerns state power over local school districts. When the Tenth Amendment to the Constitution was adopted, because there was no reference to education in the Constitution, the responsibility for education went automatically to the states. Each state became a unit for the organization and administration of education within its boundaries. Under this policy, the federal government had divested itself of control over a most important and costly social responsibility. The problem of how the state power over education should be exercised became, and to an extent continues to be, a problem for each state and, inasmuch as each state differs from the others, the problem was, and remains, in some measure unique with each state.

with each state.

In the beginning the policy of the state was largely a let-alone laissez-faire policy. To start with, the Commonwealth of Massachusetts adopted what seemed to be the simplest solution by establishing very small school districts. Massachusetts' early system largely became the pattern for educational organization throughout the land. The citizens of the small administrative units truly exercised direct power over their schools. With time and changing social conditions, however, this simple solution became more and more impracticable and unacceptable. The various state legislatures had to face the problem of change, and the only direction that change could take was the removal of certain powers from the local school districts. Of course, when you begin to take powers from one group and give them to another, you introduce a degree of conflict. From the beginning to the present, one of the most difficult educational problems of the states has had two aspects: What powers can and should be removed from local districts? What procedures should be used to accomplish the change? At the center of the difficulty the enduring issue is: What degree of centralization of power should the state attempt to promote? Or, to put it a different way: To what degree and in what ways should the state proceed to decrease local control over public education?

A state can move control over education farther from the people in two principal ways. It can pass more mandatory laws naming specific functions to be administered at the state level (taxation, pupil transportation, and the certification of teachers are examples). Also, it can reorganize the public elementary and secondary school districts to make them much larger and more consistently able to maintain a full and complete system of elementary and secondary education. Many mandatory laws take much of the control of a function, although not necessarily complete control, out of local hands; they thus always reduce the extent of local control. Enlargement of public school districts, as previously discussed, would keep control over education in the hands of local people, but in the hands of fewer people.

Minimum Standards

The state departments of education establish minimum standards which local schools must meet or else suffer such penalties as may be stated in the law—cutting down on state financial aid, for instance. As an example, a school may be required to employ only those teachers who possess minimum qualifications of training for state certification. Schools may be required to have pupils in attendance a minimum number of days each year. Some states require that certain subjects, like United States history or health education, be taught. Some states have established a minimum salary for beginning teachers. If a teacher, under contract, should perform services for a local school board and receive less compensation than the minimum prescribed by law, he is entitled to recover the deficiency.

When the state establishes minimum standards, in theory it guarantees the individual pupil a basic standard of education regardless of where he lives or which school he attends. All the states do not, of course, provide equal minimum standards.

Foundation Program

Despite the establishment of certain minimum standards, studies show that marked inequalities in educational opportunity characterize the schools in all the states. The discrepancy in educational opportunities between the poorest schools and the best schools in a state is, in some cases, so great as to constitute a social threat. The discrepancies in some states are greater than in others, but they are wide in all states. It might logically appear that poor schools are in communities of substandard wealth and that the discrepancy can be explained by lack of money. When we consider, however, that the entire state is an educational unit, it seems clear that it is not the substandard wealth of a community that is responsible. It is the policy of the state toward raising and distributing revenue for public school purposes that creates and perpetuates the discrepancies. The state organizes school districts. If a school district has low taxing ability and insufficient income to support the schools, the state has the responsibility for equalizing the educational opportunities. This can be done, if the state desires, by first establishing a foundation program for every district and then adopting a policy of school support which will ensure each district's ability to maintain the foundation program.

How can a state do this? The state must begin by defining its foundation program—the minimum program of education to be available to each child in the state. Every state now prescribes some kind of foundation program for its schools, often a bare minimum, but many of these programs have been developed haphazardly, almost without plan. In many states, they have grown out of a long list of separate legislative actions. A legislature may decree, for instance, that every school in the state shall be open for a minimum of 180 days, that United States history shall be taught in all the secondary schools, and that all eighth-grade pupils shall be required to pass examinations testing knowledge of the federal and state constitutions as a condition for admission to the ninth grade. But can one call legal prescriptions such as these a "program"? Sometimes such foundation programs, if they deserve that name, do very little to reduce educational inequalities in a state. They may be legislated mainly to satisfy the passing fancy of legislators or to placate the persistent pressures of some highly vocal organized group.

The foundation program that will reduce educational discrepancies and equalize opportunities must be expertly planned and must be broadly acceptable to the school public. The state can act in either of two general directions. It can pass legislation defining in detail the standards each school district must meet. These standards might prescribe a school session of 180 days, a specified minimum salary for beginning teachers, and buildings and equipment which must meet definitive quantitative and qualitative standards. The maximum size of a class might be established and the maximum teaching load stipulated. Many details of the state program are thus settled. They are defined by state fiat.

A simpler way, and one that is more in line with American local school tradition, is to set a minimum expenditure per pupil as the standard for all school districts. This leaves the planning of the details to the local district with a minimum of state intervention. The standard of expenditure may be changed from time to time as the occasion requires and as the state feels it is warranted.

Once the state requires that each public school district shall maintain a foundation program for all the children in the school district, it must collect and distribute school revenues so that the financial burden for this foundation program is no heavier in the districts of low taxing ability than in the districts with higher taxing ability. The cost factor must be equalized. (In fact, in 1968 the Detroit school system sued the State of Michigan in a demand for an *unequal* distribution of state school funds, with more money going to big cities, so that larger amounts could be spent there in building good schools in poor areas.)

Financial Policy

What policy should the states follow in attempting to achieve a minimum program and at the same time to equalize the cost? It will require, initially, that each district in the state will make an effort to support the foundation program equal to the effort of every other district. The local tax rate for the foundation program in a poor district will be exactly the same as the local tax rate in a wealthier district. Obviously the returns from taxes will be much greater in the wealthier than in the poorer districts. The wealthier districts will be able to support the minimum program with considerable ease. They probably will pay for the entire foundation program and will go as far beyond the program as they wish and further tax themselves accordingly. No limit is set on how much they spend on their schools or how good they make them.

The poorer districts, when taxed uniformly with the rest of the state, may find that they have collected insufficient funds to meet the cost of the foundation program. Funds from the state, called state aid, make up the difference. The poorer districts will receive larger sums from the state than districts with more taxable wealth. All districts make an equal effort to pay, but some must receive more state aid than others. This is not consistent with general state practice, which is to base state sunds solely on average daily attendance.

State aid equalizes the cost of education for the foundation program but leaves the control of schools in local hands. The state remains the unit for providing school revenue. The words "state aid" are appropriate, since they imply that the state will assist local school districts but will not dominate them.

The state has the major responsibility for a financial policy that will eradicate many of the inequalities in educational opportunity within the state. By first defining the foundation program that all public schools must provide, it lets the people of the state know the minimum education they can expect from any school. This minimum standard will be tailored to the state's over-all potential. Next, by establishing a foundation of financial support, the state will ensure that local public elementary and secondary school districts can maintain at least the accepted minimum program. Where a public school district is unable, through its own taxing powers with its own resources only, to support the foundation educational program, the state will provide the additional financial support needed. Wealthier districts may still, if they wish, provide education beyond the foundation minimum. The variable among the states will be the minimum or foundation program. This is a generally accepted plan, in broad outline. Working out the details of such a policy involves technicalities that require educational experts to formulate the foundation program and experts in state school finance to evolve the pattern for financial support.

In 1968-1969, state aid to local schools averaged about 40 percent of available local funds, with a range from 84.8 percent in Hawaii to 9.1 percent in New Hampshire. Perhaps, as a beginning, all the states should move up to or above the 50-percent point in providing state revenue. This might make a satisfactory start toward the ideal of satisfactory educational opportunity for *all* children.

Sources of State School Revenue

Where does a state get the money for its education program, including state aid? It is not possible to give a detailed analysis of all the sources of public school revenue in each of our 50 states. In any case, the picture is rapidly changing. A general trend is discernible, however: an increasing proportion of the financing of education in public elementary and secondary school districts is being assumed by the state governments. Nevertheless, the states, in varying degrees, still place a heavy responsibility for financing public schools on local governments. In the school year 1968-1969, for example, nationwide, about 53 percent of revenue receipts for public elementary and secondary schools came from local sources, with a range from 86 percent in New Hampshire to 5.2 percent in Hawaii.

The principal source of these local revenues is the property tax, both personal and real estate, a tax presumably conditioned on ownership of property and measured by its value. (The personal property tax is a tax on automobiles, furniture, jewelry, and the like.) Although specialists are generally agreed that the personal property tax is outmoded, it is still collected in some states, Illinois, for example. Making the real estate tax the principal source of school revenue also is seriously questioned, partly because the tax tends to be rather inflexible and also because accurate and fair valuations of real estate are difficult to achieve. The property tax has become increasingly inadequate as real estate has become less of an income-producing item in the economy. Many groups who have studied tax problems over the years advocate diversifying sources of public school revenue, but the property tax remains the principal local base for support of schools in public school districts.

School costs are a large part of the budgets of local governments. Although the property tax burden increases during an inflation, American citizens, in many cases, continue to approve raising the property tax ceiling and issuing bonds for school improvements. In time of inflation, the problem of adjusting to increased school costs is especially difficult because few items in the budget can be reduced. Often the only alternatives are to make needed faculty replacements from younger, inexperienced teachers who are lower on the salary scale, to increase class size, or to eliminate or reduce the services of such personnel as psychologists, fine arts teachers, or supervisory help.

Where does the state go for its revenue to distribute to the local school districts? State plans vary. Revenue from almost any state tax source may be used for school purposes if the state legislature desires. There is more and more dependence on general sales taxes. Sometimes excise taxes are levied on special products like alcohol or tobacco. The objection to the general sales tax is that it imposes a greater burden on the lower-income group which spends a larger proportion of its income on necessary items for daily living and thereby pays proportionately more of the tax. Theoretically, the income tax is considered most equitable. State constitutions and public opinion, however, sometimes make it difficult for a state to impose a state income tax. Up to now, the reforms have developed at a snail's pace, probably because such reforms may call for constitutional changes which are difficult to get passed.

The whole problem of state revenue, and especially of providing funds for public education, is a difficult one, the foremost problem in all the states. That education should be equalized throughout a state, and throughout any of the state's school districts, seems an essential, democratic principle. How to define the foundation program and how to raise the money to maintain it are, however, issues which arouse heated debate.

Policies of State Aid

All the states have programs of state aid, but the amount of state aid and the policy of distribution to the local public school districts differ vastly with the states.

Some states have moved further toward equalizing the cost of education than have others. In all probability, the state that has a lower level of state aid has had to reduce its minimum education program in order to avoid putting an impossible tax burden on some of the poorer local school districts.

It is not difficult to reason logically that the state aid fund in any particular state should be larger, that improved foundation programs should be required, or that the brunt of the burden for local and state school support should not be concentrated on property taxes. Methods for making such changes, however, are not so readily apparent. Should the local school districts be further modified? Should the kind of taxes levied be changed? Should the methods of assessing, levying, collecting, and distributing tax money be improved, and if so, how? Should the authority and functions of the divisions of the state school system be clarified, simplified, and made generally more effective? Where should we look for intelligent and dynamic leadership for necessary reorganization of a state school system? These are, as yet, unanswered questions.

The state is the educational unit. What may be done locally depends upon what the state constitution permits and what the state legislators feel inclined to do. The variations among the states regarding all details of state public school systems are imposing. Some states have advanced in their reorganization efforts, usually by gradual and continuous means. Some states have set up a permanent group, such as a commission on the reorganization of public school districts, to work on the problem.

From 1955 to 1964, the percentage of public school revenue from local, state, and federal sources remained fairly constant—about 4 percent from federal, 40 percent from state, and 56 percent from local sources. By 1968-1969, the percentage from the federal government had risen to more than 8 percent.

Summary

Each of our 50 states is the unit responsible for the administration of education within its boundaries. The states vary greatly in their policies toward education, some states placing a much higher priority on education than others. State educational policies vary in leadership, public school districting, financial aid to districts, how revenue is raised and distributed, the manner in which local citizens are involved, the transportation of pupils, and many other aspects of state and community interrelationships.

Each state has a constitution (some are considered quite antiquated) and this, together with laws passed by the legislature and decisions by courts, forms an extensive legal structure that determines policies for conducting education within the state. When laws concerning education have become part of this legal structure—known as the school code—they tend to be solidified and difficult to change.

Not all state educational problems are financial, although financial policy is perhaps the most important element in determining the quality of education within a state. Also of great importance is a state's policy toward districting. Of the three basic types of public elementary and secondary school districts—large-city, suburban, and agricultural-center—the agricultural-area districts seem to have evolved a better climate for education than either of the other two. Even in agricultural districts, however, when older ones are reorganized, the relocation of individual schools, the problem of transportation, and the difficulties of obtaining adequate specialized services have been and remain pressing administrative problems. In other words, the many perplexing questions presented by districting are far from being answered. Each kind of district has crucial problems that, in fact, may not be solved by the present generation.

FOOTNOTE

[1]This discussion is limited to public elementary and secondary school districts.